The Word from Below

Books by Robert Langbaum

*The Poetry of Experience: The Dramatic
    Monologue in Modern Literary
    Tradition*
*Isak Dinesen's Art: The Gayety of
    Vision*
*The Modern Spirit: Essays on the Conti-
    nuity of Nineteenth- and Twentieth-
    Century Literature*
*The Mysteries of Identity: A Theme in
    Modern Literature*

As Editor

Shakespeare's The Tempest
*The Victorian Age: Essays in History
    and in Social and Literary Criticism*

The Word from Below

Essays on Modern Literature
and Culture

Robert Langbaum

THE UNIVERSITY OF WISCONSIN PRESS

Published 1987

The University of Wisconsin Press
114 North Murray Street
Madison, Wisconsin 53715

The University of Wisconsin Press, Ltd.
1 Gower Street
London WC1E 6HA, England

First printing

Printed in the United States of America

Library of Congress Cataloging-in-Publication Data
Langbaum, Robert Woodrow, 1924–
   The word from below.
   Includes index.
   1. English poetry—19th century—History and
criticism.   2. English literature—20th century—
History and criticism.   3. American literature—
20th century—History and criticism.   I. Title.
PR583.L36   1987   820'.9   87-40140
ISBN 0-299-11180-6
ISBN 0-299-11184-9 (pbk.)

To Fredson Bowers

Does the Eagle know what is in the pit?
Or wilt thou go ask the Mole?
                    —Blake, *The Book of Thel*

There hath he lain for ages and will lie
Battening upon huge seaworms in his sleep,
Until the latter fire shall heat the deep;
Then once by man and angels to be seen,
In roaring he shall rise and on the surface die.
                    —Tennyson, "The Kraken"

Wherever, in a person or in a work of art, an
expression of spirituality (in the intellectual, not the
supernatural sense) came to light, [Freud] suspected it,
and insinuated that it was repressed sexuality.
                    —C. G. Jung, *Memories, Dreams, Reflections*

Contents

Acknowledgments   xi

Preface   xiii

Freud and Sociobiology: Reflections
on the Nature of Genius   3

Can We Still Talk about the
Romantic Self?   20

The Epiphanic Mode in Wordsworth
and Modern Literature   33

Wordsworth's Lyrical Characterizations   58

The Victorian Idea of Culture   78

Is Guido Saved? The Meaning of
Browning's Conclusion to *The Ring
and the Book*   89

Browning and the Question of Myth   110

A New Look at E. M. Forster   130

The Importance of Trilling's *The
Liberal Imagination*   147

The New Nature Poetry   159

Mailer's New Style   180

Pound and Eliot   195

Notes   221

Index   233

Acknowledgments

With one exception, earlier versions of the essays in this volume appeared elsewhere:

"Freud and Sociobiology: Reflections on the Nature of Genius," in *The Kenyon Review*, 3:3 (Summer 1981), 105–20.

"The Epiphanic Mode in Wordsworth and Modern Literature," in *New Literary History*, 14:2 (Winter 1983), 335–58.

"Wordsworth's Lyrical Characterizations," in *Studies in Romanticism*, 21:3 (Fall 1982), 319–39.

"The Victorian Idea of Culture," as introduction to *The Victorian Age: Essays in History and in Social and Literary Criticism*, ed. Robert Langbaum, 3d ed. rev. (Chicago: Academy Chicago, 1983), 9–19.

"Is Guido Saved? The Meaning of Browning's Conclusion to *The Ring and the Book*," in *Victorian Poetry*, 10:4 (Winter 1972), 289–305.

"Browning and the Question of Myth," in *PMLA*, 81:7 (December 1966), 575–84.

"A New Look at E. M. Forster," in *Southern Review*, 4:1 (Winter 1968), 33–49.

"The Importance of Trilling's *The Liberal Imagination*," in *Salmagundi*, Lionel Trilling issue, 41 (Spring 1978), 55–65.

"The New Nature Poetry," in *American Scholar*, 28:3 (Summer 1959), 323–40.

"Mailer's New Style," in *Novel*, 2:1 (Fall 1968), 69–78.

"Pound and Eliot," in *Ezra Pound among the Poets*, ed. George Bornstein (Chicago and London: University of Chicago Press, 1985), 168–94.

The following essays were collected in my earlier volume *The Modern Spirit* (1970): "The Victorian Idea of Culture," "Browning and the

Question of Myth," "A New Look at E. M. Forster," "The New Nature Poetry," "Mailer's New Style." The other essays are collected here for the first time. "Can We Still Talk about the Romantic Self?"—read in a much shorter version at the Modern Language Association meeting on 29 December 1984—is published here for the first time.

Preface

ALL the essays collected in this volume have been revised and updated in varying degrees. Although the
subjects and occasions of the individual essays are
diverse, the reader will I hope notice that certain themes recur, partly
because of my preoccupations, partly because of the nature of the material—the literature and culture of the nineteenth and twentieth-centuries.
Some recurring themes are: the romantic self; the epiphanic mode in literature with the related themes of psychological associationism, fragmentation in literary form, and the mythical method; the romantic and modern idea of culture as organic; the emphasis in our literature and culture
on unconsciousness and sexuality, deriving from the impact especially of
Darwin and Freud.

But the theme I think most fundamental, that underlies and perhaps
accounts for the others, is the theme I have abstracted for the book's title.
Traditionally, or at least since the victory of the sky gods or the higher
religions, people looked upward for the truth—God, spirit, goodness,
purity were conceived of as dwelling up there; while fleshliness, impurity,
unconsciousness, evil were conceived of as dwelling down here or even
lower. One of the most distinctive features of modern culture (beginning
with Enlightenment philosophy but entering literature with romanticism) is the reversal of this diagram. We now look downward for the
Word—downward to the origins of the earth and the cosmos, to our own
origins in single-cell organisms hardly distinguishable from inanimate
matter, to the unconscious motives that are the real origins of our
"noble" endeavors. Thus we come by Nietzsche's trick of "unmasking"
the "higher" motive to reveal the "lower." In Darwinian and post-
Darwinian thought, we look back to our animal origins and to the most
primitive units of life—the cell, the gene, DNA—to understand ourselves

biologically. In Marxist thought, our ideals are a "superstructure" masking economic and aggressive motives. In Freudian thought, our ideals are sublimations of unconscious sexual desires.

In literature, as I shall show, this reversal of the traditional diagram has by no means been reductive. Writers have found in it a refreshing source of imagery; the reversal has led to an imagery of regression that has had the effect of renewing spirituality through intensification rather than elevation—a way convincing to modern sensibilities. "Romanticism," I write in the Freud essay, "teaches that a work of art is not diminished but is enriched through its lowly origin in the artist's sexual desire or desire for power. Romanticism dissolves the distinction between high and low." "The Epiphanic Mode" argues that modern epiphany differs from traditional vision in that epiphany always derives from physical sensations and often from trivial details out of proportion to the sublime epiphanic moment.

In "Is Guido Saved?" I show that for Browning's Guido, in *The Ring and the Book,* the way up is through the way down. Guido is saved not through renouncing, but through realizing to the full, his base nature. Let me "Glut the wolf-nature," he says, let me grow worse so that I may grow better: "grow / Into the man again." In "Browning and the Question of Myth," I show how Browning, in defending nude painting in "Parleying with Francis Furini," says in effect that "in symbolism, there is no high or low; symbolism demonstrates that we can know the so-called high only by knowing the so-called low. There you have the error of the Darwinians . . . who think that their knowledge of man's low origin negates his spirituality."

The ending of Forster's *A Passage to India* teaches, to quote Wilfred Stone, that "Redemption is of the earth, earthy, and of the water, watery; it is full of filth and disorder." The new nature poetry, as I suggest in the essay of that title, is even more regressive in its imagery than Wordsworth's because it "deals often with the line between nonliving and living unconsciousness—as its way of evoking "the life of things."

In Mailer's *An American Dream,* we come to realize that "the Devil dwells on top, on top of the power structure. It is God who dwells, if anywhere, on the bottom." "The spiritual essence that in *American Dream* is suggested through somatic and animal imagery is evoked in Mailer's *Why Are We in Vietnam?* through the rendition of actual animals." On the hunt we find ourselves "in an intensified Wordsworthian world where smell and the ability to smell is an index of spirit; so that D. J. moves, through his question about odor, into intimations of immortality and divinity."

In conclusion, I want to thank the generous people who took time to read parts of this book and offer valuable suggestions: George Bornstein, Morris Dickstein, Lewis S. Feuer, E. D. Hirsch, Jr., Cecil Lang, James Laughlin, Lionel Rebhun, Richard Rorty, M. L. Rosenthal, Nathan A. Scott, Jr., Harvey Shapiro, Anthony Winner. Thanks also to Sylvia Adamson and John Woolford who suggested "The Kraken" for the epigraph, and to the following who answered questions: Ralph Cohen, Donald Gallup, Valerie Eliot, Walter Sokel, Diana Trilling. I cherish the memory of Irvin Ehrenpreis, Marianne Moore, and Victor Turner, who answered questions.

Thanks to Michael Coyle for invaluable help with research on Pound; and to my research assistants: Kevin Nevers, Suzanne Johnson, Paul Youngquist. Thanks to Atheneum Publishers, Inc. for permission to quote W. S. Merwin's "The Mountain" from *Green With Beasts* (© 1955, 1956 by W. S. Merwin) in W. S Merwin, *The First Four Books of Poems,* (copyright © 1975 by W. S. Merwin); and to New Directions and Faber and Faber for permission to quote from *The Cantos of Ezra Pound* (copyright © 1934, 1937, 1940, 1948, 1956, 1959, 1962, 1963, 1965, 1968, 1970 by Ezra Pound), from *Personae* (copyright © 1926 by Ezra Pound), from *Selected Letters* (copyright © 1950 by Ezra Pound). Thanks for help received from the following libraries: University of Virginia's Alderman Library; Wordsworth Library, Dove Cottage, Grasmere; British Library, London; New York City Public Library. Thanks to the University of Virginia for help with research expenses. Thanks finally to my dear wife Francesca who, as for all my books, gave me encouragement and prepared the index.

Charlottesville, Virginia
February 1987

The Word from Below

Freud and
Sociobiology:
Reflections on the
Nature of Genius

IT is a sign of Freud's greatness that a century after his first psychological publications we still can't get over him. We are still quarreling with him, still revising our understanding of his life and theory in order to reconcile Freud with our other preoccupations. There has been the attempt by the postwar German school of Adorno and Marcuse to reconcile Freud with Marx. There has been the attempt by the French psychoanalyst Lacan to reconcile Freudian psychoanalysis with the latest linguistic theory, and the attempt by the contemporary French philosopher Ricoeur to reconcile the hermeneutical or interpretive with the scientific aspects of Freudian psychoanalysis. There have been attempts, in books like Henri Ellenberger's *The Discovery of the Unconscious* (1970), to question Freud's originality by recalling the scientific and intellectual milieu from which he drew his ideas.

A major revisionist book is Frank J. Sulloway's *Freud, Biologist of the Mind: Beyond the Psychoanalytic Legend* (1979). Sulloway continues Ellenberger's work of deflating the so-called myth of the hero, but he does it for a polemical purpose—to justify the controversial new discipline, sociobiology, by showing Freud as the link between Darwin and the sociobiologists' aim to synthesize biology with sociology and psychology. A Harvard historian of science, Sulloway supports Harvard's Edward O. Wilson, whose *Sociobiology: The New Synthesis* has stirred up much discussion since its publication in 1975.

Sulloway's claim to have written an intellectual biography of Freud makes his book a critique of the monumental three-volume *Life and Work of Sigmund Freud* written by Freud's disciple, the British psychoanalyst Ernest Jones (1953–57). Yet Sulloway's book cannot compete with Jones's, because it is not really a biography but an informative,

3

polemical account of Freud's strictly scientific development inasmuch as it bears upon his debt to Darwinian evolutionary biology. The book that can compete with Jones's, in that it is a comprehensive biography, is Ronald W. Clark's *Freud: The Man and His Cause* (1980). Although Jones had the advantage of knowing Freud and participating in the events described, Clark has the advantage of impartiality. Jones is suspect in places just because he was still fighting Freud's battles. Clark has had access to documents unavailable to Jones, and is like Sulloway able to invoke the latest scientific opinion and draw upon the recent research of Ellenberger and others. Unlike Sulloway, however, Clark is critical without being revisionist—without challenging the portrait of Freud and the assessment of his genius and originality that emerge from Jones's pages. Sulloway's is therefore the controversial book that has to be coped with.

Sulloway's book seems more polemical than biographical because Sulloway lacks the literary skill to project a portrait of Freud that can embrace the many contradictions in Freud's life and character—the contradiction, for example, between Freud's generosity and vindictiveness. As a result Sulloway oscillates between deflation and reconstitution of Freud's image; whereas Jones and Clark absorb Freud's inconsistencies into a vitally unified portrait of the many-sided, self-contradictory nature of genius. Sulloway lacks an adequate understanding of genius, because he lacks the imagination to understand imagination—genius's distinguishing quality. As polemic, however, Sulloway's book is illuminating—deepening our understanding of Freud's Darwinian side—and at least partly convincing.

Sulloway argues convincingly against the tendency of Freud studies to trace a fortunate evolution in Freud from biologist to psychologist. This myth of Freud as pure psychologist relates, Sulloway argues less convincingly, to the myth of Freud as a hero who, after standing bravely alone against anti-Semitic, prudish, and scientifically reactionary enemies, singlehandedly brought forth psychoanalysis out of his own head. Freud and his disciples have, in other words, exaggerated the opposition to Freud and deliberately concealed his debt to biology in order to promote the myth of his heroism and absolute originality. This notion of a conspiracy cannot, as I shall show, stand up against the evidence that Clark's biography adds to Jones's. Nor is the conspiracy theory necessary to the valuable part of Sulloway's argument. Sulloway is valuable when he shows through a description of Freud's scientific milieu how much he owes to the medical, biological, and psychological research of his time and to the Darwinism permeating the late-nineteenth-century atmosphere. The big change in Freud, Sulloway argues convincingly, is not from biology to psychology but from his early mechanistic physiology to a Darwinism that combined biology with psychology.

Why, we may well ask, should Sulloway think it important to launch such an argument just now—especially since Freud and his disciples have never denied his intellectual debts, even if their emphasis differs in places from Sulloway's? Ernest Jones, in his "Biology" chapter, discusses at length Freud's connection with biology—citing Freud's insistence "on the genetic nature of his work, which was in line with the developmental studies in biology," and Freud's hint that Haeckel's law "'Ontogeny [the development of a single organism] is a repetition of phylogeny [the evolutionary development of the species]' might well prove to be true of mental process also." Jones says that Freud completed Darwin's work by showing how man's highest attributes, including even the religious instinct, could be accounted for in strictly evolutionary terms without invoking supernatural intervention. "By so doing," says Jones, Freud "closed the still remaining gap in the doctrine of human evolution," and "it was for this reason that I bestowed on Freud the title of the Darwin of the Mind." [1] In other words, Freud achieved that synthesis of biology, psychology, and sociology which has come to be called sociobiology— the difference being that Freud wrote mainly about humans on whom he did all his clinical work, while the sociobiologists write, or ought to write, mainly about animals on whom they do all their experimental work: the sociobiologists wander beyond their proper depth when they attempt to write directly, rather than inferentially, about humans.

Sulloway merely elaborates Jones's description of Freud as "Darwin of the Mind," giving less attention than Jones to Freud's Lamarckism— the nowadays discredited theory partly adhered to by Darwin himself, which claims that an animal's needs and acquired habits can produce variations in its heredity. Darwin believed only in the hereditability of acquired habits, but Freud insisted that Lamarck's "concept of 'need,' which creates and modifies organs, is nothing else than the power unconscious ideas have over the body of which we see the remains in hysteria— in short, the 'omnipotence of thoughts'" (Jones, 3:312). The difference between Sulloway's book and Jones's "Biology" chapter is that Jones emphasizes Freud's *contribution,* while Sulloway emphasizes Freud's *debt,* to biology.

Sulloway makes an issue of Freud's debt to biology because he wants to argue that "Freud stands squarely within an intellectual lineage where he is, at once, a principle scientific heir of Charles Darwin and other evolutionary thinkers in the nineteenth century and a major forerunner of the ethologists and sociobiologists of the twentieth century." [2] Sulloway is arguing for sociobiology; and the result is that the attacks on his book form part of the controversy that swirls around sociobiology, especially around Wilson's *Sociobiology: The New Synthesis*.

No one objects to the fruitful way in which Wilson studies animal behavior by relating the animals' biological equipment to their social organizations, systems of communication, mating rituals, care of young, and even expressions of emotion. The thing that disturbs social scientists, leftists, and to a lesser degree humanists is Wilson's final chapter on man, and even more important the implied parallel throughout, in which Wilson tries to apply to man the principles evolved from his study of animals—especially the principle that social and psychological characteristics are mainly determined by the organism's need to win out in the Darwinian process of natural selection through "maximizing" its "gene flow" or reproductive success. They all see a threat of encroachment in Wilson's imperialist statement—an imperialism like that of psychoanalysis—that "sociology and the other social sciences, as well as the humanities, are the last branches of biology waiting to be included in the Modern Synthesis."[3] Unfortunately Wilson, collaborating with Charles J. Lumsden, concentrates on human sociobiology in subsequent books: *Genes, Mind, and Culture* (1981) and *Promethean Fire* (1983); so that an authoritative biologist like Stephen Jay Gould, after praising Wilson's early *Insect Societies* (1971), condemns "the false bridges constructed by sociobiologists between Darwinian imperatives and human ethics." "We cannot conclude," for example, "that such a belief [in God] arose by natural selection directly *for* religious ardor."[4]

The sociologists and anthropologists who feel particularly threatened by sociobiology are the followers of Durkheim, who are committed to the principle that culture is discontinuous with nature—that man is human just to the extent that he has liberated himself through culture from biological laws. The case is argued most succinctly by Marshall Sahlins in *The Use and Abuse of Biology: An Anthropological Critique of Sociobiology* (1976). Sahlins insists that "there is no necessary relation between the phenomenal form of a human social institution and the individual [or biological] motivations that may be realized or satisfied therein"—that soldiers are not satisfying their aggressive or territorial instincts, that the reasons animals or individual humans fight "are not the reasons wars take place."[5] Such an abstract view is open to question, and it is certainly reasonable to test it against the evidence of equally abstract wars between biologically determined ant colonies; or against the contrary evidence of Nazi Germany, where Hitler and a lot of Germans derived more emotional satisfaction from the nationally organized slaughter of Jews than was good for the abstract interests of the German state.

Sahlins criticizes Wilson's use of anthropomorphizing terms like "polygyny," "castes," "slaves," to prove that animal "societies" are comparable to ours (7). Yet we can hardly think about nonhuman phenomena except through such metaphorical comparisons. Sahlins's most convincing argument against the comparison of animal and human societies is that variation in animal societies always accompanies biological differences; whereas the single human species exhibits a rich variety of cultures and social organizations—even within the same race. It must be said in Wilson's defense that his mainly implied comparisons of animal and human psychological and social characteristics reveal differences even more vividly than similarities, and that in his final chapter on man he grants the incalculable range of man's evolutionary leap. His final chapter is the least interesting just because he repeats what has been better said by social scientists and humanists.

Leftists object to sociobiology because they see in it a revival of the Victorian social Darwinism that used Darwin's biological concepts of "natural selection," "struggle for existence," and "survival of the fittest" to justify the brutal competitiveness of free-market capitalism. Sahlins, who writes from a leftist point of view, sees sociobiology as even more capitalistic than social Darwinism, because the sociobiologists emphasize individual over group selection and conceive the individual organism as *using* natural selection to "maximize" its gene flow—and not as being used *by* natural selection. Sahlins, however, is quarreling over metaphors. Darwin admits that the necessities of language force him to speak metaphorically, as though natural selection had a will. It is unfortunate that the sociobiologists have chosen to use the jargon of economics to describe an unconscious process. But their choice of metaphor, in addressing citizens of a free-market economy, doesn't necessarily indicate a capitalist bias in what they are actually saying.

Although Wilson uses "profitability" to describe an animal's weighing of the "cost" of altruism against its own genetic advantage, he gives as many examples of inherited "altruism" as of inherited "selfishness" (also anthropomorphic metaphors). Sahlins could find a model for communism in Wilson's admiration for the perfect cooperativeness of ant and wasp societies and in his statement that of the mammals only man approaches—as far as he can, given his individuality and free will—that much cooperativeness. Wilson makes it clear that man's victory in the struggle for existence comes of his ability to cooperate—an ability maximized by language. But in speaking of the individual organism as though it had a will which could affect evolution, Wilson is being more Lamarck-

ian and therefore more Freudian than Darwin; and this brings us back
to Sulloway's interposition of Freud between Darwin and the sociobiologists. It is because Sahlins ignores the way in which the Freudian unconscious infuses animal life with mind that he overlooks the humanist element in sociobiology.

Humanists are or should be less disturbed by sociobiology to the
extent that they understand Freud and understand what modern literature has been saying since the early-nineteenth-century appearance of
romanticism. For romanticism teaches that a work of art is not diminished but is enriched through its lowly origin in the artist's sexual desire
or desire for power. Romanticism dissolves the distinction between high
and low. Coleridge taught that the imagination is richest when it embraces the widest possible contradictions. The Coleridgean or romantic
theory of imagination prepares us for evolutionary biology, because it
describes the movement from sensation to thought back to sensation—
the movement of the poetic image. The poet, said Wordsworth in the
early nineteenth century, remembers his childhood more vividly than
other people and can combine those memories with his highest thoughts.
The poet, said T. S. Eliot in the early twentieth century, is at once more
primitive and more civilized than other people. Freud said much the same
thing in *Three Essays on the Theory of Sexuality* (1905), where he wrote
that the importance for psychoanalysis of childhood memory and childhood sexuality "increases in proportion to the degree of individual
culture"[6]—in proportion, in other words, to the degree of repression, of
uneasy combination with civilization.

Freud confirmed the romanticists' intuitions through what he taught
about the origins of art in the artist's unconscious. He is biological in his
theory that the sex drive or libido is the force behind all human endeavor.
But in his idea of sublimation, of the way in which frustrated libido is
rechanneled into cultural achievement, Freud is sociobiological and hu-
manistic. He teaches us to value the highest manifestations of libido all
the more because of the price paid in sexual privation. The ultimate implication of Freud and of romantic literary theory is that the work of art
ought to contain the evolutionary history of the artist, the race, and the
species.

In his essay "Freud and Literature," Lionel Trilling tells us that
Freud's contribution to literature lies not in his direct remarks on it; for
Freud finally speaks of literature with contempt, as mere wish-fulfilling
illusion, with the artist in the same category as the neurotic. Freud's contribution rather lies in this—that "of all mental systems, the Freudian
psychology is the one which makes poetry indigenous to the very constitution of the mind,"[7] in that it shows the mind as operating naturally
through the images and symbols that are the stuff of poetry.

I would add Freud's other major contribution to literature. He confirmed and elaborated through analysis the romantic intuition and Darwin's suggestion that there is no clear line between thinking and non-thinking. Once we possess the notion of unconscious thought, we can understand that we are thinking even when we suppose we are not think-ing—when we dream, feel an emotion, or receive sensations—and that some mode of thought goes on even in the lowest organisms, even in single cells which seem to "know" what to do. Darwin demonstrates how tenuous is the line between what we call "instinct" and what we call "thought." Freud therefore justifies literature's way of communicat-ing through emotion and sensation. He also justifies the respect shown in romantic and modern literature and in modern culture generally for the mental life of children, primitives, and even animals. All this partly accounts for our current worry over endangered species and our interest in the songs of whales and the intelligence of porpoises and chimpanzees. The striking thing about Wilson's book is not, as his opponents think, that he downgrades man but that he upgrades animals—showing the liveliness and variety of their mental and emotional life, systems of com-munication, and social interaction. Freud, inasmuch as he supplements Darwin, is responsible for this. But Wilson makes his contribution too. For Wilson extends Freud's notion of unconscious memory to include the memory locked up in our genes.

Freud is at least partly responsible for that reversal of the Victorian reaction to Darwin which manifests itself in the enthusiasm for socio-biology and for the upgrading of animals. The Victorians were distressed by the news of our animal descent. We instead are proud of our animal descent, because Freud has taught us that the deeper the unconscious roots of a cultural flowering, the more substantial and precious is that flowering. We are proud of our descent from animals who are under-stood to be unconsciously thoughtful—not, as the Pavlovian behaviorists would have it, mechanically conditioned. We positively seek evidence of our animal descent because it saves us from that other, more threatening model of man as a machine.

All this is congenial to the literary mind. In "The New Nature Po-etry" (below), I discuss the new importance of animals in twentieth-century nature poetry as symbolizing, more vividly than landscapes, the vitality of our unconscious life. The issue is between rationalistic dualists who see abrupt discontinuity between man and nature (for the seven-teenth-century dualist Descartes, only man *thinks*, therefore animals are machines), and the romanticists who see continuity. We favor the roman-tic view because we have seen that rationalistic dualism can, when di-vorced from religion, turn man too into a machine.

Both utopian leftists and Marxists oppose any theory, whether it be the theory of original sin or of our ineradicable animal heritage, which limits man's perfectibility and malleability. The literary mind, instead, has been prepared by the greatest literature for the more complex tragic view of man as torn between his aspirations and the limiting conditions of society, heredity, circumstance—as torn, in the Greek tragic view, between free will and fate. That is why Freud is so appealing to literary people. He has reconfirmed the old tragic view that man is mainly not governed by reason; and he has, at the same time, increased man's stature—after science's reduction of it—by enlarging the dimensions of his psychic life and by showing that his psychic conflicts are objectified in myth. Paradoxically, Freud enriches our humanity by showing that we are capable of the most degrading desires and actions; the degradation can be enriching if reconciled to our capacity for the highest thoughts. Freud traces our highest achievements back to the primeval ooze, showing that our thoughts like our bodies recapitulate the history of the species, and this imaginative appropriation of evolutionary biology awakens in us a sense of awe before the miracle of culture—as a flower growing out of the mud.

It is out of this imaginative synthesis of man's biological, psychological, and social history that Freud has created in books like *Totem and Taboo* (1913) and *Civilization and Its Discontents* (1930) two great epic poems in prose. Epic poems have always dramatized the legendary origins of the tribe or nation. Freud has used the Darwinian "legend" to dramatize the origin of our species, and he has imbued his accounts with the resonances of Greek tragedy. In *Civilization and Its Discontents,* Freud suggests that man first committed the tragic sin of *hybris* or pride when he dared to stand erect and consequently repressed his sense of smell, especially as a sexual stimulus. Out of repression—disgust over "bad" smells and shame over his newly exposed genitals—came the diverted libido that produced civilization. But man pays a tragic price for civilization in the repression that causes mental illness.

In its last chapter, *Totem and Taboo* takes off from Darwin's hypothesis that primal human groups must have resembled ape hordes in which one old male dominates the females and drives out the sons, who then form an all-male group. Freud imagines a phylogenetic human drama, which would have occurred repeatedly, in which the expelled sons combine to kill and eat the father and possess the females. Smitten by guilt (or fear of the dead father's avenging spirit), the victorious sons deny themselves the females. They regularly recall—at a feast where they consume the totem animal, which as Freud proves symbolizes the father— they recall their parricide and their vow never to repeat it and never to commit incest. The totem feast is the origin of religious ritual. Freud's

Darwinian "plot"—what he acknowledged as his "Just-So-Story"—explains the connection between totemism, with its ban on marriage within the totem clan, and the incest taboo fundamental to all human societies. His "plot" arouses the pity and terror of the great epic and tragic plots, and also the sense of their psychic, if not historical, truth—for Freud's primal drama objectifies a psychic pattern, the Oedipus complex.

Freud is Darwinian as well in his treatment of our individual sexuality as an evolution toward the capacity for heterosexual genital intercourse—with the perversions, like homosexuality and sadism, explained as fixations at earlier stages when the erotic zones are distributed throughout the body; so that infantile sexuality is polymorphous, recapitulating the sexual experiences of our animal ancestors. Freud accounts for culture by three biological phenomena in addition to man's erect posture. The first is permanent libido which keeps male and female together. The second is the long period of human childhood, which gives time for education and which produces through involvement with the parents the Oedipus complex, entailing guilt and idealism. The third is the interrupted sexual development distinctive of human beings. The period of uninhibited polymorphous infantile sexuality is followed, after the age of five, by the latency period—a period of repression during which infancy is blotted from memory and the restraints of civilization are acquired; there follows puberty with its development of genitality and retention of the latency period's guilt and amnesia. Freud remained so Darwinian that he went on to speculate, in *Moses and Monotheism* (1939), that "the human race is descended from a species of animal which reached sexual maturity in five years," and that this "postponement of sexual life and its diphasic [two-wave] onset" is connected with the process of becoming human (*SE,* 23:75). Sulloway makes clear a biological point in Freudian theory that even attentive readers of Freud may have missed—that the repression of the latency period need not be culturally acquired, that it is an inherited recapitulation of the instinctual renunciations necessary for human psychosexual evolution.

In arguing that Freud did not singlehandedly give birth to psychoanalysis, Sulloway shows how many of Freud's fundamental ideas were already in the air of the 1890s. There was, for example, the work of the sexologists—Krafft-Ebing's famous catalogue of perversions, *Psychopathia Sexualis* (1886); Havelock Ellis's *Man and Woman* (1894); Albert Moll's 1891 book on homosexuality and his *Libido Sexualis* (1897), which according to Sulloway influenced Freud's abandonment in a September 1897 letter to Fliess of his theory that neuroses are caused by seductions in childhood. In *The Assault on Truth: Freud's Suppression of the Seduction Theory* (1984), Jeffrey M. Masson created a stir by arguing, on the evidence of unpublished material in the Freud Archives, that Freud abandoned his seduction theory in order to cover up the ineptness of Fliess's nose surgery on Freud's patient, Emma Eckstein, and in order to avoid shocking his medical colleagues. Although Fliess as it turned out had neglected to remove a bandage from Emma's nose, Freud considered her nearly fatal postoperative hemorrhaging a hysterical symptom and concluded that her memories of childhood seduction must also be fantasy. Anyone acquainted with Freud's way of thinking must doubt that he would have abandoned a major theory on such flimsy evidence. As for the second charge, the alternative theory of infantile sexuality, which regards children as sexually active, is surely more shocking than the seduction theory which regards them as presexual victims. The logic of psychoanalysis required the rejection of a theory which made the cause of neuroses entirely objective, leaving no room for fantasy and the development of the fundamental doctrine of the Oedipus complex. "I argue, in direct opposition to Masson and others," wrote William J. McGrath in 1986, "that this step [Freud's rejection of the seduction theory] represented an advance in both theoretical and personal insight."[8]

In any case a Vienna that was reading Krafft-Ebing, Sulloway argues, would not have been shocked by Freud's revelations. Sulloway forgets, however, that Freud's sexual revelations raised and continue to raise more opposition than those of sexologists for at least two reasons. First, Freud uses abnormal cases to throw light on normal sexuality, thus involving us all. Second, his literary talent makes scientists suspicious of his methods and insures that his ideas will reach laymen and reach them at a depth to stir up their defenses. It is because Freud's intellect and imagination enable him to connect sexuality with every other aspect of life that people, quite justifiably, feel threatened. Freud's system-building genius makes him the begetter of the current sexual revolution, though he would hate its promotion of promiscuity and its mechanization of sex.

Freud was ready enough to acknowledge a debt for his early biophysics to Helmholtz and Brücke. He also repeatedly acknowledged a debt to Josef Breuer, his friend and collaborator on *Studies in Hysteria* (1895). Breuer discovered that hysterical symptoms can arise from unconscious ideas, and can be made to disappear through the "cathartic" method of allowing the patient to bring these ideas into consciousness by talking out his or her problems. Freud broke with Breuer when Breuer refused to support publicly Freud's conclusion that *all* cases of hysteria and, indeed, *all* psychoneuroses have a sexual cause. Contrary to the usual view that Breuer refused to accept the sexual cause of neurosis,

Sulloway demonstrates convincingly through quotations that Breuer accepted sexual causation but thought Freud went too far in *universalizing* the principle.

The real issue, argues Sulloway in trying to right the balance in favor of Breuer, was "Breuer's relative caution in matters scientific" (85). The real issue, it seems to me, is the difference between mediocrity and genius. It is in the nature of genius to search for the single law—one thinks of Newton, Darwin, Marx, Einstein. Sulloway paraphrases Freud to this effect: "To marry an idea, as Freud liked to say, was quite a different matter from recognizing it in passing" (76). "'They regard me,'" Freud complained, "'rather as a monomaniac'" on sexuality (86). Einstein, as I recall, suggested that only monomaniacs accomplish anything important. We have to fit into such an understanding of genius Freud's unattractive vindictiveness against Breuer and other erstwhile friends after a break over principles. Men of genius are often great haters, principles being more important to them than mere agreeableness.

Sulloway only half recognizes the issue between mediocrity and genius. Or why is he at such pains to justify Breuer? He vacillates curiously by speaking of Freud's "fanaticism" (89) about sexual causation, while admitting that the sexual principle gives mental illness the biological determinism he (Sulloway) approves of. Although Sulloway sets out to deflate the myth of the hero, he actually reconstitutes it by portraying Freud as heroic in temperament and achievement. He tells us that Freud's birth with a caul gave him the sense that he was singled out for a special destiny. And as a contrast to Breuer's caution, he quotes Freud's description of himself:

> I was always the *bold oppositionist,* always on hand when an extreme
> had to be defended. . . . I have often felt as though I had inherited all the
> defiance and all the passions with which our ancestors defended their
> Temple and could gladly sacrifice my life for one great moment of history.
> (86)

Even while insisting on Freud's scientific debts, Sulloway repeats that Freud's "conceptual transformations" of what he borrowed show his originality. If we recall that Shakespeare borrowed almost all his plots, we realize that it is not only "revolutionary advances in science" that consist of such "transformations" (474–75). In the end Sulloway surprisingly admits that "after all, Freud really was a hero. The myths are merely his historical due" (503).

Before arriving at this conclusion, Sulloway tries to minimize the amount of Freud's persecution in order to minimize the amount of his heroic resistance. He insists that the reviews of *The Interpretation of Dreams* were more numerous and favorable than is generally believed, and that anti-Semitism was not a serious problem for Freud. He argues unconvincingly that it was not anti-Semitism but a reduction in the number of positions that accounts for the protracted blocking of Freud's promotion at the university—this though men of lesser achievement were passed over him for those fewer positions. Anti-Semitism was in fact so widespread in the Vienna of the 1890s that a notorious anti-Semite, Karl Lueger, was elected mayor in 1895. The Emperor, says Carl E. Schorske in *Fin de Siècle Vienna* (1980), refused to confirm the election (the anti-monarchist Freud celebrated this autocratic veto), but two years later even the Emperor had to give way to the popular anti-Semitic tide. Freud begins his *Autobiographical Study* (1925) by alluding to the anti-Semitism he encountered as a university student, saying that it prepared him for "the fate of being in the Opposition and of being put under the ban of the 'compact majority'" (*SE*, 20:9)—for the role, in other words, by which he defined his heroic stance. As for reviews of *Interpretation of Dreams*, reviews containing mixed judgments always seem unfavorable to the author.

Although Clark, too, says that the hostility and anti-Semitism were not quite so implacable as Freud thought, he shows us a Freud so continuously embattled until 1914 that Sulloway's theory of a conspiracy to exaggerate the opposition to Freud seems absurd. Here is how Clark explains the ministry's steady rejections of the university's nominations of Freud for a professorship: "while a Jew" or "a man who saw sex at the root of most things" might have been approved, "the combination of both was too much for the authorities." Even when "in 1920 Freud was . . . at last made a full professor at the university, . . . it was not an appointment that gave him a seat on the board of the faculty."[9]

It is a sign of Freud's continuing obsession with anti-Semitism that he later fought to get Jung elected President of the International Psychoanalytical Association, because he thought he needed Jung and the Swiss to provide "Aryan" cover for what would otherwise seem a Jewish movement, and that he subsequently complained of Jung's "'anti-Semitic condescension towards me.'" As for opposition on professional grounds, Clark tells us that in turn-of-the-century Vienna Freud's name raised a laugh like a dirty joke and that medical circles dismissed him "as someone who could not be taken seriously" (243, 191). The letters to Fliess (1887–1904) record Freud's chagrin over the reception of his early psychoanalytic writings.

The issue of Freud's debt to biology hangs largely on our assessment of the influence on him of the Berlin nose specialist and biologist Wilhelm

Fliess, who replaced Breuer as Freud's confidant during the crucial years when Freud was laying the foundations of psychoanalysis. Fliess belonged to the same Jewish professional middle class as Freud and Breuer; he was introduced to Freud by Breur. They exchanged letters and manuscripts and met at intervals for intense conversational sessions which Freud called "congresses." A selection of Freud's side of the correspondence (Freud destroyed or lost Fliess's letters) was published in 1954 under the title *The Origins of Psychoanalysis*, a fascinating, revealing book despite the editors' censorship of the original documents. We now have *The Complete Letters*, edited by Jeffrey Moussaieff Masson (1985), based on a new and presumably more correct German text; I will cite the letters from this text.

Since Freud's break with Fliess was even bitterer than his break with Breuer, involving an ugly dispute over who thought of what first, Freud and his disciples have, according to Sulloway, minimized the importance of Fliess's influence on Freud. Jones, Ernst Kris in his introduction to *Origins of Psychoanalysis*, and even Clark insist that during Freud's most creative and neurotic years Fliess fulfilled a psychological need that made Freud overrate him intellectually—especially since Freud required from Fliess biological confirmation of his emerging psychoanalytic theories. But Sulloway proves convincingly through quotations that Fliess combined biology and psychology in just Freud's way; so that far from being, as Jones puts it, "a drag on Freud's painful progress from physiology to psychology" (1:300), Fliess helped Freud forge those links between the two disciplines that were to emerge as psychoanalysis.

Fliess drew a connection between nose and genitals which was psychoanalytic, since smell is the primary sexual stimulant among mammals and since Fliess successfully analyzed certain nasal disturbances—including Freud's—as neurotic. Fliess is responsible for the importance Freud gave smell as the most repressed sense. Also psychoanalytic is Fliess's theory that we are all constitutionally bisexual and his theory of periodicity—that males are governed by a twenty-three-day cycle equivalent to the female twenty-eight-day menstrual cycle, that our lives are governed by cycles accordant with the tides and moon. Both men took seriously Darwin's tantalizing suggestion that human beings are descended from a bisexual, tide-dwelling marine animal whose feeding and reproductive habits depended on changes of tides and moon. (What a poem on life's rhythms might be made out of that suggestion!) Fliess was as Darwinian in his thinking and as imaginatively speculative as Freud; Freud called him "an even greater fantasist than I am." [10]

They began to differ when Fliess suggested that the appearance and disappearance of neuroses might have more to do with periods than with pathology and therapy, and when Fliess began juggling numbers to con-

struct a pseudomathematical system by which he claimed he could predict crucial events in people's lives, including their death dates. At this
point each began to feel that the other disapproved of his work—Fliess
that Freud disapproved of his numbers, Freud that Fliess considered his
work unscientific. In a letter of 19 September 1901, Freud tries to answer
Fliess's accusations: "You know that I lack any mathematical talent
whatsoever. . . . Perhaps you have been too quick to give up on me as a
confidant." He goes on to accuse Fliess:

> You are ready to agree that the "reader of thoughts" perceives nothing in
> the other, but merely projects his own thoughts, you really no longer are
> my audience either and must regard my entire method of working as
> being just as worthless as the others do. (450)

If the difference between Freud and Breuer was the difference between genius and mediocrity, the difference between Freud and Fliess was
the difference between genius and pseudogenius—a difference more easily distinguishable by final results than by the freewheeling, speculative
quality common to both types of mind. Freud himself barely evaded
crackpottery throughout his career; and he always liked to have a speculative friend (later it was Ferenczi) on whom he could try out his wilder
surmises. The genius, whether artist or scientist, must, if he is to stay alive
intellectually, keep himself open to nonsense; for the innovations and discoveries of genius often look at first *like* nonsense. The fact that Fliess's
ideas later rigidified into actual nonsense does not invalidate their earlier
speculative phase.

The friendship with Fliess was fruitful for Freud because of the concepts which Jones admits he got from Fliess—bisexuality, latency period,
sublimation—and because Fliess encouraged Freud's imaginative powers. The letters to Fliess contain passages that might have been written
by a romantic poet—this one, for example, of 3 December 1897:

> Every now and then ideas dart through my head which promise to realize
> everything, apparently connecting the normal and the pathological, the
> sexual and the psychological problem, and then they are gone again and I
> make no effort to hold onto them because I indeed know that neither
> their disappearance nor their appearance in consciousness is the real
> expression of their fate. On such quiet days as yesterday and today, how-
> ever, everything in me is very quiet, terribly lonely. I cannot talk about it
> to anyone, nor can I force myself to work, deliberately and voluntarily as
> other workers can. I must wait until something stirs in me and I become
> aware of it. And so I often dream whole days away. (284)

It was because the friendship ran so deep and may have contained, as Freud suspected, "some pieces of unruly homosexual feeling," that Fliess was involved in the famous self-analysis during which Freud discovered his hostility to his father and thus the Oedipus complex. Their emotional involvement explains why the break between them was so ugly that Freud evolved his theory of paranoia from Fliess's behavior. But Freud's own behavior in their priority dispute was not attractive; and he may have deceived himself in saying in a letter of 1910 to Ferenczi that in his case "a part of homosexual cathexis has been withdrawn and made use of to enlarge my own ego. I have succeeded where the paranoiac fails" (*Letters*, 3n).

Sulloway charges that Freud and his disciples have concealed Fliess's priority in the discovery of infantile sexuality, that Fliess was writing about infantile polymorphous sexuality at a time when Freud still believed in the seduction theory and therefore in childhood asexuality, since it was only after puberty that the memory of childhood seductions supposedly became meaningful and caused neurosis. When Freud came to realize that many of his patients' stories of childhood seduction by parents were fantasies that revealed their infantile sexual desire for a parent, he was on the way to discovering the Oedipus complex. Sulloway quotes a passage Fliess published in 1897—just before Freud's abandonment of the seduction theory—which, with its interest in infantile sexuality and in etymologies, might have been written by Freud. Fliess suggests that the word "sweet" is in many languages formed by the motion the lips make in sucking:

> The sucking movements that small children make with their lips and tongue . . . as well as thumb-sucking, must be considered as an equivalent of masturbation. . . . The role which the word "sweet" [*süss*] later plays in the language of love has its initial physiological root here. With lips and tongue the child first tastes lactose [*Milchzucker*] at his mother's breast, and they provide him with his earliest experience of satisfaction. "Sweet" [*süss*] is related to the French *sucer* (to suck) and to *Zucker, suggar, sugere.* (73–74)

The discussion of Fliess's influence on Freud is Sulloway's most interesting and persuasive section. But Freud's debt to Fliess as well as to Breuer, the sexologists, and Darwin does not—as Sulloway argues—disprove, it rather proves Freud's genius and originality. For supreme genius, I would add, is never eccentric; it rides the main stream of its age, combining and transforming the age's truths in such a way as to make them accessible to the future. Shakespeare, for example, made standard Elizabethan ideas and theater conventions accessible to the future as the other Elizabethan dramatists could not.

Darwin's case is analogous to Freud's. For Darwin drew on a rich store of evolutionary theory; and his contribution, the idea of natural selection, was conceived independently by Alfred Russel Wallace. Yet Wallace, as he himself admitted, had not the genius to give the idea the world-shaking impact that Darwin gave it by working out all its ramifications. For one thing it was Darwin who coined the term "natural selection," and the ability to coin illuminating terms is a sign of genius. The difference between the two men appears in the papers by which they announced at the same scientific meeting their coincidental discovery. Wallace writes about natural selection without using the term; and he did not see, as did Darwin, that its principles could be derived from the breeding of domestic plants and animals for desirable qualities (the term "natural selection" derived from analogy with artificial selection). Instead, Wallace writes: "what applies to the one [domestic animals] is almost sure not to apply to the other [wild animals]." [11] The ability to see ever wider connections is another sign of genius.

Since Sulloway gives so much attention to Freud's breaks with Breuer and Fliess, it is surprising that he says so little about the main rupture in Freud's life—the break with Carl Jung, the brilliant Swiss psychiatrist whom he had chosen as his successor. Sulloway's neglect is all the more surprising since Jung's objection to Freud's emphasis on sexuality parallels the current attacks on sociobiology as destructive of all that distinguishes humans from animals. At their first meeting in 1907, Jung—Clark tells us in his detailed account of Freud's relations with Jung—already had reservations: "I could not swallow his so-called science positivism, his merely rational view of the psyche and his materialistic point of view." Later Jung complained that "wherever, in a person or in a work of art, an expression of spirituality (in the intellectual, not the supernatural sense) came to light, he suspected it, and insinuated that it was repressed sexuality" (240–41). This Jung argued—as do the opponents of sociobiology—devaluated culture as no more than a pathological consequence of repressed sexuality.

Sulloway does, however, quote, at greater length than Clark, Jung's account of a conversation with Freud from which one can infer why Freud insisted on the sexual cause of neurosis.

> I can still recall vividly how Freud said to me, "My dear Jung, promise me never to abandon the sexual theory. That is the most essential thing of all. You see, we must make a dogma of it, an unshakable bulwark." He said that to me with great emotion . . . In some astonishment I asked him,

"A bulwark—against what?" To which he replied, "Against the black tide of mud"—and here he hesitated for a moment, then added—"of occultism." (362)

Jung suggests that the sexual theory derived from some peculiar emotional need of Freud's. But Freud's admonition is from his point of view logically sound. For Freud the sexual theory was a guarantee that the "unconscious" would not turn into another word for soul, that it would not be divorced from body. Early in his career, in the unpublished "Project for a Scientific Psychology," he tried to construct a psychology entirely derived from physiological functions. He failed. But he never ceased to feel that psychology was but a name for what we still do not know about biology. "The deficiencies in our description [of mind]," he wrote as late as 1920, in *Beyond the Pleasure Principle,*

> would probably vanish if we were already in a position to replace the psychological terms by physiological or chemical ones. . . . Biology is truly a land of unlimited possibilities. We may expect it to give us the most surprising information and we cannot guess what answers it will return in a few dozen years to the questions we have put to it. (*SE,* 18:60)

The Jungian system did in fact turn the unconscious into soul, and did in fact retreat beyond Cartesian to Christian dualism and to a renewed support for religion, mysticism, occultism. By deriving neuroses from sexuality merged with memory, Freud was doing what Wordsworth did in deriving imaginative experiences from physical sensation merged with memory. Freud was reaffirming a monism that is scientific, romantic, and to some extent Jewish and anti-ascetic (as compared to Christian dualism)—a monism that makes Freud, with his new way of connecting body to mind through the unconscious, the link between the romanticism and Darwinian biology that precede him and the sociobiology that follows him.

Can We Still Talk about the Romantic Self?

I ask the above question because the latest theoretical criticism has all but wiped out the self as a legitimate subject for literary discourse. It therefore becomes necessary to see if we can justify a forum such as this one, which presumes to discuss the self in its most blatant manifestation—the romantic self or ego.*

The attack on the self as an attack on the manifestation of the author's self in his work is not of course new. It began with Flaubert and Mallarmé. Most of the literary modernists, taking their cue from these two formidable Frenchmen, advocated an impersonal literature into which the author's life and personality do not intrude. Their advocacy, however, turns out to have been more theoretical than practical, in that so many modernist classics are in fact thinly veiled autobiographies—Proust's *A la recherche du temps perdu,* Lawrence's *Sons and Lovers,* Joyce's *Portrait of the Artist as a Young Man* and *Ulysses.* T. S. Eliot, the most eloquent advocate of an impersonal poetry, traces through his principal poems a story of autobiographical development from disbelief and despair to Christian faith which corresponds to the development traced in Wordsworth's principal poems from political radicalism to pantheism to Christianity. To be properly understood, the poems of both poets must be read in chronological order and with reference to real men named William Wordsworth and Thomas Stearns Eliot.

Samuel Beckett, especially in his novels, comes closest to fulfilling the prescriptions for impersonality of the modernists and the contemporary theoretical critics. Beckett is apparently absent from his novels

* This essay is a revised and expanded version of a paper read for the session, "The Romantic Ego," at the Modern Language Association meeting on 29 December 1984.

(though he seems less absent as we learn more about his life), and his featureless characters are little more than vehicles of an endless discourse; it is only through speaking that they know they are alive: "I'm in words, made of words," says the voice in *The Unnamable*.[1] The French theorist Michel Foucault ends the essay I will discuss, "What Is an Author?" by paraphrasing Beckett: "What difference does it make who is speaking?"[2] You could not find a question that annihilates more smashingly the topic of the romantic self.

The New Critics, those followers of Eliot who dominated Anglo-American criticism during the 1940s and 1950s, anticipated many of the principles of the contemporary theoreticians. The New Critics made us sophisticated enough to distinguish between the poet as man and the speaker of his first-person poems, whom we understood to be an artistic construct usefully referred to as a *persona* and not as Wordsworth or Keats. The New Critics subordinated (they did not ignore) outside information about the poet's life, ideas and historical period to the evidence of the text itself. They believed that the attempt to fathom the author's intention, called the "Intentional Fallacy," could be irrelevant or downright misleading. A favorite pedagogical game of the time was to give students poems to analyze without the authors' names, in the naive belief that the text tells us all we need to know. In *Practical Criticism* (1929), I. A. Richards, a founder of the New Criticism, reported the results of such an experiment; most of his Cambridge students misread and misevaluated the poems. The truth is that to omit the author's name is like omitting the poem's first two lines. The author's name is part of what the poem is saying, while awareness of his period in literary history indicates the conventions by which his poem is to be read. Foucault confirms this truth by showing that what he calls the "author-*function*," as distinguished from the author, is a principle *within* the text.

The New Critics, however, did not make a metaphysical attack on the author's selfhood. They believed that the author as author had an existence outside the text but that he ought deliberately to exclude signs of himself from it. The metaphysical attack begins with Heidegger in, for example, "The Origin of the Work of Art" (1960):

> On the usual view, the work arises out of and by means of the activity of the artist. But by what and whence is the artist what he is? By the work . . . it is the work that first lets the artist emerge as a master of his art. The artist is the origin of the work. The work is the origin of the artist. Neither is without the other.[3]

This is still a sensible position with which we can easily agree. It is less easy to agree with Foucault's complete effacement of the authorial self when he says, in his characteristically brilliant shocking manner, that "the author does not precede the works," that he comes into being only as we read, that the "author-function" is a *way* of reading (159). Surely a person, to create the kind of text we call literary, must begin by thinking of him or herself as an author, or, more complexly, must cease while writing to be the person friends know, having donned, in Yeats's words, the authorial mask.

The attack on the self in literature from Eliot through the New Critics to the theoretical critics is always understood to be a reaction against romanticism. Indeed, the self would not be an issue in literary discussion were it not for the romanticists. That is because the romanticists were the first literary generation to regard the self as problematical. They asserted the self so extravagantly in order to answer an attack on the self almost as devastating as the attack launched by the theoretical critics and their philosophical forebears, Husserl and Heidegger. The romanticists faced the attack on the self by Locke and the even more radical attack by Hume, who wrote: We "are nothing but a bundle or collection of different perceptions, which succeed each other with an inconceivable rapidity, and are in a perpetual flux and movement." We arrive at the sense of self through error, through the process of association; and in order to justify this absurdity, says Hume, "we feign the continu'd existence of the perception of our senses, to remove the interruption," or we imagine "something unknown and mysterious, connecting the parts," and thus "run into the notion of a *soul,* and *self* . . . to disguise the variation."[4] That "something unknown and mysterious, connecting the parts," will be aggressively asserted as the romantic self, what the deconstructionist critic Paul de Man, in "The Rhetoric of Temporality," calls "the mystified self."[5]

It was against such formidable attacks as Hume's, which explained their own experiences of diminished self, that the romanticists reconstructed the validity of the self on *new* grounds—grounds not deriving from the self's creation by God, the grounds under attack. Wordsworth's reply is the most philosophical in verse; for he begins by insisting that the mind is part of nature and therefore fitted to perceive the external world, just as a plant is fitted to receive sunshine and rain. Every genuine experience of the external world is thus a new validation of the integrity of the perceiving mind. To Descartes' "I think therefore I am," the romanticists added, "I *experience* therefore I am," thus including thinking in a larger awareness of bodily sensations and the external physical world. This larger awareness bridges the gap bequeathed by Descartes between mind and matter.

In "Tintern Abbey" and elsewhere Wordsworth blends thought, sensation and emotion as inseparable phases of a single biological process:

sensations sweet,

Felt in the blood, and felt along the heart;
And passing even into my purer mind.[6]

And in *The Prelude* he shows how every deep experience is assimilated into a continuously evolving self which transforms the quality of that experience. After describing a particularly frightening childhood experience, Wordsworth reflects, as though answering Hume on the self's discontinuity:

there is a dark

Inscrutable workmanship that reconciles
Discordant elements, makes them cling together
In one society. How strange that all
The terrors, pains, and early miseries,
Regrets, vexations, lassitudes interfused
Within my mind, should e'er have borne a part,
And that a needful part, in making up
The calm existence that is mine when I
Am worthy of myself!

(1.341–50)

Disparate experiences are reconciled and given value by the self to whose evolution they contribute.

In Book 14 we find the ultimate valorization of self. The perceiving mind has just been apotheosized as imagination. "Such minds," we are told,

are truly from the Deity,

For they are Powers; and hence the highest bliss
That flesh can know is theirs—the consciousness
Of *Whom they are,* habitually infused
Through every image and through every thought,
And all affections.

(14.112–17, my italics)

"Through every image" means through all they *see,* and their affections are for the external *physical* world. This is important in understanding how "the consciousness / Of Whom they are" informs and gives value to experience, which is why that consciousness of self is the highest spiritual achievement. "Such minds are truly from the Deity," not primarily in the Christian sense, but mainly because "they are *Powers*"—because they have validated *themselves* and therefore share in divinity. This new insight confirms, as we see at the end of *The Prelude,* the Christian view of soul.

Byron is less interested than Wordsworth in the epistemological validation of self. He is more interested in declaring the self's moral autonomy, its independence of any external system of rewards and punishments. He makes Manfred say:

> The mind which is immortal makes itself
> Requital for its good or evil thoughts,—
> Is its own origin of ill and end—
> And its own place and time.[7]

The reaction against romantic subjectivism which began with the Victorians, in Arnold's criticism for example, and continued into the twentieth century with Eliot and the New Critics, turns into thorough rejection in the philosophy of Heidegger and in the criticism of his followers, the theorists. Heidegger's attack on "metaphysics" is an attack on the Western world-picture since Plato, on an organization of reality according to which subjectivity is set off against objectivity with language the mediator between the two. Heidegger replaces the subject-object split and the "mystified self" with his even more mystifying concept of *Dasein* or "being there," a condition manifested in language. "Language," he writes in "Letter on Humanism," is "the house of Being. In its home man dwells" (*Basic Writings,* 193).

To try to understand how language protects us against the subject-object split, we must recall Heidegger's remark "*Die Sprache spricht*" or "Language speaks." In the essay "Language" (1950), in which this remark is often reiterated, he explains oracularly that the view of language as expression

> already presupposes the idea of something internal that utters or externalizes itself. If we take language to be utterance, we give an external, surface notion of it at the very moment when we explain it by recourse to something internal.

If in the usual way we say, "man speaks," then we cannot say, "language speaks," for to say the latter is to say: "It is language that first brings man about, brings him into existence"[8]—the implication being that our thoughts and feelings and therefore our humanity do not come into being until they are articulated according to the preestablished channels of language from which they emerge not as our thoughts and feelings but as language. We are asked to conceive of the self as a series of states and sentences but not as something that *has* those states and sentences.

In "Language" Heidegger admits that the commonsense views of language are pragmatically right, but "despite their antiquity and despite their comprehensibility, they never bring us to language as language" (193). Where does language speak? In poetry. Heidegger quotes a symbolist poem by Trakl and reads it, in the Mallarméan manner, as though it had no author.

> As the calling that names things calls here and there, so the saying that names the world calls into itself, calling here and there. It entrusts the world to the things and simultaneously keeps the things in the splendor of the world. The world grants to things their presence. Things bear world. World grants things. (201–2)

Heidegger's later thought seems to have become aesthetic, deriving from symbolist poetics. The epiphanic mode of romantic and symbolist poetry provides the imagery for Heidegger's notion of language as "the home that preserves the ecstatic for [man's] essence. Such standing in the lighting of Being I call the ek-sistence of man" (*Basic Writings*, 204). In "The Thinker as Poet" (1954), he writes:

> Only image formed keeps the vision.
> Yet image formed rests in the poem.

In "The Thing" (1950), he distinguishes between the metaphysical-scientific "object" and the artistic "thing." His notion of the thing sounds symbolist or imagist, except that the thing's thinginess does not derive from an observer: it is rather "the made thing's standing forth into the unconcealedness of what is already present" (*Poetry, Language, Thought*, 7, 168).

Just as Heidegger sinks the self in language and the author in his text, so do his followers, the theoretical critics. I shall take as brilliant examples of the author's effacement two essays I have already cited, Foucault's "What Is an Author?" and de Man's "The Rhetoric of Temporality." In "What Is an Author?" Foucault begins by asserting that the idea of the author is a recent invention, already on the way out: "The coming into being of the notion of 'author' constitutes the privileged moment of *individualization* in the history of ideas" (141). To understand that the effacement of the author implies the effacement of the self, we must realize that this statement is a special application of the statement in Foucault's preface to *The Order of Things* that it is "a source of profound relief to think that man is only a recent invention, a figure not yet two centuries old, a new wrinkle in our knowledge, and that he will disappear again as soon as that knowledge has discovered a new form." [9] By "man," as he explains in the penultimate chapter, Foucault means individualized man whose ego is "contained within his organism, inside the shell of his head," as contrasted to the traditional "human being" whose selfhood derived from his appointed place in the external order of things (318). In "What Is an Author?" Foucault continues as follows:

> It would be worth examining how the author became individualized in a culture like ours, . . . in what kind of system of valorization the author was involved, at what point we began to recount the lives of authors rather than of heroes. . . . I want to deal solely with the relationship between text and author and with the manner in which the text points to this "figure" that, at least in appearance, is outside it and antecedes it. Beckett nicely formulates the theme with which I would like to begin: "'What does it matter who is speaking. . . .'" In this indifference appears one of the fundamental ethical principles of contemporary writing. (141)

Contemporary writing, in other words, as opposed to romantic writing, anticipates an antihumanist future to which Foucault looks forward eagerly, but which makes most of us shudder. "As our society changes," he concludes, "the author-function will disappear, and in such a manner that fiction and its polysemic texts will once again function according to another mode, but still with a system of constraint—one which will no longer be the author, but which will have to be determined or, perhaps, experienced." The principle of order would no longer derive from a text interpreted as the expression of a single subjectivity.

> We would no longer hear the questions that have been rehashed for so long: "Who really spoke? Is it really he and not someone else? With what authenticity or originality? And what part of his deepest self did he express in his discourse?" Instead, there would be other questions, like these: "What are the modes of existence of this discourse? Where has it been used, and how can it circulate, and who can appropriate it for himself? What are the places in it where there is room for possible subjects? Who can assume these various subject-functions?" And behind all these questions, we would hear hardly anything but the stirring of an indifference: "What difference does it make who is speaking?" (160)

One wonders why the "indifferent" future would be looking for "subject-functions."

The last question, "What difference does it make who is speaking?" reverses Foucault's description in *The Order of Things* of Nietzsche's psychological relativism: "For Nietzsche, it was not a matter of knowing what good and evil were in themselves, but of . . . *who was speaking*"

(305). Nietzsche's psychological relativism explains such romantic I-centered poetic forms as the dramatic lyric and the dramatic monologue. Foucault traces the reaction against such romantic I-centeredness when he continues, "To the Nietzschean question: 'Who is speaking?,' Mallarmé replies . . . the word itself—not the meaning of the word, but its enigmatic and precarious being" (305).

In "What Is an Author?" Foucault argues that the "author-function" resides strictly *within* the text, giving it a special organization and status: "In a civilization like our own there are a certain number of discourses that are endowed with the 'author-function,' while others are deprived of it. A private letter may well have a signer—it does not have an author" (148). Unless, I would add, the letter writer is already an "author," in which case we presumably find in it the author-function and publish his letters as part of his complete works. Foucault's concept of the author-function is useful in that it leads us to reexamine our concept of the oeuvre or literary work. What would we include in an author's complete works? Certainly his letters, probably his notebooks and marginalia inasmuch as they relate to his authorial writing, certainly not his laundry lists and checks. Yet the checks may be most important of all in the person's life. The author-function is a principle within the text that gives it a privileged status, qualifying it for inclusion in an author's oeuvre.

All this implies an attack on the romantic notion of the author as the person outside, who precedes the poem or novel and creates it by letting his or her excess vitality, his or her experiences or powerful feelings, overflow into it. A poet, says Wordsworth in the Preface to *Lyrical Ballads,* "is a man speaking to men: a man, it is true, endowed with more lively sensibility, more enthusiasm and tenderness . . . than are supposed to be common among mankind." "All good poetry," he says, "is the spontaneous overflow of powerful feelings" (453, 448).

To show that the romantic self is already on the way out, Foucault writes:

> Today's writing has freed itself from the dimension of expression. Referring only to itself, [it creates] a space into which the writing subject constantly disappears. . . . The work, which once had the duty of providing immortality, now possesses the right to kill, to be its author's murderer, as in the cases of Flaubert, Proust, and Kafka. . . . This relationship between writing and death is also manifested in the effacement of the writing subject's individual characteristics. (142)

Dramatic words like "kill" and "murderer" yield an irresistible modernist pathos—the pathos of the author dying into his work. We have heard many such author-killing statements since Flaubert and Mallarmé; but they cannot, as I have already suggested, be applied to many modern authors. Certainly Marcel Proust is a bad example for Foucault's argument. Not only has Proust, like Flaubert and Kafka, gained personal immortality from his writing, but we know through his novel, in which the first-person narrator is called Marcel, more about his "individual characteristics" than about those of almost any other writer you could name, including the romanticists. All these autobiographical writings refer to publicly available legends of their authors' lives, which are artistic constructs peripheral to their texts—constructs which go on developing even after their deaths. The fact that Foucault reaches as far back into the nineteenth century as Flaubert for an example of "today's writing" shows that he is attacking the romantic self.

Common sense rejects Foucault's most striking statement: "The author does not precede the works, he is a certain functional principle by which, in our culture, one limits, excludes, and chooses" (159). Now we all know, and M. Foucault knew, that the person who writes the work must necessarily precede it and must think of himself as an author before beginning to write and while writing; that is why he puts into the text the "author-function" that readers perceive. But if we play temporarily Foucault's metaphysical game, we can learn a good deal about reading.

We can understand, for example, the illuminating statement that those

> aspects of an individual which we designate as making him an author are only a projection, in more or less psychologizing terms, of the operations that we force texts to undergo, the connections that we make, the traits that we establish as pertinent, the continuities that we recognize, or the exclusions that we practice. (150)

We can understand his valuable remarks that "the author's name is not . . . just a proper name like the rest," that it characterizes "a certain mode of being of discourse," conferring "a certain status." He defines the author, quite brilliantly, as "the principle of thrift in the proliferation of meaning" (146–47, 159). It is true that if we see the name Wordsworth on a poem, we know in advance that certain meanings are excluded. We will not read that the city is better than the country, that art is better than nature, that insincerity is better than sincerity—we will not read the kinds of things we expect when we see the name Oscar Wilde at the head of a text. Paradoxically, however, one of the meanings excluded by the name Wordsworth is just Foucault's definition of the author as "the principle of thrift in the proliferation of meaning." And one of the meanings included is the definition Foucault rejects—the definition of the author as "the genial creator of a work in which he deposits, with infinite wealth and generosity, an inexhaustible world of significations" (159).

For it is the *art* of romantic poetry to suggest "an inexhaustible world of significations." This is especially true of dramatic lyrics, of those "placed poems," like "Tintern Abbey," "Frost at Midnight," "Mont Blanc," "Ode to a Nightingale," in which a poet, whom we associate with Wordsworth, Coleridge, Shelley, Keats, seems to make the poem before our eyes by projecting himself into a natural object through a dialogue with it. The dramatic lyric, a specifically romantic innovation, specializes in evoking an infinite suggestiveness which is in the romantic sense symbolic.

The word *symbolic* leads me to Paul de Man's essay "The Rhetoric of Temporality," in which he argues for an inversion of the romantic and modernist preference for symbol over allegory. De Man prefers allegory, because symbol relies on the romantic projective self to unite subject and object and to establish a continuity between experience and its representation in language. Allegory, instead, "suggests a disjunction between the way in which the world appears in reality and the way it appears in language" (191).

De Man makes a similar point in the key essay of *Blindness and Insight*, "The Rhetoric of Blindness," in which he says that

> the status of Rousseau's language is not to be found in his consciousness, in his greater or lesser awareness or control over the cognitive value of his language. It can only be found in the knowledge that this language, as language, conveys about itself, thereby asserting the priority of the category of language over that of presence [the author's and his intuition of reality]—which is precisely Derrida's thesis. (119)

He makes the point again in a later essay, "Shelley Disfigured," where he interprets the shape of light that comes and goes in Shelley's *The Triumph of Life*

> as the model of figuration in general. By taking this step beyond the traditional conceptions of figuration as modes of representation, as polarities of subject and object . . . the way is prepared for the subsequent undoing and erasure of the figure.[10]

We are left in the position proper to allegory, with no continuum between the thing seen and its meaning. "The figure is not naturally given or produced"; its "signification . . . is posited by an arbitrary act of language" (62). The position is opposite to the one described in Coleridge's great remark that "a Symbol . . . always partakes of the Reality which it renders intelligible".[11]

In "The Rhetoric of Temporality," de Man uses the symbol-generating dramatic lyric as a prime example of what is wrong with romantic symbol and its interpreters. "Anglo-American criticism," he says, uses "the symbol as the unit of language in which the subject-object synthesis can take place." The symbol therefore requires a "mystified self" as the synthesizing force (*Blindness & Insight,* 199–200). The romantic self can withstand de Man's criticism, because it was originally asserted against such attacks—Hume's for example: in order to justify this absurdity, the sense of self, we imagine "something unknown and mysterious, connecting the parts."

De Man argues that we have been misreading romantic dramatic lyrics, that they are to be read allegorically. The much touted specific place of romantic poems ("a few miles above Tintern Abbey") turns out through "spatial ambiguities" to be an allegorical place; and the early romanticists, in a "negative moment" ("in Wordsworth that of the loss of self in death or in error"), actually renounced the projective self, opening the way for allegory which "prevents the self from an illusory identification with the non-self, which is now fully, though painfully, recognized as a non-self" (206–7).

The flaw in this brilliant argument is that de Man is simply not describing the story of these romantic dramatic lyrics, the speakers of which do not in the least want to renounce what de Man calls "the desire to coincide" with the nonself (207). I can think of no instance where Wordsworth renounces this desire. In the poem de Man analyzes, "A Slumber Did My Spirit Seal," the dead girl is so completely merged in the rolling life of nature ("Rolled round in earth's diurnal course / With rocks, and stones, and trees") that she need no longer willfully make the identification. In the first stanza the poet says that in his failure of vision he had thought the girl immortal, beyond "the touch of earthly years," but now that she is dead (in the second stanza) he realizes that she is immortal in a sense he had not foreseen, through merger with the earth—the agent, in the first stanza, of mortality. It is significant that the girl is a "thing" in the first stanza where she is alive, but a "she" in the second stanza where she is dead and apparently inanimate.

Coleridge, it is true, in "Dejection," despairs that he can no longer coincide with the nonself, with nature. But this is no voluntary renunciation; it is a disability resulting from loss of inner vitality:

> Ah! from the soul itself must issue forth
> A light, a glory, a fair luminous cloud
> Enveloping the Earth.[12]

The romanticists were not babies; they knew perfectly well that the self is different from the nonself. But they also knew from experience that the imagination operates by merging the two in an alliance in which the distinction is not lost but bridged—temporarily.

As for place in romantic dramatic lyrics its specification in the title or subtitle or in the poet's legend is, like the author's name, part of what the poem is saying. Readers have always understood the importance of romantic place specification; hence all the literary pilgrimages to the very place where the poet had the experience and even seems to have composed the poem. Hardy thought it necessary to visit Leghorn where Shelley saw his skylark, as though there were a guarantee he would see another such skylark there. Hardy's placed poem "Shelley's Skylark" both criticizes and praises Shelley's "To a Skylark." Wordsworth's "Lines Composed a Few Miles above Tintern Abbey" has nothing to do with the Abbey, which is not mentioned in the text. Nor does the poem indicate that the Abbey is in view. Tintern Abbey is named in the title only to locate the poem.

In *The Prelude* Wordsworth says that his experiences have been objectified in specific places: "The sands of Westmoreland, the creeks and bays / Of Cumbria's rocky limits, they can tell" of the experiences I had there (1.567–68). These specific places remain sacramentalized (Geoffrey Hartman describes Wordsworth's obsession with the "spirit of place . . . familiar to archaic religion")[13] like the biblical places where Abraham sojourned.

If we return now to my original question, whether we can still talk about the romantic self in the face of all the recent and not so recent attacks on it, I would answer that we can and should talk about the romantic self for several reasons. We should talk about it, first (here de Man would have accused me of mere historicizing), because it really existed for the romanticists and their readers; so whatever we believe now (de Man notwithstanding), there is no way of talking convincingly about romantic poetry without talking about the selfhood that gives it validity. In addition, the romantic self remains valid even today for those who feel it in themselves or are at least attuned to it as readers of nineteenth and even twentieth-century romantic writing (Lawrence's, for example). The romantic self remains valid because it came into being as a reaction against attacks on the self almost as devastating as today's attacks, and thus contains a protection against such attacks. Twentieth-century writers—as I suggest in the previous essay and elsewhere in this volume—have made the romantic self more ruggedly substantial by working into it ideas of unconsciousness and primitive instincts derived from Darwin and Freud.

Even more important, we should go on talking about the romantic self as a necessary critique of current philosophy and criticism. If it is not presumptuous to say so, I find myself of Nietzsche's mind when he says that it matters less to know what good and evil are in themselves than to know *who is speaking*. Having lived long enough to see several intellectual fashions come and go, I find myself less interested in the truth or falsity of propositions than in the question of *who is speaking* and why the speaker wants to believe such a proposition. Thus I wonder why so many of our most brilliant and articulate writers take such savage delight in sinking the self in its own creations—in sinking humanity in the language it created, in sinking the author in the text he or she created. This seems to me a kind of idolatry. We have come full circle from Blake's declaration in *The Marriage of Heaven and Hell* that "All deities reside in the human breast." The romanticists knew they were stamping their image on the external world, but they never lost sight of the self that did the stamping.

Finally, why do so many professors nowadays like to shock each other by declaring their "antihumanism"? Surely they are playing games. I know many of these professors—some are friends—and I suspect that their sense of themselves does not differ radically from my sense of myself. I also suspect that they would no more than I desire the state of things that would come to pass should they and the rest of us take their declarations seriously. For if you deprive the individual of the sense of his own sovereignty, you take away his last protection against the state, you prepare the way for a totalitarian society—not I am sure what any of us desires.

The Epiphanic Mode in Wordsworth and Modern Literature

WHEN Hazlitt in *The Spirit of the Age* said that Wordsworth had made poetry democratic, had taken it off stilts, he put his finger on Wordsworth's essential contribution to modern poetry. "Mr. Wordsworth's genius," says Hazlitt speaking with the authority of a contemporary,

> is a pure emanation of the Spirit of the Age. Had he lived in any other period of the world, he would never have been heard of. . . . His homely Muse can hardly raise her wing from the ground. . . . He has "no figures nor no fantasies," . . . neither the gorgeous machinery of mythologic lore, nor the splendid colors of poetic diction. His style is vernacular: he delivers household truths. He sees nothing loftier than human hopes; nothing deeper than the human heart. . . . He takes the simplest elements of nature and of the human mind, . . . and tries to compound a new system of poetry from them.

"It is," Hazlitt comments, "one of the innovations of the time. It partakes of, and is carried along with," he says thinking of the French Revolution,

> the revolutionary movement of our age: the political changes of the day were the model on which he formed and conducted his poetical experiments. *His Muse . . . is a levelling one.* It proceeds on a principle of equality, and strives to reduce all things to the same standard. It is distinguished by a proud humility. . . . Hence the unaccountable mixture of seeming simplicity and real abstruseness in the *Lyrical Ballads.* Fools have laughed at, wise men scarcely understand them.[1]

Hazlitt explains the innovations of *Lyrical Ballads*—the point of which, as indicated in the Preface, is this: that poetry is not determined by a formal structure, by meter or rhyme, nor by a special kind of subject matter and language. Poetry, in other words, is determined not by external signs but by a kind of mental operation that Wordsworth and Coleridge called "imagination." Imagination is democratic because it can turn any subject matter poetic through intensification and transformation. Imagination operates best through a plain style that allows intensification to take place, that does not rely on the artificial elevation of rhetoric. It operates best on realistic material that requires transformation, and helps us believe that the transformation really does take place.

What we have here is a magic realism—the *natural supernaturalism* of the plan according to which Wordsworth and Coleridge cooperated on *Lyrical Ballads*. According to the plan as Coleridge describes it in *Biographia Literaria* (chap. 14), Wordsworth was to choose subjects from "ordinary life" and excite in us "a feeling analogous to the supernatural" by lifting "the film of familiarity" from our eyes. Coleridge was to start with supernatural or partly supernatural incidents or characters and make them seem natural through the psychological truth of the emotions involved. The final effect of both kinds of poems would be both natural and supernatural or, in other words, *imaginative.*

The plan for *Lyrical Ballads* suggests that imagination operates most obviously and effectively within a new realistic mode that Wordsworth in *The Prelude* called "spots of time" and that Joyce a century later called "epiphanies." I take over Joyce's term in order to show the long-range significance of Wordsworth's innovation, which has influenced not only poetry but also modern fiction, especially the modern short story. My purpose is not merely to show that epiphanies exist in romantic and modern literature. I argued this in *The Poetry of Experience* (1957), and the connection is by now generally accepted—see, for example, Morris Beja, *Epiphany in the Modern Novel* (1971), and M. H. Abrams, *Natural Supernaturalism* (1971, 385–427). My purpose is to do what has not yet been done: to examine the *structure* of epiphany, to analyze the ways in which the various kinds of epiphany operate so as to distinguish modern epiphany from traditional vision, and to show how epiphany as a necessary concomitant of realism determines the structure of many romantic and modern poems and fictions. My analysis will suggest that the epiphanic mode is to a large extent the romantic and modern mode—a dominant modern convention.

An epiphany is the manifestation of a god, or of spirit in body. The Christian Epiphany is the manifestation of Christ to the Magi. In a letter of 1904, Joyce uses the analogous term *epicleti* to explain the liturgical origin of his own magic realism. His projected volume of short stories

Dubliners is, he writes, "a series of epicleti," an error for *epicleses*, an invocation in the Greek Orthodox mass that the Holy Ghost transform the host into the body of Christ. Joyce further explains epiphany by saying that his method is to give "my idea of the significance of trivial things."[2] In the autobiographical novel *A Portrait of the Artist as a Young Man*, Stephen resents the fact that his girlfriend reveals her soul to a priest of the Church rather than to him, "a priest of eternal imagination, transmuting the daily bread of experience into the radiant body of everliving life."[3] By way of epiphany, Joyce goes farther than even Pater and Yeats in articulating the religion of art. Pater and Yeats use art to bring us back to religion or mysticism, but Joyce establishes art as a rival religion.

In *Stephen Hero*, the first draft of *Portrait*, Joyce makes even clearer the connection of the term *epiphany* with the innovativeness of his fiction. We are told how Stephen heard in the street one evening a "fragment of colloquy out of which he received an impression keen enough to afflict his sensitiveness very severely. . . . This triviality made him think of collecting many such moments together in a book of epiphanies."[4] Joyce actually did make such a collection, which Stephen Dedalus remembers in *Ulysses* as his "epiphanies . . . deeply deep."[5] The forty manuscript epiphanies so far known have been published in *The Workshop of Daedalus*, edited by Robert Scholes and Richard M. Kain.

In his introduction to the epiphanies, Scholes says that for Joyce "Epiphany" referred "to life only, not to art. An Epiphany was life observed. . . . [it] could not be constructed, only recorded." Scholes suggests that the term is inapplicable to *Dubliners*, since no "known Epiphany has been discovered in that collection of stories."[6] My quotations above, however, show that Joyce himself applied the concept of epiphany to *Dubliners*, and Scholes contradicts himself by indicating in his notes to the epiphanies how carefully Joyce wrought them for a specific effect. It is true that epiphanies give the *impression* of having happened to the author. Like all romantic artists, Joyce dissolves the distinction between life and art: the epiphany apparently occurs in the author's life, and the author expends art to make it occur in the reader's life as well.

Besides, not all Joyce's epiphanies are notations of objective details; some, especially the so-called dream epiphanies, are prose poems. In *Stephen Hero*, Joyce distinguishes two kinds of epiphany. "By an epiphany," Stephen "meant a *sudden* spiritual manifestation, whether in the vulgarity of speech or of gesture or in a memorable phase of the mind itself. He believed that it was for the man of letters to record these epiphanies with extreme care, seeing that they themselves are the most delicate and evanescent of *moments*" (211, my italics). The epiphany reveals spirit, and breaks—whether, as in the plan for *Lyrical Ballads,* we start with fact or a phase of the mind—*suddenly,* in a *moment* of insight, upon a sensitive observer and through him upon the reader. In art, epiphany is something that happens to the reader.

The truth is that most of Joyce's notebook epiphanies are the raw material of epiphanies, requiring a context to produce in the reader the turn of mind that would make them manifestations of spirit. None of the notebook epiphanies is so perfect an example of the type as the epiphany that ends "The Dead" in *Dubliners.* The fully developed epiphanies usually combine "the vulgarity of speech or of gesture" with "a memorable phase of the mind"—the former producing the latter. The combination is expressed by Stephen's remark in *Ulysses,* "That is God. . . . A shout in the street" (34). At the end of "The Dead," Gabriel transforms the evening's scraps of conversation and of his own thoughts—just such scraps as appear in the notebook epiphanies—first, into a vision of snow falling over Ireland, and then: "His soul swooned slowly as he *heard* the snow falling faintly through the universe and faintly falling, like the descent of their last end, upon all the living and the dead."[7] Gabriel experiences a Wordsworthian epiphany of cosmic process; and like Wordsworth, Joyce brings off the transformation by moving from the visual to the auditory senses. Epiphany and irony are the alternate modes by which realistic notation achieves form and significance. In the ironic mode the author gives significance to the details through the distance which implies adverse comment. In the epiphanic mode the author relies on the reader's sympathetic projection to transform the details into visionary significance—a visionary significance that cannot be stated as a meaning. When the transformation does not come off, it is because the author has not supplied the necessary structure for transformation. I shall examine that structure later, especially in connection with Wordsworth.

Let us return to the scrap of dialogue in *Stephen Hero,* which gave Stephen the idea of "collecting many such moments together in a book of epiphanies."

> The Young Lady—(drawling discreetly) . . . O, yes . . . I was . . . at the . . . cha . . . pel . . .
> The Young Gentleman—(inaudibly) . . . I . . . (again inaudibly) . . . I . . .
> The Young Lady—(softly) . . . O . . . but you're . . . ve . . . ry . . . wick . . . ed . . . (211)

It is easy to understand through the whisperings and innuendoes the nature of the young couple's relation. But haven't fiction writers and dramatists always operated through such characterizing dialogue?

The relatively new thing for fiction is this; that the dialogue has significance only because it registers upon Stephen, who, when he hears it, is disapproving of the combination in his girlfriend of sexual suggestiveness and elusiveness, just the qualities of the lady in the dialogue. It is the sensitized condition of the observer that brings on epiphany, and the art of epiphany consists in establishing this sensitized condition. For epiphany offers an insight into the observer as well as into the object observed. Stephen, we are told in *Portrait*, "wanted to meet in the real world the unsubstantial image which his soul so constantly beheld" (65). The Stephen of *Stephen Hero* says that he could pass the clock of the Ballast Office "time after time, allude to it, refer to it, catch a glimpse of it. It is only an item in the catalogue of Dublin's street furniture. Then all at once I *see* it and I know at once what it is: epiphany" (211, my italics). The difference between habitual and epiphanic seeing is the essence of Wordsworth's art, as is the momentaneousness of the epiphanic experience.

Joyce is usually considered the first to use the theological term *epiphany* to denote a psychological and literary mode of perception. But Emerson in 1838 gives the term the same psychological meaning, even showing how epiphany rises out of vulgar fact: "Day creeps after day, each full of facts, dull, strange, despised things. . . . presently the aroused intellect finds gold and gems in one of these scorned facts, then finds . . . that a fact is an Epiphany of God."[8] Wordsworth refers to this mode of perception in life and art as "spots of time" (*Prelude*, 12.208), and many writers since Wordsworth have spoken of such privileged moments. The most famous statement is that of Pater, who in the Conclusion to *The Renaissance* says that the multiplication of privileged moments ought to be the purpose of life and that art is the surest source of such moments: "For art comes to you proposing frankly to give nothing but the highest quality to your moments as they pass, and simply for those moments' sake"—for those moments' sake because art does not teach doctrine or ask for commitment. Dissolving the distinction between life and art, Pater sees epiphany as both encapsulated in the work of art and as taking place in the beholder of art.

The epiphanic mode has pervaded poetry and determined its structure since Wordsworth. It shapes the Victorian dramatic monologue, which is an epiphany of character and a slice-of-life in just the manner of the modern short story, which appeared soon after the dramatic monologue. The epiphanic mode determines such modernist forms as imagism and symbolism. Pound's definition of the image is a definition of epiphany:

> An "Image" is that which presents an intellectual and emotional complex in an instant of time. . . . It is the presentation of such a "complex" instantaneously which gives that sense of sudden liberation; that sense of freedom from time limits and space limits; that sense of sudden growth . . .

He also defines epiphany in describing the "'magic moment' or moment of metamorphosis" in the *Cantos* as a "bust thru from quotidien into 'divine or permanent world.'"[9] Stevens's "freed man" is freed from doctrine by epiphany:

> It was how the sun came shining into his room:
> To be without a description of to be,
> For a moment on rising, at the edge of the bed, to be,
> . . . .
> It was everything being more real, himself
> At the centre of reality, seeing it.
> It was everything bulging and blazing and big in itself.
>
> ("The Latest Freed Man")

But in Stevens and other modernists, like Beckett, epiphanies are sometimes negative—insights into the abyss. In "The Snow Man," Stevens achieves a negative epiphany by reversing Wordsworth's idea that mind and nature are admirably suited to each other. "One must have a mind of winter," says Stevens, one must have not a human mind but the mindless mind of a snow man, to be

> the listener, who listens in the snow,
> And, nothing himself, beholds
> Nothing that is not there and the nothing that is.[10]

Joyce's epiphany of snow in "The Dead" is, by contrast, romantically vital.

With very few exceptions, the epiphanic mode of romantic poetry does not appear in fiction until the turn of the century with James, Conrad, Proust and with the development of the modern short story by Chekhov, Joyce, Lawrence. James writes of the "imaginative" mind as able to convert "the very pulses of the air into revelations." Conrad's

Marlow speaks in *Lord Jim* of "one of these rare moments of awakening when we see, hear, understand ever so much—everything—in a flash—before we fall back again into our agreeable somnolence." Virginia Woolf speaks of the novelist's art as the attempt "to reconstruct . . . in words" the moment when "a tree shook; an electric light danced; . . . a whole vision . . . seemed contained in that moment." Faulkner believes the novelist's "craft" is "to arrest for a believable moment" the experience of life. Fitzgerald writes that what he, Wolfe, and Hemingway have in common is their attempt "to recapture the exact feel of a moment in time and space," an attempt he associates with "what Wordsworth was trying to do." [11]

The most thorough practitioner in fiction of the epiphanic mode is Proust, whose vast novel *A la recherche du temps perdu* is built upon moments of what Proust calls "involuntary Memory," moments in which the past returns and overwhelms the present. Proust's epiphanies are closest to Wordsworth's in that they are mainly delayed epiphanies, epiphanies of recollection, moments triggered by a present event and occurring after the original experience, which was not itself an epiphany. The psychological association between present and past events causes the original experience to return as a delayed epiphany—a moment of recollection in which spatial reality is dematerialized through the free-floating perspective of time. Proust suggests that only the *absent* can be imagined; and Wordsworth says many times in *The Prelude* that only the "unremembered," which is to say the unconsciously remembered, can be remembered in a way that counts imaginatively. Proust's epiphanies are like Wordworth's in that they operate through carefully delineated psychological association. Realism and psychology make epiphany a modern mode as distinguished from traditional *vision*.

The concept of epiphany is useful only to the extent that we recognize epiphany as distinctively modern. Otherwise we may as well scrap the term and speak only of *vision*. I insist that we need the term to understand one line of innovation in nineteenth- and twentieth-century literature. In order to understand *epiphany*, we must realize that Vaughan's seventeenth-century lines, "I saw eternity the other night / Like a great ring of pure and endless light" (in "The World"), make a statement about *vision* not epiphany, because nothing is physically sensed—eternity is merely likened to a ring of light. The opening lines of Blake's "Auguries of Innocence," instead, make a statement about *epiphany* because there are physically sensed objects: "To see a World in a Grain of Sand / And a Heaven in a Wild Flower, / Hold Infinity in the palm of your hand." But we need to make still another distinction between Blake, who makes statements about epiphany, and his younger contemporaries Wordsworth and Coleridge, who create structures that produce epiphanies in the reader.

In his excellent book *Epiphany in the Modern Novel*, Morris Beja distinguishes modern epiphany from traditional vision by two criteria: the Criterion of Incongruity (the epiphany is irrelevant to the object or incident that triggers it) and the Criterion of Insignificance (the epiphany is triggered by a trivial object or incident). Dante in his vision at the end of *Paradiso* "sees God in all His magnificence," but the modern epiphany, says Beja, is out of proportion to its cause (16–17).

I would add four more criteria. The first is the Criterion of Psychological Association: the epiphany is not an incursion of God from outside; it is a psychological phenomenon arising from a real sensuous experience, either present or recollected. The second is the Criterion of Momentaneousness: the epiphany lasts only a moment, but leaves an enduring effect. The third is the Criterion of Suddenness: a sudden change in external conditions causes a shift in sensuous perception that sensitizes the observer for epiphany. The fourth is the Criterion of Fragmentation or the Epiphanic Leap: the text never quite equals the epiphany; the poetry, as Browning put it, consists in the reader's leap.[12] Hence the deliberate fragmentation of modernist literature, which blocks grammatical or logical organization in order to enforce psychological organization. All these criteria, Beja's and mine, are illustrated by the epiphany at the end of "The Dead," when suddenly: "A few light taps upon the pane made him [Gabriel] turn to the window. It had begun to snow again" (287).

All these criteria are strikingly illustrated by Wordsworth's Lucy poem "Strange Fits of Passion Have I Known." The narrator, Lucy's lover, is riding horseback to her cottage. He keeps his eyes fixed on the moon, and this fixity, together with the regularity of the horse's hoofbeats, throws him into a kind of hypnotic trance which prepares him for epiphany. It is, however, the sudden disruption of this pattern, the sudden dropping and disappearance of the moon behind Lucy's roof that wakes him out of his sweet dream and makes him suddenly associate the disappearance of the moon with the possibility of Lucy's death. Here are the last three stanzas.

> In one of those sweet dreams I slept,
> Kind Nature's gentlest boon!
> And all the while my eyes I kept
> On the descending moon.

My horse moved on; hoof after hoof
He raised, and never stopped:
When down behind the cottage roof,
At once, the bright moon dropped.

(Ll. 17–24)

"What fond and wayward thoughts," he says—and "fond" has its older
meaning *mad* as well as its newer meaning *affectionate*—

What fond and wayward thoughts will slide
Into a Lover's head!
"O mercy!" to myself I cried,
"If Lucy should be dead!"

(Ll. 25–28)[13]

In the first stanza, the narrator calls this epiphany a strange fit of passion
which he will confide to "the Lover's ear alone"; for emotional predis-
position is required if the reader is to make the epiphanic leap. Wordsworth often specifies the kind of reader he requires, for the epiphanic
poem is a joint venture of poet and reader.

Note that the narrator's sweet dream is a trance or waking dream.
Dreams proper cannot, for the most part, be fitted into a workable definition of *epiphany*—unless, like dreams in the opening pages of Proust's
Swann's Way, they arise from physical sensations or body positions.
Wordsworth's dream of the Arab in *The Prelude,* Book 5, arises from
experience—the sight of the sea and the reading of *Don Quixote*—but
the dream is too drawn out and allegorical to be epiphanic. Epiphany is
the opposite of allegory, conceit, metaphor; it really happens. Joyce's so-
called dream epiphanies in the notebook raise problems for his own definition of *epiphany;* for in defining the term for life or art, Joyce never
takes dreams into account. Nor is it certain that all the epiphanies which,
in his transcription of his brother's epiphanies, Stanislaus Joyce calls
dreams really are dreams; some could just as easily be understood as
imaginatively perceived reality. Number 8: "Where three roads meet and
before a swampy beach a big dog is recumbent . . ." appears as a real
incident in *Stephen Hero* (38); while number 32: "The human crowd
swarms in the enclosure, moving through the slush. . . . A little old man
has mice on an umbrella. . . . A beautiful brown horse, with a yellow
rider upon him, flashes far away in the sunlight" (*Workshop of Daedal-
uls,* 18, 42) is less imaginative than the epiphany in *Portrait,* certainly
not a dream, where a girl bathing in the sea appears to Stephen as a
mythological bird-girl (171).

When Joyce in *Stephen Hero* applies the concept of epiphany to art, we realize that an epiphanic art is object-oriented and therefore static and lyrical rather than moving and dramatic. It is significant that the epiphanic mode begins with the romantic poets, for whom lyric becomes the dominant genre. It is also significant that the epiphanic mode appears in fiction at just the time when fiction begins to approximate the intensity of the lyric. "The third quality," says Stephen, "is the moment which I call epiphany," when "we recognize that the object . . . is *that* thing which it is. Its soul, its whatness, leaps to us from the vestment of its appearance. The soul of the commonest object, the structure of which is so adjusted, seems to us radiant. The object achieves its epiphany" (213). Note the combination of realism with radiance and the suggestion that the radiance is produced by a structure.

In revising this passage for *Portrait,* Joyce omitted the word "epiphany"; but he clearly had epiphany in mind, for he makes Stephen say that the object is "that thing which it is and no other thing." He also expands the notion of "radiance": it is the intensification of the object's realistic quality, its "whatness," as revealed in an instant: "The instant wherein that supreme quality of beauty, the clear radiance of the esthetic image, is apprehended luminously by the mind which has been arrested by its wholeness and fascinated by its harmony in the luminous silent stasis of esthetic pleasure" (213). Note how difficult it is to distinguish the *radiance* of the object from the *luminousness* of the mind that beholds it. That is because the object's radiance is its inwardness, which is to say the beholder's inwardness projected into it. The object is beheld at that point of intensity where it becomes an equivocally subjective-objective *image.* The word "stasis" refers to the reader's response; but we can infer from it the structure that produces such response, and that structure is, I would suggest, lyrical. For the epiphanic story or poem (even when the poem is narrative) is devoted to intensifying an object into radiance rather than to telling a story with a beginning, a middle, and an end. Even narrative, in other words, is lyricized and rendered relatively static. Wordsworth's "Strange Fits of Passion" is a good example of lyricized narrative; there is very little linear movement, just enough to prepare for the epiphanic final stanza.

In the Victorian dramatic monologue, we see how drama is lyricized. Very little happens; there are no reversals; there is simply the static intensification of character. Joyce's *Ulysses* is the most conspicuous example of lyrical stasis in fiction. For such a big novel very little happens. There is very little linear movement, either spatial or temporal. The whole gigantic novel takes place in Dublin during twenty-four hours. Someone is buried; someone is born; Molly Bloom commits adultery without any consequences; Stephen Dedalus and Leopold Bloom meet and part. The novel's movement is mainly in depth; vast reaches of time converge in a limited present. Virginia Woolf's novels follow the same pattern; *The Waves* is an extreme example of the static lyrical novel.

My idea of lyrical stasis is supported by the pregnant metaphor "spatial form" advanced by Joseph Frank in his influential essay "Spatial Form in Modern Literature." Frank considers spatial form the distinguishing sign of twentieth-century modernist literature. We apprehend spatial form, Frank argues, by piecing together a deliberately fragmented modern work as though the parts existed simultaneously: "The meaning-relationship is completed only by the simultaneous perception in space of word-groups that have no comprehensible relation to each other when read consecutively in time. . . . Modern poetry asks its readers to suspend the process of individual reference temporarily until the entire pattern of internal references can be apprehended as a unity"—as, in my terms, a static retrospective flash. "The reader," says Frank, "is forced to read *Ulysses* in exactly the same manner as he reads modern poetry, that is, by continually fitting fragments together and keeping allusions in mind until, by reflexive reference, he can link them to their complements. . . . Joyce cannot be read—he can only be reread." Frank's persuasive argument would be even stronger if he employed the concepts of epiphany and lyrical stasis; for he would then realize that the phenomenon he is describing is not distinctively twentieth-century but begins in English literature with Wordsworth. In his later essay "Spatial Form: Some Further Reflections," Frank says he has learned from the structuralists that "the emergence of spatial form in twentieth-century narrative should no longer be regarded as a radical break with tradition. Rather, it represents only what Jakobson would call a shift in the internal hierarchy of the elements ["causal-chronological" versus "spatial"] composing a narrative structure."[14] Frank still does not see that romanticism caused the shift; he therefore cannot account for the shift, cannot see that it derives from a changed world view that values experience over system, whether the system be causal-chronological, logical, theological, or ethical.

If we take as models of the modern short story Joyce's stories in *Dubliners,* as well as Chekhov's stories, we see that the modern short story is plotless and apparently pointless in order that it may be epiphanic. Once we realize this, we can understand that one origin of the modern short story is in *Lyrical Ballads,* in the plotless and apparently pointless story, for example, of Simon Lee. This is a poem about a tall, vigorous huntsman who is so reduced by poverty and old age that he is too weak to work the "scrap of land" left to him. The poem tells a realistic story about old age and the passing of the feudal economy that could support liveried huntsmen. In strikingly realistic detail, we are told that Simon's "body, dwindled and awry, / Rests upon ankles swoln and thick." In the end the narrator sees him trying in vain "To unearth the root of an old tree," and taking Simon's mattock cuts the root for him. The old man's eyes fill with tears of gratitude, a gratitude that leaves the narrator "mourning." For Simon's tears are an epiphany of his reduced condition.

I am reminded of Joyce's story "Clay" (in *Dubliners*), where in the end Joe's eyes fill with tears when Maria, the poor, old, ugly, unmarried servant to servants, sings, all oblivious of her condition, "I dreamt that I dwelt in marble halls." Wordsworth has, in Joyce's phrase, merely traced "the curve of an emotion." But in doing so, in getting the appearance just right, he has worked a transformation; he has made the appearance yield its radiance or essence, the essence of a whole life or condition—the condition, as in "Clay," of old age and poverty.

The epiphany registers, however, not on Joyce's Maria or on Wordsworth's Simon but on the beholder, and through him, on the reader. This "is no tale," says Wordsworth, once again enlisting the reader's cooperation, "but should you [the reader] think, / Perhaps a tale you'll make it." The tale resides not in the events but in the quality of the imagination that produced it and that receives it. The author does not *tell* the reader the story, but plays upon him as though he were a musical instrument—making him move through a series of associations that will produce the epiphany in *him*. "The feeling therein developed," says Wordsworth in the Preface to *Lyrical Ballads*, "gives importance to the action and situation, and not the action and situation to the feeling." Wordsworth reverses Aristotle's prescription for the primacy of action. He lyricizes narrative and gives lyric a narrative form: hence *lyrical* ballads. No wonder Joyce wrote: "I think Wordsworth of all English men of letters best deserves your word 'genius.'" [15]

So far I have concentrated on short poems and stories where the epiphany occurs at the end, reordering and rendering static all that has preceded. In longer poems and in novels, epiphanies occur successively, reordering the parts backward and forward in the direction of lyrical stasis. In Virginia Woolf's *To the Lighthouse*, epiphanies reduce the action to a series of still, silent moments that give the text a fragmented quality. Mrs. Ramsay, stopping her knitting, has an epiphanic vision of "the steady [i.e., still] light" from the lighthouse; and her stillness breaks upon Mr. Ramsay as an epiphany: "He turned and saw her. Ah! She was lovely." Mrs. Ramsay suddenly sees her dinner party as a static moment, rising, despite the talk, "in this profound stillness. . . . Of such moments, she thought, the thing is made that endures." Lily Briscoe, the painter, arrives at a theory of epiphany by asking: "What is the meaning of life?

. . . The great revelation perhaps never did come. Instead there were little daily miracles, illuminations, matches struck unexpectedly in the dark." Mrs. Ramsay unconsciously does in life what Lily necessarily does in painting and what Virginia Woolf chooses to do in this novel: they give meaning to life by spatializing and silencing it, while suggesting its noisy movement. "Beauty," Lily thinks, "stilled life—froze it." Lily reduces to stasis even the sight of Mr. Ramsay's boat sailing at last to the lighthouse: "the sea and sky looked all one fabric." And she completes her spatializing "vision" of the Ramsays when "with a sudden intensity, as if she saw it clear for a second, she drew a line there, in the centre" of her canvas. Mrs. Ramsay earlier understood that her stilled vision of the dinner party was organized around a spatial center—"the still space that lies about the heart of things." [16]

Wordsworth moves toward stasis in his relatively long narrative poem "The Thorn," which raises a problem of interpretation that illustrates the difference between traditional and epiphanic narrative. If we read the poem the way people used to, as an objective story told by a reliable narrator, it becomes a melodramatic, social-protest story about a wronged woman, jilted at the altar, who is driven to murder her illegitimate infant. If, however, we take seriously Wordsworth's note to the poem—as Stephen Parrish says we should[17]—we read an unreliable narrative by a sea captain, newly arrived in the district, who hears the story of Martha Ray through village gossip and associates it with an earlier epiphanic experience of a thorn tree. The poem, which carries later information back into an earlier experience, substitutes for temporal sequence a psychological organization around a center, thus showing in an experience of nature the psychological genesis of the village legend that Martha sits beside the thorn wailing for her dead infant. This reading throws doubt on the story of Martha—on whether she murdered, or even gave birth to, a baby, and whether she really does sit wailing beside the thorn.

The interest shifts to the narrator and, as Wordsworth says in his note, to "the general laws [of association] by which superstition acts upon the mind." The only thing certain is the narrator's experience of the thorn; so that the poem evolves through epiphanic intensification of the thorn, as it evolved in Wordsworth's own experience of the thorn. The poem, says Wordsworth, "arose out of my observing, on the ridge of Quantock Hill, on a stormy day, a thorn which I had often passed in calm and bright weather without noticing it. I said to myself, 'Cannot I by some invention do as much to make this Thorn permanently an impressive object as the storm has made it to my eyes at this moment?'"

Here are the stanzas about the narrator's epiphanic experience of

the thorn in a storm on a mountaintop, which took place "Ere I had
heard of Martha's name."

> "'Twas mist and rain, and storm and rain:
> No screen, no fence could I discover;
> And then the wind! in sooth, it was
> A wind full ten times over.
> I looked around, I thought I saw
> A jutting crag,—and off I ran,
> Head-foremost, through the driving rain,
> The shelter of the crag to gain;
> And, as I am a man,
> Instead of jutting crag, I found
> A Woman seated on the ground."
>
> (Ll. 177–87)

What he probably finds is the thorn; what he probably hears is the sound
of the wind:

> "I did not speak—I saw her face;
> Her face!—it was enough for me;
> I turned about and heard her cry,
> 'Oh misery! oh misery!'"
>
> (Ll. 188–91)

All has been hearsay; no one in the village has actually seen Martha on
the mountaintop. This is the one time the narrator claims to have seen a
woman there; yet it is the time when visibility is poorest. The poor visibility could have produced an anthropomorphic illusion to which he
later attached the name Martha. Blake's dictum that every intense experience of nature is anthropomorphic accounts for the origin of legends
and myths. If the narrator really does see Martha, then the poem is not,
as Wordsworth said it was, a study of superstition. However we interpret
these lines—and it is enough that we read them as ambiguous to make
the poem a lyrical rather than an objective narrative—the shift in the
next lines to present and future tenses indicates that the narrator could
not possibly see such a timeless scene:

> "And there she sits, until the moon
> Through half the clear blue sky will go;
> And, when the little breezes make
> The waters of the pond to shake,
> As all the country know,

She shudders, and you hear her cry,
'Oh misery! oh misery!'"

(Ll. 192–98)

"As all the country know" shows that the narrator is carrying later information about Martha back into his account of the earlier experience and assimilating that experience to the legend—a nature legend deriving Martha's "shudders" from shaking waters.

Like other Wordsworth narratives, like "Michael" which begins with a heap of stones, this poem begins with a thorn which is so intensely seen as to seem ready to give birth to Martha's woeful story.

"There is a Thorn—it looks so old,
In truth, you'd find it hard to say
How it could ever have been young,
It looks so old and grey.
Not higher than a two years' child
It stands erect, this aged Thorn;
No leaves it has, no prickly points;
It is a mass of knotted joints,
A wretched thing forlorn.
It stands erect, and like a stone
With lichens is it overgrown.

"Like rock or stone, it is o'ergrown,
With lichens to the very top,
And hung with heavy tufts of moss,
A melancholy crop:
Up from the earth these mosses creep,
And this poor Thorn they clasp it round
So close, you'd say that they are bent
With plain and manifest intent
To drag it to the ground;
And all have joined in one endeavor
To bury this poor Thorn for ever."

(Ll. 1–22)

These stanzas are not epiphanic because there is no moment of observation, no sudden shift in perception. They seem to crystallize the results of epiphany—Wordsworth's and the narrator's—and to explain why in his epiphanic experience the narrator turns the thorn into a woman. The opening and the epiphanic stanzas make "The Thorn" a lyrical nature poem in which the story is half objective and half a way of dramatizing Wordsworth's and the narrator's feelings about the thorn. The assimilation of Martha's story to natural forces works, as in other Wordsworth narratives, to give the story its lyrical quality and save it from sentimentality and melodrama the way music saves an opera from its melodramatic libretto.

Wordsworth's most characteristic nature passages are organized as epiphanies. In the midst of his eighteenth-century-style early poem *Descriptive Sketches* (1793), with its generalized descriptions of nature ("And what if ospreys, cormorants, herons cry, / Amid tempestuous vapours driving by"), one passage points toward the romantic Wordsworth. In the contrast between this passage and the rest we see the difference between description, which relies on rhetoric, and epiphany, which relies on dramatic organization.

This romantic passage is organized around a sudden change as, after rain, the sun appears over the Swiss lake, imbuing the whole landscape with its light:

> But what a sudden burst of overpowering light!
> Triumphant on the bosom of the storm,
> Glances the wheeling eagle's glorious form!
> Eastward, in long perspective . . .

The perspective locates an observer, who adds a tactile perception of the sun's heat to the visual perception of its light:

> Eastward, in long perspective glittering, shine
> The wood-crowned cliffs that o'er the lake recline;
> Those lofty cliffs a hundred streams unfold,
> At once to pillars turned that flame with gold.

A new agent of perception is introduced:

> Behind his sail the peasant shrinks, to shun
> The *west,* that burns like one dilated sun,
> A crucible of mighty compass, felt
> By mountains, glowing till they seem to melt.
>
> (Ll. 254–55, 274–84)[18]

The peasant completes the internalization of the scene; for we, by way of the observer, project ourselves into the peasant's feeling of heat to sense the mountains' internal glowing. The sudden climactic enlargement of the scene's unity as "one dilated sun," burning externally and internally and uniting human beings with the landscape, is precisely epiphanic.

"A Night Piece," written in 1798 when Wordsworth's style was securely romantic, is organized in the same way. The moon, which has been hidden by clouds, suddenly appears; and "the pensive traveller," whose "unobserving eye" has been "bent earthwards," suddenly

> looks up—the clouds are split
> Asunder,—and above his head he sees
> The clear Moon, and the glory of the heavens.

He experiences an epiphany of the distant, silent motion of the stars. The auditory sense is added to the visual, in that the silence of the stars is distinctly contrasted to their motion and to the sound of the wind: "the wind is in the tree, / But they are silent;—still they roll along / Immeasurably distant." This is a typically Wordsworthian epiphany of cosmic process, characterized by Wordsworth's favorite verb *roll,* a word that adds the tactile to the visual and auditory senses—the auditory sense is sometimes invoked through its unexpected absence. "At length the Vision closes," we are told. The epiphany lasts a moment, and is usually defined at both ends. "The great discovery of the eighteenth century," writes Georges Poulet in *Studies in Human Time,* "is the phenomenon of memory." Nineteenth-century romanticism adds to that *"experienced continuity,"* mingling "human time and cosmic time . . . in a sole continuity."[19] This is a way of accounting for Wordsworth's epiphanies of cosmic process.

De Quincey records Wordsworth's statement about the shift in perception that produces such epiphanies. Wordsworth said that from his earliest days he had observed that if "the attention is energetically braced up to an act of steady observation, or of steady expectation, then, if this intense condition of vigilance should suddenly relax, at that moment any beautiful, any impressive visual object, or collection of objects, falling upon the eye, is carried to the heart with a power not known under other circumstances." Wordsworth cites as illustration the beautiful passage in *The Prelude,* Book 5, on the Boy of Winander, Wordsworth himself. This boy liked at evening on the lake to imitate the hootings of owls "that they might answer him," and they did. But sometimes they did not, and the unexpected silence would come as "a gentle shock of mild surprise" that

> carried far into his heart the voice
> Of mountain torrents; or the visible scene
> Would enter unawares into his mind,
> With all its solemn imagery, its rocks,

Its woods, and that uncertain heaven, received
Into the bosom of the steady lake.

(Ll. 374, 382–88)

The scene figures as "imagery" because it is both external and internal. De Quincey notes spatialization of the experience in the word "far," and goes on to describe his own epiphanic response: "This very expression, 'far,' by which space and its infinities are attributed to the human heart, and to its capacities of re-echoing the sublimities of nature, has always struck me as with a flash of sublime revelation."[20] The heaven, in Wordsworth's last two verse lines, is "uncertain" because reflected in the fluid lake—a sign of how precisely sensuous are the perceptions that produce epiphanies.

Epiphanies produce an effect that might be called "the modern sublime." For while they produce in the reader the emotions named by writers on the sublime—Longinus's "transport," Burke's "terror" and "astonishment"—they add an awareness of disparity between the diction and visualization, on the one hand, and the sublime effect on the other. The sense of disparity is particularly acute in Joyce. Wordsworth often employs Miltonic diction and many of the visual devices named by Burke—obscurity, heights, boundariless expanses suggesting infinity. Joyce, however, usually produces the sublime effect out of small, sharp details delivered in a flat diction—though such details combine in "The Dead" to produce an epiphany that is exceptional in Joyce for the Wordsworthian and Burkean quality of its sublimity.[21]

In his prose fragment "The Sublime and the Beautiful," Wordsworth says that "whatever suspends the comparing powers of the mind & possesses it with a feeling or image of intense unity, without a conscious contemplation of parts, has produced that state of mind which is the consummation of the sublime."[22] The statement applies, I think, to Joycean epiphanies—except for the phrase "without a conscious contemplation of parts," for Joycean epiphanies usually derive from sharply etched details that are transformed into unity without our losing consciousness of the details.

Wordsworth analyzes the "sensation of sublimity" into "three component parts: a sense of individual form or forms; a sense of duration; and a sense of power." The only way, he continues,

in which such an object [a mountain] can affect us, contemplated under the notion of duration, is when the faint sense which we have of its individuality is lost in the general sense of duration belonging to the Earth itself. Prominent individual form must, therefore, be conjoined with duration . . . [to] impress a sense of sublimity [or cosmic process]. (2:351)

Wordsworth's "duration" seems to anticipate Bergson's *durée,* which means just that and which Bergson uses to denote psychic as contrasted to clock time. More than a hundred years after Wordsworth had composed his "spots of time," Bergson in his chapter "L'idée de durée" (in *Essai sur les données immédiates de la conscience,* 1912) wrote what is in effect a metaphysical description of them. Bergson distinguishes between *durée,* where states of consciousness penetrate each other and occupy the same space, and space, where material objects cannot penetrate each other and must be lined up successively. "Pure *durée,*" he writes, "is the form taken by our successive states of consciousness when the self relaxes, when it abstains from making a separation between our present state and past states." It is not necessary for the self "to forget the past as long as, in remembering, it does not juxtapose past and present states of consciousness as distinctively successive points, but blends them like the notes of a melody." [23] Music, we are told, is the purest expression of *durée.*

Language, instead, is geared to the spatial realm of succession, so that it is almost impossible to represent *durée* in words without using spatial metaphors. *Durée* is mainly represented by a space-time symbolism that tries to transform succession into simultaneity through intensification. How aptly all this accounts for Wordsworth's space-time metaphor "spots of time," and for the structure of epiphanies. In his preceding chapter, "On the Intensity of Psychological States" ("De l'intensité des états psychologiques"), Bergson beautifully writes what might be a description of a Wordsworthian epiphany:

> Our ideas and sensations succeed each other with increased rapidity. . . .
> Finally, in extreme joy, our perceptions and memories acquire an indefinable quality, comparable to heat or light, and so new, that at certain moments, returning upon ourselves, we experience an astonishment of being. (8)

The sensuous shifts that produce the transformations of Wordsworth's epiphanies are described in Wordsworth's "I saw them [natural objects] feel" (*Prelude,* 3.132), and are concisely illustrated in the three best known "spots of time" in *The Prelude.* In the episode of the stolen rowboat in Book 1, it is the sudden appearance of a mountain, hitherto unseen as the boy rows away from the shore, which creates the optical illusion that the mountain is striding after him like a punishing deity. The ice-skating episode in Book 1 is the best example of synesthesia, the employment of all the senses to produce an epiphany. The steel of the ice skates and "the polished ice" are tactile equivalents of the cold night.

The metallic sounds are auditory equivalents of the cold: "the precipices rang aloud; / The leafless trees and every icy crag / Tinkled like iron" (1.440–42). The visual equivalent of the cold night as a gleam in darkness becomes apparent when we are told that sometimes the boy would leave "the tumultuous throng" to skate "across the reflex of a star" (ll. 449–50). The shift from group to private experience prepares the epiphany of cosmic process, when suddenly the boy would stop short, producing the optical and tactical illusion that

> still the solitary cliffs
> Wheeled by me—even as if the earth had rolled
> With visible motion her diurnal round!
>
> (Ll. 458–60)

The richness of sensuous texture makes it possible for us to participate in this epiphany of cosmic process, because we feel the interplay on our own senses.

The climactic epiphany on Mt. Snowdon in Book 14 begins with optical illusion. The sudden appearance of the moon makes the mist around seem a "still ocean" (l. 44), with the surrounding hills static billows. This illusory ocean stretches out to the real Atlantic in the distance. The optical illusion is reinforced by an auditory illusion, by the roar of inland waters that sounds like the ocean roaring. This sensuous transformation produces the epiphany of the moon shining on waters: "the emblem of a mind" brooding "over the dark abyss"—waiting, like Milton's God in the opening passage of *Paradise Lost*, to bring forth the world. This epiphany of the creative imagination is accomplished through the blending of sight and sound, out of which the whole episode has been woven:

> the emblem of a mind
> That feeds upon infinity, that broods
> Over the dark abyss, intent to hear
> Its voices issuing forth to silent light
> In one continuous stream.
>
> (14.70–74)

Note how in the last two lines sound and sight blend with touch as the "*voices* issuing forth to *silent light*" become a wet "stream."

In tracing the art of epiphany to our own time, I must point out that Wordsworth invented the epiphanic or modern sonnet. Wordsworth wrote two kinds of sonnet—the Miltonic or discursive and the epiphanic sonnet. The best example of Wordsworth's Miltonic sonnet is "London, 1802": "Milton! thou should'st be living at this hour"—which, like Milton's sonnets, says something, makes a point. The best example of Wordsworth's epiphanic sonnet is "Composed upon Westminster Bridge," which does not *say* anything. This sonnet does more than describe London at sunrise; it evokes the city's life. It produces an epiphany of human as distinguished from natural life, through the implied contrast between human activity and natural stillness. The whole sonnet operates like a spring wound up in the direction of silence and stillness, so that it can be released into the opposite direction of activity and noise.

The octave gives a visual and auditory description of the sun rising over the empty, silent city, the beauty of which is continuous at this hour with the beauty of the country. The coming discontinuity is broached, however, in the eighth line: "All bright and glittering in the smokeless air," which suggests the smoke to come. Internalization begins in the sestet, which introduces the tactile sense: "Never did sun more beautifully steep / In his first splendour, valley, rock or hill." A sensibility not only sees the sun but also feels its warmth from within the landscape. This is the sensibility, as the next line indicates, upon which the epiphany will register: "Ne'er saw I, never felt, a calm so deep!" The internalization—as evidenced by the combination of visual, auditory, and tactile senses—comes to a climax in: "The river glideth at his own sweet will." "Sweet will" gives us—through the line's delicate anthropomorphization—the internalized, tactile sense of a peace so perfect that the only motion and will are the river's. Yet the river's silent gliding prepares for the epiphany of power, for the mighty life that will spring into action when the city awakens: "Dear God! the very houses seem asleep; / And all that mighty heart is lying still!"

In "It is a Beauteous Evening, Calm and Free," the epiphany occurs in the middle, when the sea's silence and calm make audible its surprising, distant roar:

> Listen! the mighty Being is awake,
> And doth with his eternal motion make
> A sound like thunder—everlastingly.

The rest of the sonnet reflects on this epiphany of deity.

Such sonnets gave rise to Keats's sonnets, which are almost all epiphanic—illustrating Keats's phrase in a letter about "coming continually on the spirit with a fine suddenness."[24] "On First Looking into Chapman's Homer," a sonnet about sudden discoveries, reveals in its last lines the structure of epiphany; for "Cortez" stares *outward* upon the Pacific,

while his men look *inward*—looking "at each other with a wild sur-
mise." Involved in all epiphanies is both discovery and the shock of recognition—recognition of the self in the external world. Keats's "bright
star," in the sonnet of that name, might be considered the eye transformed by epiphany, beholding natural process as a stilled moment. Rossetti—whose sonnet "Silent Noon" is a fine example of synesthetic
stilled epiphany ("Deep in the sun-searched growths the dragon-fly /
Hangs like a blue thread")—defined the modern sonnet stemming from
Wordsworth when he wrote in the introductory sonnet to *House of Life:*
"A Sonnet is a moment's monument."

Hopkins's sonnet "The Windhover" raises an interesting problem of
interpretation. If we make the subtitle "To Christ our Lord" apply from
the beginning and read the bird throughout as an emblem of Christ, we
have the extended conceit of a metaphysical poem. But if, as seems more
likely, we read the bird as really observed, we have a romantic nature
poem; and it is only in the moment of epiphany, when the falcon gains
power through buckling or diving, that he is transformed for the poet-
priest into an emblem of Christ, who gained power through a downward
movement into martyrdom: "Buckle! AND the fire that breaks from thee
then, a billion / Times told lovelier, more dangerous, O my chevalier!"
The analogy is emotional not logical, since the observer stops short of
considering the predatory purpose of the bird's dive; that is why we have
epiphany, not conceit. Epiphany and conceit exclude each other.

Yeats's sonnet "Leda and the Swan" is literally about the manifestation of a god as a bird and the impregnation of flesh by spirit through
Zeus's rape of Leda. The whole sonnet is an epiphany, culminating in the
moment of orgasm when Leda may or may not know, but the poet
knows, that she is being impregnated with a historical cycle:

A shudder in the loins engenders there
The broken wall, the burning roof and tower
And Agamemnon dead.

"Leda and the Swan" raises a problem, however, for my definition of
epiphany, in that there is no observer on the scene, so that we must read
the poem as visionary. Yet the vision is so sensuously conceived as to
make an effect unlike that of traditional visions and like that of modern
realistic epiphanies (which are themselves sensuously vivid fictions); I am
tempted therefore to suggest a category of visionary epiphanies. Such a
category could account for the modern effect of an internally glowing
vision like Blake's "The Tyger," which projects the vitality of a real tiger,
stilled, as in a picture: "Tyger! Tyger! burning bright."

Let me conclude this tracing of epiphany from Wordsworth to the present by pointing out the evolution in Eliot's poetry from romantic to Christian epiphany. Eliot's early poems inhabit the scientific, romantic world of nonbelief checkered by inexplicable moments of spiritual insight. The best example is the scene in *The Waste Land* where a real girl carrying hyacinths becomes the occasion for a vision so profound that the protagonist spends the rest of the poem trying to recover that vision, thus making an analogue to the legendary Quest for the Grail:

> —Yet when we came back, late, from the hyacinth
>   garden,
> Your arms full, and your hair wet, I could not
> Speak, and my eyes failed, I was neither
> Living nor dead, and I knew nothing,
> Looking into the heart of light, the silence.[25]

Even so early, Eliot goes beyond Wordsworth in trying to stabilize the effect of epiphany; Wordsworth is content to remember, Eliot wants to recover, the vision.

Eliot deals with the Christian Epiphany in "Journey of the Magi," written in 1927, the year he converted to the Anglican Church. The Magi behold the manifestation of God as an infant, know that something irrevocable has happened, but do not understand it and cannot change their lives to accord with it. Not until *Four Quartets* (1943) is Eliot able to stabilize epiphanies through theological interpretation of them. In the first poem, "Burnt Norton," he deals with romantic epiphany:

> But only in time can the moment in the rose-garden,
> The moment in the arbour where the rain beat,
> The moment in the draughty church at smokefall
> Be remembered.
>
> (Pt. 2)

"Only through time," through such privileged moments, "time is conquered." He associates such moments in and out of time with the Incarnation, the Word, "the still point of the turning world," which gives pattern to life, stillness to movement. Nevertheless, "Burnt Norton" ends with another epiphany that only reminds the poet of the "Ridiculous . . . waste sad time / Stretching before and after" the privileged moment.

In the second poem, "East Coker," Eliot demands more than the privileged moment:

> Not the intense moment
> Isolated, with no before and after,
> But a lifetime burning in every moment
> And not the lifetime of one man only
> But of old stones that cannot be deciphered.

(Pt. 5)

Religion and the sense of tradition are ways of stabilizing epiphany, of objectifying intensity. This possibility is explained in the third poem, "The Dry Salvages":

> But to apprehend
> The point of intersection of the timeless
> With time, is an occupation for the saint—
> . . . .
> For most of us, there is only the unattended
> Moment, the moment in and out of time,
> The distraction fit, lost in a shaft of sunlight.

Such privileged moments "are only hints and guesses." But

> The hint half guessed, the gift half understood, is
>   Incarnation
> Here the impossible union
> Of spheres of existence [flesh and spirit] is actual.

(Pt. 5)

Epiphany, the romantic substitute for religion, becomes the means of returning to and revalidating dogma as experience.

In the last poem, "Little Gidding," the sensuous transformations of romantic epiphany become mystical. The spring holiday Pentecost—another Christian Epiphany, celebrating the descent of the Holy Spirit upon the disciples—is experienced in winter as "midwinter spring" because frost and fire are magnified by the sun-reflecting ice:

> Midwinter spring is its own season
> . . . .
> When the short day is brightest, with frost and fire,
> The brief sun flames the ice . . .

(Pt. 1)

This is "pentecostal fire / In [winter] the dark time of the year"—and the dark time of England's history, World War II. "This is the spring time / But not in time's covenant." Where, asks the poet, is redemption: "Where is the summer, the unimaginable / Zero summer?"—"zero" because not in time's covenant. The answer lies in the collapsing of the whole year and the whole of England's history within that stilled moment of pentecostal illumination. The passage takes its structure from romantic epiphany. Eliot is a great poet because he embraces the whole of the poetic tradition up to his time and takes it a step forward. Wordsworth is the great seminal romantic poet who revolutionized the tradition of his time, giving rise to much that is most innovative in romantic and modern literature.

Wordsworth's Lyrical Characterizations

SINCE we generally think of Wordsworth as a lyrical and autobiographical nature poet, we are apt to forget that he is also a great narrative poet and that he is as much interested in character as in nature. Even the poems we consider lyrical usually tell a story. "Tintern Abbey" tells a story of autobiographical development. The Lucy poems tell the story of the death of a beautiful young woman. Sometimes—as in the Lucy poem called "Strange Fits of Passion Have I Known" or in "Resolution and Independence"—it is difficult to decide whether the poem is narrative or lyrical. Such poems are narrative to the extent that we read them as dynamic or moving through time. They are lyrical to the extent that we read them as static, as organized around a moment of illumination—the narrator's sudden premonition in "Strange Fits" of Lucy's death, or in "Resolution" the poet's sudden transforming vision of the old leech-gatherer as a Messenger sent to teach him the value of endurance. The same ambiguity as between narrative and lyric applies to the kind of modern short story introduced by Chekhov and Joyce, which ends in a moment of insight, an epiphany.

The question arises: these poems may be narratives, but are they fictions? The poems that are properly lyrical ballads are certainly fictions, even when they take off from real incidents as do so many novels and short stories. The poet himself does not appear in these poems; the narrators are fictitious. The Lucy poems present a more difficult case, because we think of the poet as speaking all of them except "Strange Fits of Passion" in which the narrator is Lucy's lover. Yet Lucy herself is apparently a fictitious character, even if we speculate on whom in real life she may represent. In "Resolution and Independence," we take the narrator to be the poet; but the considerable difference from the account in

Dorothy's journal of the actual meeting with the leech-gatherer shows that Wordsworth took the liberties of the fiction writer in composing the poem. He omits Dorothy herself, and omits most of her details about the leech-gatherer in order to concentrate on the man's extreme old age. Such changes help, as I shall show, to internalize the experience for the poet.

Even the patently autobiographical *The Prelude* displays in its arbitrary omissions, selections and rearrangements of the incidents of Wordsworth's life the freedom and narrative line of fiction. Many of the episodes are constructed like short stories. The episode of the stolen rowboat is an example. Another is the awesome meeting with the discharged soldier at a moment when the youth Wordsworth is returning from an evening party in high spirits. The sudden shift from high to low spirits and the transformation of consciousness occasioned by the meeting give the episode a structure similar to that of Joyce's story "An Encounter" or of "Resolution and Independence." In portraying people other than himself in *The Prelude* and the shorter autobiographical poems, Wordsworth faces the same problems of characterization as the fiction writer. Indeed autobiography must be considered—as Northrop Frye has pointed out—a form of fiction; for we must ask about autobiography, once we analyze its *artistic* qualities, many of the same questions that we ask about fiction.

If we ask then about Wordsworth's characterizations, we must ask the same questions about his autobiographical as about his fictitious poems. In both kinds of poem, Wordsworth's *successful* characterizations are mainly what I would call lyrical rather than dramatic. Wordsworth is relatively unsuccessful when he tries conventionally dramatic characterizations—as in his pseudo-Shakespearean early tragedy *The Borderers,* or in his late narrative "The White Doe of Rylstone" where the only successful character is Emily Norton, the one character, as I shall show, who is characterized lyrically. In his dramatic characterizations, Wordsworth portrays social class and what Aristotle calls *ethos* or moral choice. In his lyrical characterizations, Wordsworth alludes to social class only to show its unimportance for the kind of spirituality he is portraying. *Ethos* is also negated; moral quality in Wordsworth's lyrical characterizations derives not from conscious choice but from a state of being.

In his lyrical characterizations, Wordsworth gives very few individualizing traits: very few details of appearance and dress, eccentricities of manners and speech, complex motivations. Wordsworth eliminates almost all external details in order to portray the character's inner life— not psychologically, not as a stream of consciousness, but as a quality of soul or imagination. Most typically Wordsworth portrays character not through action or dialogue but through visual impression—an impression that often includes the figure's setting in a landscape and that characterizes the figure by characterizing the landscape. In the Lucy poems, for example, Lucy is never described; we get an impression of her shy, reclusive beauty through descriptions of the mild beauty of English landscape. Indeed, Wordsworth is most effective when he treats character like landscape—as a pole for projection and therefore as a way of intuiting the "life of things" through finding there his own life. The figure becomes part of the general life and therefore the opposite of an individual life. Wordsworth's most effective characterizations approximate pure being. That is why his most effective characterizations are solitaries; for only the solitary figure can be treated like a landscape and evoke pure being. In groups, social interaction takes over.

In order to understand the innovativeness of Wordsworth's lyrical characterizations, let us consider the analogous case of Henry Moore, who in *Henry Moore on Sculpture* shows that he is a romantic organicist who treats the human figure in Wordsworth's manner:

> Wordsworth often personified objects in nature and gave them the human aspect, and personally I have done rather the reverse process in sculptures. I've often found that by taking formal ideas from landscape, and putting them into my sculpture I have, as it were, related a human figure to a mountain.

The remark suggests likeness rather than difference, especially since Moore accounts for Wordsworth's personifications of nature but not his naturalization of human figures—the way, for example, the leech-gatherer is related to a huge stone. The similarity to Wordsworth emerges from Moore's further remarks:

> I realized what an advantage a separated two-piece composition could have in relating figures to landscape. Knees and breasts are mountains. Once these two parts become separated you don't expect it to be a naturalistic figure; therefore, you can justifiably make it like a landscape or a rock.[1]

Both Moore and Wordsworth endow their figures with a larger-than-life, mythical dimension by treating them like landscape. They are following at least one theory about the origin of myths as anthropomorphizations of landscape—the theory set forth by Wordsworth in *The Excursion,* Book 4. In two lines excised from *The Prelude,* Wordsworth refers to his kind of lyrical characterization as a "border" figure, an organic (Moore-like) statue: "A Borderer dwelling betwixt life and death, / A living Statue or a statued Life."[2]

The old leech-gatherer is just such a border figure; the details of the actual meeting are manipulated in order to place him on the border between life and death. Here is the account of the actual meeting in Dorothy's Grasmere Journal entry of 3 October 1800:

> When William and I returned from accompanying Jones, we met an old man almost double. He had on a coat, thrown over his shoulders, above his waistcoat and coat. Under this he carried a bundle, and had an apron on and a night-cap. His face was interesting. He had dark eyes and a long nose. John, who afterwards met him at Wytheburn, took him for a Jew. He was of Scotch parents, but had been born in the army. He had had a wife, and "a good woman, and it pleased God to bless us with ten children." All these were dead but one, of whom he had not heard for many years, a sailor. His trade was to gather leeches, but now leeches are scarce, and he had not strength for it. He lived by begging, and was making his way to Carlisle, where he should buy a few godly books to sell. He said leeches were very scarce, partly owing to this dry season, but many years they have been scarce—he supposed it owing to their being much sought after, that they did not breed fast, and were of slow growth. Leeches were formerly 2s. 6d. [per] 100; they are now 30s. He had been hurt in driving a cart, his leg broke, his body driven over, his skull fractured. He felt no pain till he recovered from his first insensibility. It was then late in the evening, when the light was just going away.[3]

The omission of Dorothy from the poem produces an encounter between two solitary figures—the observer and the observed—which resembles the subject-object relation of the landscape poems. The relation makes the observed, the leech-gatherer, a pole for projection and therefore an ambiguously external-internal, natural-supernatural figure.

Dorothy gives the leech-gatherer the individualizing, socially determined traits that would be given by a realistic novelist, down to the price of leeches. Wordsworth's figure, instead, is immediately transcendent because seen in connection with a landscape that does not appear in Dorothy's account. One is struck by the enormous expansion of the scene in the poem. The sight of the old man breaks upon the observer suddenly, as an epiphany:

> Beside a pool bare to the eye of heaven
> I saw a Man before me unawares:
> The oldest man he seemed that ever wore grey hairs.

(Ll. 54–56)[4]

The man is supernaturally old, hanging onto life by a thread: indeed, "A Borderer dwelling betwixt life and death." His unawareness of being seen gives him in his stillness the appearance of a natural object or a Moore-like statue modeled on a natural object. He is in the next stanza compared to "a huge stone" (l. 57) that in its isolation seems half animate because it seems to have moved itself to that unlikely place; the stone is in turn compared to a sea-beast which seems inanimate because undistinguishable from the rocky shelf on which it reposes. The old man's existence shifts between the animate and the inanimate.

The comparison is complex, first because the poem does not specifically locate a boulder on the landscape. Yet the "huge stone" exists as a *presence* (we half assume it is there)—as though the old man *were* the stone in human shape. The sea-beast, an even more remote allusion, has relevance only to the extent that we think of the stone geologically, as remaining from a time when sea covered the land. The pool, as Geoffrey Hartman suggests in *The Unmediated Vision,* would be another such reminder; so that the leech-gatherer's dependence on a dwindling supply of water creatures takes on symbolic as well as economic significance. Since the narrator is worrying about old age and poverty at just the moment when he meets the old man, there emerges still another reason why this transcendentalized figure seems at once a projection of the narrator's mind and a supernatural Messenger evoked in both cases to answer the narrator's problem. The old man teaches the lesson of endurance—the lesson of ancient stones and Christianity. The one lesson confirms the other.

Only a concept of lyrical characterization can explain so unusual a portrayal as that of the leech-gatherer. The lyrical characterization parallels the dramatic characterization of the leech-gatherer as beset by old age and by an economic problem, the disappearance of leeches. The dramatic characterization omits many of Dorothy's details (for example, "He lived by begging"), and makes others seem different because they blend with the lyrical characterization. Wordsworth follows Dorothy, for example, in saying that the old man's "body was bent double" (l. 66); yet the detail, which stands out in Dorothy's account, gets overlooked in the poem because curiously at odds with the lyrical impression of the old man as upright in his fortitude. Other details, also implied in Dorothy's account, that the old man is Scottish, pious, with "stately speech" (l. 96), define him culturally and therefore fit into the dramatic characterization. Yet these details blend with the lyrical characterization to reinforce the impression of the old man's upright posture, and to take on a symbolic significance that directs the poet to the next stage in his own spiritual development. For the cultural details show that the old man draws upon powers which are distinctively human and divine and therefore beyond what nature can supply. In "Resolution and Independence," the lyrical and dramatic characterizations blend admirably. The blend is not always so perfect in other poems, as we shall see.

How about the character of the narrator? He is obviously identifiable with Wordsworth. From their artfulness, we might suppose that the opening stanzas, which sensitize the narrator for the encounter through rapid shifts from depression to elation back to depression, are fictitious. Yet Wordsworth later told Isabella Fenwick, "I was in the state of feeling described in the beginning of the poem." The case shows that the autobiographical and fictitious elements are not always separable. The narrator has the character of all Wordsworth's self-portrayals—self-portrayals which are selective enough to be at once autobiographical and fictitious. The narrator is a sensitive, solitary, meditative poet with a poet's preoccupations; he is a lover and keen observer of nature and of the solitary figures encountered in natural settings. But his character is in flux; the experience of each autobiographical poem—"Tintern Abbey," "Resolution and Independence," "Immortality Ode," "Elegiac Stanzas"—is a way station in the narrator's development.

To what extent are the characterizations of Wordsworth's narrators lyrical? They are lyrical to the extent that the narrator is identifiable with Wordsworth; they are dramatic to the extent that the narrator is someone other than Wordsworth—like the retired sea captain who narrates "The Thorn." Where the narrator is characterized lyrically—as in "Resolution and Independence" or the encounter with the discharged soldier in *The Prelude*, Book 4—the observed figure becomes a projection of himself; so that the two solitaries become in effect one figure. Such poems point toward the dramatic monologue. But Wordsworth in criticizing the ancient Mariner for having the same qualities as his own lyrical characterizations—for having "no distinct character . . . he does not act, but is continually acted upon"[5]—showed that, like many poets, he did not understand the theoretical implications of his own practice. Coleridge showed equally reactionary obtuseness when he attacked certain of Wordsworth's dialogues as "a species of ventriloquism, where two are represented as talking, while in truth one man only speaks."[6] In attacking self-projection as "ventriloquism," Coleridge showed no recognition of the innovating structure of dramatic lyric which would lead to dramatic monologue.

In "The Thorn," if we read it as an epiphanic poem, the relation between the narrator and Martha resembles the subject-object relation of the nature poems, which makes Martha and her story partly objective and partly a projection of the narrator's mind. Martha according to this reading is characterized lyrically. Her dramatic characterization is not excluded; it is blended with the lyrical characterization to increase the poem's imaginative intensity.

We gather from Wordsworth's note that he intended to organize the poem around a point-of-view character in a manner pointing toward Browning's dramatic monologues and Henry James's fiction. He has not quite accomplished his purpose because he introduces the narrator too late, long after we have been taking the narrator to be Wordsworth. We do not pay attention to the quotation marks until a dramatized speaker emerges in stanza 16 where we finally learn that the speaker is a newcomer who, the day he experiences the thorn, climbs the mountain to view the ocean with his telescope. But we do not learn as much about him from the poem as from the note in which Wordsworth tells us that the narrator is "a Captain of a small trading vessel," who has "retired upon an annuity" and has "become credulous and talkative from indolence" and therefore "prone to superstition." The prosaic details recall Dorothy's account of the leech-gatherer, and are in any case inappropriate to the quality of imagination that enables the narrator to blend the lyrical and dramatic characterizations of Martha almost as completely as the two kinds of characterization are blended in "Resolution and Independence." The difficulty of "The Thorn" arises from the conflict between the narrator's dramatic characterization and his quality of imagination, which is clearly the poet's and which gives him a lyrical characterization at odds with his dramatic characterization.

What then are the dramatic and lyrical characters of Martha and the leech-gatherer? They have surprisingly little character. They have benevolence and an ability to suffer and endure. As in all sublime art, the fewer the details the greater the depth of characterization. In place of details we have the character's connection with, his apparent emergence from, the landscape. The lack of individualizing details reminds us that the characters are vessels of the same force that runs through nature, that they are vessels of pure being. "What is brought forward?"—Wordsworth wrote in explaining his method in "Resolution and Independence"—"'A lonely place, a Pond' 'by which an old man *was,* far from all house or home'—not stood, not sat, but '*was*'—the figure presented in the most naked simplicity possible." "In the heart of lyrical stasis," says Daniel Albright in an observation applicable to Wordsworth's statement, "there is a peculiar indifference to the emotional content, although a kind of general suggestiveness, suggestive of nothing in particular, is usually desirable." [7]

In his earliest romantic poems—the "Salisbury Plain" poems (1793– c. 1799), published as "Guilt and Sorrow" (1842); and "The Ruined Cottage" (1797–98), published as *The Excursion*, Book 1 (1814)—Wordsworth tried to combine his interests in social reform and nature by placing his socially deprived characters on a landscape that dramatizes their suffering and enlarges their dimensions. Wordsworth was trying already to produce twin characterizations, both dramatic and lyrical. The poems fail to the extent that the characters and their stories are so detailed that we lose sight of the characters' connection with nature. The characters are insufficiently simplified to serve as vessels of natural force, and are therefore insufficiently archetypalized. The result is, as I shall show, sentimentality.

The first relative successes in blending character with landscape are "The Old Cumberland Beggar" and "Animal Tranquillity and Decay," written in 1797. The former is the more complex, but is not completely successful because it does not completely blend its dramatic and lyrical characterizations; the latter is completely successful because it projects a purely lyrical characterization. In "The Old Cumberland Beggar," Wordsworth archetypalizes the beggar by simplifying him, by giving him a minimum of consciousness. The old beggar is a borderer between nature and humanity—Wordsworth begins here his exploration of the minimum level of consciousness at which humanity can be discerned. The beggar is also, like the old leech-gatherer, a borderer between life and death: he is so supernaturally old that he "seems not older now" (l. 23) than when the narrator knew him as a boy. Like so many of Wordsworth's archetypal figures, the old beggar is a solitary wanderer in nature; his lyrical characterization is largely achieved through the refrain "He travels on, a solitary Man" (l. 24 and elsewhere). Yet he moves so slowly that he has also the stillness of Martha and the leech-gatherer: "he is so still / In look and motion" that "all pass him by" (ll. 60–65). The oxymoron of stillness and motion is a favorite device of Wordsworth's for lyrical characterization—for example, the rock that seems to have moved and the apparent stillness of the moving cloud to which he compares the leech-gatherer's stillness.

Like Martha and the leech-gatherer, the beggar is benevolent and has the capacity to suffer and endure. But his benevolence is unconscious—he *unwittingly* feeds the birds from the leavings of his own meal; his benevolence is largely reflected from the benevolence he awakens in others. He affects the villagers as nature affects them, in that he predisposes them to charity through their pleasurable associations with him. The beggar's shred of humanity is portrayed powerfully in the passage which says that whatever consciousness he has is concentrated on the small patch of ground upon which in his bent-over posture his eyes are fastened, and that whatever will he has is devoted to the agonizing effort of taking the next step:

> His age has no companion. On the ground
> His eyes are turned, and, as he moves along,
> *They* move along the ground; and, evermore,
> Instead of common and habitual sight
> Of fields with rural works, of hill and dale,
> And the blue sky, one little span of earth
> Is all his prospect. Thus, from day to day,
> Bow-bent, his eyes for ever on the ground,
> He plies his weary journey; seeing still,
> And seldom knowing that he sees.
>
> (Ll. 45–54)

The last line and a half place the beggar on the border between consciousness and unconsciousness.

The beggar's lyrical characterization is one of Wordsworth's first great successes. But it combines uneasily with the didactic purpose of the dramatic characterization, which is to argue against the movement to lock up such beggars in workhouses. The bombastic rhetoric of the didactic passages—"But deem not this Man useless.—Statesmen!" (l. 67); "May never HOUSE, misnamed of INDUSTRY, / Make him a captive!" (ll. 179–80)—conflicts with the plain style of the lyrical characterization. The blend of lyrical with dramatic or social interest is perfect in "Resolution and Independence," because there is no suggestion that the economic problem, the disappearance of leeches, can be solved by social action. The blend is less perfect though still successful in "The Thorn," because it is problematic whether Martha really is a victim of social prejudice.

The short sequel, "Animal Tranquillity and Decay" (originally "Old Man Travelling"), extracts the lyrical characterization of the old beggar as a slow-moving figure of almost complete unconsciousness. Here is the whole poem:

> The little hedgerow birds,
> That peck along the road, regard him not.
> He travels on, and in his face, his step,
> His gait, is one expression: every limb.
> His look and bending figure, all bespeak
> A man who does not move with pain, but moves

With thought.—He is insensibly subdued
To settled quiet: he is one by whom
All effort seems forgotten; one to whom
Long patience hath such mild composure given,
That patience now doth seem a thing of which
He hath no need. He is by nature led
To peace so perfect that the young behold
With envy, what the Old Man hardly feels.

The young envy the composure deriving from the old man's unconsciousness of his connection with nature. Patience and endurance have gone so far that the old man, like a natural object, no longer requires them. He seems to move not with pain but with thought because, we can infer, his pain is so intense that it requires an effort of his whole being to take the next step; so that "thought" means the opposite of thought as an isolated activity—it means a manifestation of pure being.

The lyrical characterizations in "The Old Cumberland Beggar" and "Animal Tranquillity and Decay" are what I have in *The Poetry of Experience* called mute dramatic monologues, because the characters reveal themselves through visual impression. They reveal their lyrical characterization. Wordsworth's portrayals of character usually begin with a visual impression; and even when speech follows, revealing the dramatic characterization, it adds little to and often detracts from the visual impression. Thus Wordsworth wisely cut the bit of dialogue with which "Animal Tranquillity" originally ended—dialogue which provides a dramatic context by giving a most uninteresting account of where the old man is heading.

The theme of unconsciousness is carried farthest in "The Idiot Boy," Wordsworth's most misunderstood and underrated poem. In this poem we find in extreme form the problem of interpretation that appears in "The Thorn" and elsewhere—that the poem seems sentimental unless we read the main characterization as lyrical. A correct reading of "The Idiot Boy" yields a poem which, far from being sentimental, is Wordsworth's only comic triumph. "I never wrote anything," he told Isabella Fenwick, "with so much glee." The poem is comic in the romantic manner in that the comedy expands rather than diminishes imagination. "We are called on for tenderness rather than condescension," writes John F. Danby in *The Simple Wordsworth*.[8] In a letter of 1802, Wordsworth says in regard to "The Idiot Boy,"

> I have often applied to Idiots, in my own mind, that sublime expression of scripture that, "*their life is hidden with God.*" . . . I have indeed often looked upon the conduct of fathers and mothers of the lower

classes of society towards Idiots as the great triumph of the human heart.[9]

The idiot boy is not sentimentalized because he exists in a circumscribed pastoral world where simplicity is nature's simplicity and therefore profound. The other characters, Betty Foy and Susan Gale, are not much cleverer than he; and the pony is about as clever as the human beings. But they are all rich in benevolence. The moonlight provides the element in which such characters can flourish. The only cranky person is the doctor, who having some intelligence exists outside the charmed circle.

Betty, her idiot boy, and the pony are also rich in imagination. Quality of imagination is an important criterion of judgment in Wordsworth. But in the poems I have so far discussed, imagination is located in the observer-narrator and harmony with nature in the observed, with the two qualities brought together in the course of the poem. In "The Idiot Boy," the observed have more imagination and harmony with nature than the so-called author who cannot devise so good an ending for the story as do the pony and the idiot boy.

The sign of the characters' imagination and harmony with nature is joy. When the idiot boy is mounted on the pony, his joy renders him incompetent as a horseman; but his incompetence brings him into harmony with imagination and nature and produces his triumph:

> For joy he cannot hold the bridle,
> For joy his head and heels are idle,
> He's idle all for very joy.
>
> (Ll. 73–75)

His loving mother's "face with joy o'erflows," and even the pony "never will be out of humour" (ll. 88, 111). Although the pony moves, the idiot boy achieves stillness: "The Moon that shines above his head / Is not more still and mute than he" (ll. 80–81). His mother, Betty Foy, and the sick neighbor, Susan Gale, for whom he is being sent to find a doctor, are very simple dramatic characterizations in that their only characteristics are stupidity and benevolence. But the idiot boy's muteness makes him a quintessential lyrical characterization. His muteness is the sign of an imagination that blends perfectly with nature.

The quality of Betty's imagination is shown as she imagines all the things that might have happened to Johnny when he does not return. The possibilities are all poetical; yet her characterization is dramatic because she verbalizes the possibilities:

"Or in the castle he's pursuing
Among the ghosts his own undoing;
Or playing with the waterfall."

(Ll. 229–31)

The so-called author, too, strains his imagination speculating on John-ny's whereabouts: perhaps he will "lay his hands upon a star, / And in his pocket bring it home" (ll. 320–21). But when Betty finally comes upon Johnny, his situation is even more poetical then anyone imagined since he is *unconsciously* a part of the moonlit night:

Who's yon, that, near the waterfall,
Which thunders down with headlong force,
Beneath the moon, yet shining fair,
As careless as if nothing were,
Sits upright on a feeding horse?

(Ll. 347–51)

Johnny is like a figure in "romances," because "Of moon or stars he takes no heed" (ll. 354–55). His unconsciousness, muteness and stillness carry to an extreme all Wordsworth's lyrical characterizations; for they portray him as pure being. The comic mode suggests that idiocy is too high a price to pay for such pure being; yet Johnny points a direction for us.

As in all Wordsworth's characterizations by visual impression, it is a shock when Johnny finally speaks in the last stanza. But his speech is not as in other poems anticlimactic, for it is pure nonsense and therefore poetical. To Betty's question about what he has heard and seen, Johnny answers: "'The cocks did crow to-whoo, to-whoo, / And the sun did shine so cold!'" Johnny's answer is pure poetry because poetry speaks of one thing in terms of another—the owls as cocks, the moon as a cold sun. His answer is, by Wordsworth's and modern standards, better po-etry than the so-called author's eighteenth-century-style "The owls in tuneful concert strive" (l. 443). Johnny is a perfect because unconscious poet who fulfills his mission in the manner of poetry, indirectly. It is by *not* fetching the doctor that he cures Susan Gale, who forgets her pain in order to go in search of him and his mother. Wordsworth said that the poem grew out of Johnny's utterance, which he heard in a true account of an idiot. Johnny's nondiscursive speech works like his muteness to clarify the purpose of all Wordsworth's lyrical characterizations—to make our common humanity newly apparent because located where we would least expect it, at the minimum level of consciousness.

When we consider the regressiveness of Wordsworth's lyrical characterizations, we realize how remarkable technically is his characterization of
the leech-gatherer. For the leech-gatherer has all the mute existential
power of the Cumberland beggar and the idiot boy, while endowed with
consciousness and will: he draws upon human will and faith in God to
endure despite nature's niggardliness. Midway between such extremes
of unconsciousness and consciousness stands the great lyrical characterization of the discharged soldier in the closing episode of *The Prelude,*
Book 4.

The discharged soldier seems to be an attempt to achieve an effect
that Wordsworth failed to achieve in the figure of the discharged sailor
in the second version of "Salisbury Plain." Both men are penniless after
having served their country, and their plight is dramatized through solitary location on a landscape. The difference is that the story of the discharged sailor is so detailed that he emerges, despite his connection with
landscape, as a dramatic characterization, especially since he engages in
dialogue with other solitary figures whose stories are as important as his.
(The story of the female vagrant, in the same poem, is even less successful
because both detailed and detached from landscape.) Of the soldier in
The Prelude, Book 4, instead, we learn only through his indirect narration that he served in the Tropic Islands, "had been dismissed, / And
now was travelling towards his native home" (ll. 424–25). He is not
quoted until the end when he says something resembling the sailor's remark at the end of the revised version, "Guilt and Sorrow." The sailor
says, "'My trust, Saviour! is in thy name!'" (l. 657).[10] The soldier says,
"'My trust is in the God in Heaven, / And in the eye of him who passes
me!'" (ll. 459–60). Both remarks express the speakers' capacity to
endure.

The main difference between the two figures is that the sailor is not
observed. He and his story are presented objectively, and therefore seem
sentimental because unable to substantiate the affect attributed to them.
The soldier, instead, is seen by an observer whose inner situation has
been so elaborated that the soldier's affect is substantiated as the observer's projection. The soldier is an external-internal border figure, important in himself but also important in the development of the observer
who seems substantial because he is Wordsworth.

The elaboration of the observer is the innovative feature of this episode, drafted in winter 1797–98 and revised for incorporation in *The
Prelude* of 1805. Since the early draft gives as much attention to the
observer as the revised versions of 1805 and 1850, it figures as Wordsworth's earliest elaboration of the observer in a narrative. The dis-
charged-soldier episode was drafted at the same time as "A Night-

Piece"—both employ the sudden appearance of the moon,[11] with "A Night-Piece" figuring as Wordsworth's early elaboration of the observer in a lyrical nature poem. "Tintern Abbey," the nature poem which carries the elaboration of the observer farthest, was not written until July 1978.

In the context of *The Prelude,* the observer's preparation for the encounter with the discharged soldier begins in the passage in Book 4, where Wordsworth compares his pursuit of memory with the sight from a boat of objects really underwater yet mingled with deceptive reflections of mountains and sky, so that one "cannot part / The shadow from the substance" (ll. 263–64)—the subjective from the objective. Not often, he says, "have appeared / Shapes fairer or less doubtfully discerned" (ll. 273–74)—so ambiguous—than in the tale he will tell.

All that follows is indeed wrapped in ambiguity. Wordsworth speaks of his regrets for a time when he fell from his high purpose through indulgence in youthful revelry.

> And yet, for chastisement of these regrets,
> The memory of one particular hour
> Doth here rise up against me.
>
> (Ll. 307–9)

The hour is probably the incident immediately following when, returning at sunrise from a summer's night of dancing, the young Wordsworth in a burst of exultation felt himself "A dedicated Spirit" (l. 337)—dedicated perhaps to poetry. Or the hour could refer to the meeting with the discharged soldier. In both cases the significance of the hour derives from contrast with the revelry; so that the revelry proved beneficial and regret for it is chastised. Yet this meaning has to be disentangled with effort from the emotional thrust of "chastisement" and "rise up against me," which seem to be directed against the revelry. The lingering punitive meaning creates ambiguity.

"My mind was at that time," says Wordsworth, "A parti-coloured show of grave and gay" (ll. 339–40). He continues in a passage inserted later to explain the significance of the discharged soldier: "When from our better selves we have too long / Been parted by the hurrying world . . . / . . . How gracious, how benign, is Solitude," which is "Most potent when impressed upon the mind / With an appropriate human centre" (ll. 354–60). The soldier will appear as that "human centre," the embodiment of solitude that recalls the young Wordsworth to his better self. We would expect the meeting to take place at this point. But there follows, instead, the self-dedication; and the meeting with the soldier takes place in autumn after a similar night of dancing. The sliding of the one occa-

sion into the other suggests that the encounter is both historical and
typological. On the second occasion Wordsworth returns when it is still
night; so that natural-supernatural transformations can be worked. The
meeting with the discharged soldier can be understood as a repetition
and complication of the earlier self-dedication, because the young
Wordsworth learns to include pity for human suffering in the high purpose to which he so joyfully dedicated himself.

"My homeward course," says Wordsworth,

> led up a long ascent,
> Where the road's watery surface, to the top
> Of that sharp rising, glittered to the moon
> And bore the semblance of another stream
> Stealing with silent lapse to join the brook
> That murmured in a vale. All else was still.
>
> (Ll. 379–84)

We have here one of those optical illusions, dissolving the distinctions
among earth, water and light, which so often prepare Wordsworth for
epiphany. The sound of a real stream reinforces the optical illusion that
the moonlit road is a stream. The soldier appears suddenly like an ema-
nation from this mysteriously fluid landscape. He appears not as an individual but as "an uncouth shape." "Uncouth" meant for Wordsworth
strange and *unknown,* but the more modern meaning *low-class* also
applies.

"But, lo! an uncouth shape," says Wordsworth,

> Shown there by a sudden turning of the road.
> So near that, slipping back into the shade
> Of a thick hawthorn, I could mark him well,
> Myself unseen.
>
> (Ll. 387–91)

Why does the youth hide himself? The lines that follow suggest that he
feels guilty, that the desolate figure seems an almost supernatural rebuke
of his youthful, middle-class frivolity:

> He stood, and in his very dress appeared
> A desolation, a simplicity,
> To which the trappings of a gaudy world
> Make a strange back-ground.
>
> (Ll. 401–4)

Hence the youth's "self-blame" and need to subdue his "heart's specious cowardice," in order to leave his "shady nook" and hail the soldier (ll. 401–12). The encounter recalls the youth to the "grave" side of his "parti-coloured" mind (ll. 339–40).

The characterization of the soldier is even more mysterious than I have so far suggested; for he is portrayed as a ghostly figure who has the muteness and stillness of some of Wordsworth's other lyrical characterizations. Like the leech-gatherer, he is a traveler beheld at a moment of rest: the soldier is so still that "at his feet / His shadow lay, and moved not" (ll. 407–8). Yet he has been walking and will walk, making like the Cumberland beggar an impression of stillness in motion. He looks "ghastly [ghostly] in the moonlight" (l. 396); when the two walk together, "I beheld," says Wordsworth, "With an astonishment but ill suppressed, / His ghastly figure moving at my side" (ll. 432–34). The youth is astonished because the figure at his side does not seem quite alive. The soldier tells his story with

> a strange half-absence, as of one
> Knowing too well the importance of his theme,
> But feeling it no longer.
>
> (Ll. 443–45)

He has, like the Cumberland beggar, suffered so long that he is numb; he speaks like one returned from the dead. The earlier dissolution of distinctions among earth, water and light has prepared for the dissolution now of the distinction between life and death, externality and internality, which establishes the soldier on the border between these realms. All the elaborate spiritualizing techniques are designed to portray the soldier as also the youth's alter ego, the projection of his better self. The episode is in structure and purpose like "Resolution and Independence." In both, the final pious utterance gains authenticity from the visual impression. The soldier's utterance emphasizes benevolence; he places his trust not only in God, but also in human benevolence: "'in the eye of him who passes me!'" (l. 460).

The surprising thing is that the youth expresses his benevolence by commending the soldier to the charity of a third party. The youth hid in the hawthorn shade not only out of shame for his frivolity, but also out of egotism; he was subject to Wordsworth's recurring temptation to use nature as an escape from human communion—his earlier self-dedication arose from communion with the morning landscape. When the youth addresses the soldier, he discovers a human communion based on benevolence. But when he knocks on the cottage door, assuming that the cottager will take in the soldier, he discovers a social principle based on benevolence. The fact that the door is unbarred without sight of the cottager, as though it had unbarred itself, shows that a social principle rather than an individual act is at issue. (Wordsworth's final revision makes the unbarring autonomous; in the early draft and in the 1805 version, the youth knows and is quoted as speaking to the laborer who opens the door.) The youth can in the last line return to solitude "with quiet heart" (l. 469); for having seen a victim of social injustice, he has learned how to remake society by connecting nature, human suffering and benevolence.

A great weight of meaning has been placed on the figure of the soldier, all of it evolving from the complex way the figure registers upon the observer. The meaning, however, is implied; there is no didactic content to conflict, as in "The Old Cumberland Beggar," with the lyrical characterization. In "Resolution and Independence," we apprehend the evolution of meaning in the observer's mind through metamorphoses in his vision of the leech-gatherer—to stone and sea-beast, to motionless cloud, to "one whom I had met with in a dream" (l. 110), to one pacing "About the weary moors continually" (l. 130). Here, instead, the realistic and transcendental visions, the dramatic and lyrical characterizations, are contained in a single impression from the moment the soldier first appears as "an uncouth shape" that takes on individual lineaments without losing mystery.

Such human mystery is distilled in the purely lyrical characterization of the blind beggar in *The Prelude*, Book 7. The beggar is seen in connection not with nature but with a sea of London faces shown to be as mysterious as nature. Still and mute, he wears "a written paper, to explain / His story" (ll. 641–42). The spectacle leads to an epiphanic turning of the mind as awesome as an epiphany of nature:

> my mind turned round
> As with the might of waters; an apt type
> This label seemed of the utmost we can know,
> Both of ourselves and of the universe;
> And, on the shape of that unmoving man,
> His steadfast face and sightless eyes, I gazed,
> As if admonished from another world.
>
> (Ll. 643–49)

The symbolic possibilities of lyrical characterization are developed even farther in the passage on shepherds in Book 8. The passage contrasts to the conventional shepherds of pastoral poetry the hard life of a

real Cumbrian shepherd, and then transcendentalizes the real shepherd
through optical illusions caused by mists and radiant sunsets:

> By mists bewildered, suddenly mine eyes
> Have glanced upon him distant a few steps,
> In size a giant, stalking through thick fog,
> His sheep like Greenland bears; or, as he stepped
> Beyond the boundary line of some hill-shadow,
> His form hath flashed upon me, glorified
> By the deep radiance of the setting sun.

(Ll. 264–70)

Wordsworth goes so far as to turn the shepherd into an icon, into the
outdoor cross with which earlier he represented the enduring quality of
the Grande Chartreuse. The shepherd is

> like an aerial cross
> Stationed alone upon a spiry rock
> Of the Chartreuse, for worship.

(Ll. 273–75)

Although "this creature" was less "spiritual," less perfect, than the conventional shepherds "of books," he was "more exalted far; / Far more of
an imaginative form" (ll. 281–84). Wordsworth is distinguishing between the neoclassical *type,* which derives from literary convention, and
the romantic *archetype* which derives from imaginative transformation
of a realistic portrayal. Such archetypalization parallels the movement
from mourning to figuration which Peter M. Sacks, in *The English Elegy*
(1985), sees as the consolatory movement of elegies.

The momentary symbolization of character which Wordsworth
achieves through the aerial cross is sustained in the figure of the doe in
"The White Doe of Rylstone." The attempt to give a symbol a sustained
existence apart from somebody's perception circles back to the Spenser-
ian allegory (Wordsworth acknowledged Spenser's influence on the
poem), which Wordsworth had originally rejected. The doe remains romantic, however, in what she represents—the values of Wordsworth's
earlier poetry: nature, ruins, benevolence, memory, continuity. Mainly
the doe represents the imaginative retrospective vision which reconciles
opposites, in this case the historical clash between Catholics and Protes-
tants. The doe appears at Sunday services at the ruins of the now Protestant Bolton Priory:

> Comes gliding in with lovely gleam.
> Comes gliding in serene and slow,
> Soft and silent as a dream,

(Ll. 55–57)

while recalling the Priory's Catholic past when she was also present. Wandering in the end "like a gliding ghost" in Bolton's graveyard, amid "sculptured Forms of Warriors brave," the doe settles tranquilly by the grave of Francis Norton who contained the conflict within his own breast: "There doth the gentle Creature lie / With those adversities unmoved" (ll. 1883–1902).

The doe remains romantic because symbolic of Emily Norton, the poem's one lyrical characterization. I said earlier that a lyrical characterization omits moral choice. Although Peter Bell is a solitary wanderer in nature, he is a dramatic characterization because he exercises moral choice: he is evil, then converts. Lyrical characterizations—the speakers of dramatic monologues, for example—never convert; they become more intensely what they are. A Protestant, Emily, not out of choice but at her father's command, embroiders the Catholic banner around which her father and brothers rally. Her brother Francis, the other Protestant in the family, exercises moral choice in refusing to fight with his father and brothers though he is ready to share their doom. Francis, however, enjoins Emily to renounce "All prayers for this cause, or for that!" (l. 541). She is called "the consecrated Maid" (l. 591) because of her detachment.

Like all Wordsworth's lyrical characterizations, Emily exhibits a composure in suffering—"carrying inward a serene / And perfect sway" (ll. 1593–94)—and a capacity to endure: she outlives the other Nortons, enduring as "a wandering Pilgrim" (l. 1610). Emily's compassion for both sides in the conflict is represented as a principle of beauty—the doe. Wordsworth explores in this poem that question of poetry versus doctrine—the notion that poetry reconciles and transcends ideas, thus turning them into poetry—which was to fascinate T. S. Eliot. "These men, and those who opposed them," says Eliot speaking in "Little Gidding" about a later civil war in England, now "Accept the constitution of silence / And are folded in a single party" (pt. 3).[12] The lines express perfectly the significance of the white doe and her serene silence.

We can understand and admire the symbolism and artistry with which Wordsworth carries to a new extreme the implications of lyrical characterization; yet the poem is beautiful and dead, like white alabaster, because it does not emerge from vitally realistic portrayals of Emily and the doe. The ethereal doe carries the weight of more significance than she can substantiate. Emily and the doe are not in the usual Wordsworthian subject-object relation; since the doe does not exist through Emily's perception, Emily does not project significance onto her. The doe exists as an objective parallel figure that restates Emily's significance—a significance which itself seems mere sentimental wishfulness, perhaps because

Emily is insufficiently connected to a realized landscape from which she could draw value. Since the authority for the symbolism does not as in Spenser derive from a publicly acknowledged system of values, the symbolism seems arbitrary. The case shows how the romantic and modern poet cannot sustain a symbol without enveloping it in the affect projected from a dramatized observer or from a particularized eye. There is no such eye on the white doe.

But if we understand what Wordsworth is trying to do in "The White Doe," we can understand all his lyrical characterizations—that in their omission of moral choice and their portrayal of character through mystery rather than through many details, his lyrical characterizations are all designed to portray the pure being represented by the doe. We can also see how Wordsworth's lyrical characterizations are a step toward symbolist poetry and toward the new sense of character as unconscious being to be found in twentieth-century fiction and in all the advanced twentieth-century arts.

The Victorian Idea
of Culture

To understand what the Victorian age means to us today, let us take the case of E. M. Forster. The story of his family is characteristic of the century-long migration of English liberal intellectuals from Clapham to Bloomsbury. Forster was the great-grandson of the Evangelical and utilitarian M.P. Henry Thornton of Clapham; and Clapham, near London, was at the beginning of the nineteenth century the home of the so-called Clapham Sect—wealthy lay leaders of the Evangelical or Low Church reforming party within the Church of England. At Clapham resided Hannah More, who wrote pious tracts and did philanthropic work among the poor, and William Wilberforce, who led the campaign to abolish the slave trade and was aided in the campaign by such other residents as Zachary Macaulay, father of Thomas Babington, later Lord Macaulay, and James Stephen, grandfather of Leslie Stephen and great-grandfather of Virginia Woolf. These families gradually connected through marriages with Trevelyans, Huxleys, Arnolds, Darwins, Keyneses, Stracheys—all the families which, according to Noel Annan in his biography of Leslie Stephen, constitute the intellectual aristocracy of modern England.

The point is that in the early nineteenth century the upper-middle-class elite believed in piety, reform of church and state, moral action and laissez-faire economics. Their early-twentieth-century descendants, however, as represented by the so-called Bloomsbury Group (Leslie Stephen's four children formed the nucleus; Lytton Strachey and J. M. Keynes belonged; Forster was a frequent visitor), disbelieved in religion and moral action, and did believe (through their political voices, Leonard Woolf and Keynes) in a regulated economy, and in refinement of sensibility. Between Clapham and Bloomsbury stands Matthew Arnold with his admonition to liberals to be less Hebraic or moral and more Hellenic or aesthetic; for the Victorian experience had shown that moral action without self-understanding and inner refinement resulted in the hypocrisy and the damaging forms of philanthropy Dickens is so good at exposing. Thus Bloomsbury's favorite philosopher, G. E. Moore, taught that nothing mattered but "states of mind." Foster himself, in *Two Cheers for Democracy* (1951), sums up the paradoxical position of liberal intellectuals nowadays in Britain and America. We believe in government regulation of the economy, he suggests, but in a laissez-faire of the spirit; we believe in political democracy, but in an aristocracy of the spirit. Since this is the position toward which the whole Victorian literary enterprise has led us, we can see why Victorian literature matters. And, indeed, the concerted revaluation of the period that has gone on since 1940 has quite reversed the old sneering attitude exemplified by Lytton Strachey's *Eminent Victorians* (1918).

The order of perception that lay behind Arnold's attack is expressed by the remark of Arnold's contemporary Walter Bagehot that "Nothing is more unpleasant than a virtuous person with a mean mind. A highly developed moral nature joined to an undeveloped intellectual nature, an undeveloped artistic nature, is of necessity repulsive."[1] In the 1850s, the younger members of the prosperous middle class were becoming aware of the narrowness and meagerness of the middle-class tradition. The term "Victorian" or "Early Victorian" began at this time to appear in its pejorative sense, to refer to the middle-class Evangelical and utilitarian spirit. Since the best Victorian writers were on the whole anti-"Victorian," we have to read backward from their writings to discern the assumptions and tastes of the articulate public.

Thomas Babington Macaulay is the one outstanding writer who does speak for the middle class, just because he steered a Whiggish course between the Evangelical Toryism of his father, on the one side, and, on the other, the democratic politics and religious agnosticism of the Benthamites. Macaulay believed like the Benthamites in progress and laissez-faire, but was more genial, literary, conventional, and far less philosophical than they. He was in these respects—in others, he was Augustan and aristocratic through his connection with the Whig nobility—closer to popular thinking than the Benthamites. In his passion for political liberty, Macaulay represents the best of the middle-class spirit. But in his identification of reason with common sense and in his smug satisfaction with the age because it showed numerical increase in population and wealth, he displays the attitudes Arnold was to stigmatize as Philistine ("a Philistine of genius," A. L. Rowse calls Macaulay). To understand the side against which the literary men were reacting, read Macaulay's attack in 1830 on Southey's book *Sir Thomas More; or, Colloquies on the Progress and Prospects of Society.*

Southey and the other two Lake poets, Wordsworth and Coleridge,

were considered renegades, because they had started in the 1790s as radicals, supporters of the French Revolution, and later turned into Tories.
But leaving aside their personal crotchets, they are, I think, to be understood as the first Victorians, in that they realized long before Queen Victoria's accession that the nature of the enemy had changed—that the
enemy was no longer feudalism but rather the laissez-faire industrialism
that threatened to destroy the countryside and men's souls. From what
Macaulay says about Southey and what Mill in "Coleridge" (1840) says
about Coleridge, we see the makings of a peculiarly Victorian phenomenon—that the movement against laissez-faire and toward the present-
day welfare state came largely from the right, from conservatives harking
back nostalgically to a unified and more humane agrarian order. In the
early Carlyle of *Sartor Resartus* (1833–34) and *Past and Present* (1843),
we see a radical conservatism; for Carlyle wanted radical institutional
changes in order to revivify the permanent responsibility of all societies
to look after the physical, moral, and spiritual welfare of their citizens.
The economists were mistaken, said Carlyle, in supposing that they had
found a new formula through which society could now shirk its responsibility, could send its citizens into the "free market" with the pious hope
that the general good would somehow be served if each man looked after
his own interest without minding the other fellow's.

The characteristics we think of as Victorian were well established
by the time of the queen's accession in 1837. Some historians consider
the era as starting with the 1832 Reform Bill, which opened the way for
the eventual political ascendancy of the middle class and ushered in a
rapid succession of legislative reforms. Certainly the laissez-faire ideology was fully developed by 1832; whereas serious regulation of industry
began with the Factory Act of 1833—which was the first act regulating
hours and conditions of work that had teeth in it, because it provided
for inspection. There followed, in counterpoint to a continued lifting of
controls, a succession of regulatory laws; it was the pro-laissez-faire Benthamites, paradoxically, who had prepared the administrative apparatus
that made regulation possible. Victoria's reign saw, therefore, in what
was finally to prove to be the main current, a steady retreat from laissez-
faire. Again, if we associate Victorianism with prudery, gloomy Sundays,
and fear of the senses, pleasure and art—with, in other words, the Evangelical spirit—then it is also true that the Evangelical spirit had
triumphed by 1833, the year of Wilberforce's death and the abolition of
slavery, and that Victoria's reign saw a slow retreat from it, a retreat that
became apparent when aestheticism developed after the mid-century into
a conspicuous cultural force. By the 1890s the cultivated minority was
in full rebellion against prudery.

The apparent exception to the above line of development is the Free Trade principle, which did not win out until 1846 with the repeal of the Corn Laws, the tariff on wheat that seemed to protect the aristocratic or landed interest. The Free Trade principle, which had acquired the magical sanction of a religious dogma, maintained its ascendancy for the rest of the century even though British agriculture suffered badly in the last three decades from the competition of American wheat.

Another Victorian characteristic, well established before the queen's accession, resulted from the unprecedented statistical surveys that accompanied the reform movement of the thirties. The thirties was the decade of the Blue Books, the reports of parliamentary committees or royal commissions on every aspect of English life except agriculture. Engels and Marx, who settled in England in 1849 (Engels had already visited in 1843–44), used these Blue Books—Engels for *The Condition of the Working Class in England in 1844* and Marx for *Das Kapital,* the first volume of which was published in 1867. The guiding spirit behind the Blue Books was that of Bentham and his philosophic radicals or utilitarians; and they, through the Blue Books, taught the English reading public to worship—as Dickens was to put it satirically in *Hard Times*— "Facts . . . Facts . . . Facts."

The Philistine worship of facts went along with a literary reaction against Byronism that followed Byron's death in 1824. The literary reaction, as summed up by Carlyle's injunction in *Sartor* "Close thy Byron; open thy Goethe," was against self-preoccupation and for the social responsibility that Wilhelm Meister and Faust finally arrive at. As summed up by Sir Henry Taylor in the preface to his verse drama *Philip Van Artevelde* (1834), the reaction was against too much feeling and imagination at the expense of realism, intellect and morality. Passing on to Shelley, Taylor condemns him for a too exclusive pursuit of beauty and for a visionary quality that presents us forms "never to be seen through the mere medium of eyesight."[2]

It was into this hostile atmosphere that Tennyson and Browning sent their still romantic poems of 1830, with unhappy results. Tennyson, particularly, wavered throughout his career between his impulse to write poetry of private sensation and his genuine interest in writing on public issues and joining in the march of progress. In reviewing Tennyson's 1830 *Poems,* Arthur Hallam praises Tennyson for just the qualities Taylor condemns in Shelley; for Hallam classes Tennyson with Keats and Shelley, with "poets of sensation" as distinguished from a "reflective" poet like Wordsworth. Hallam's position was taken up again in the aesthetic movement—especially the later phase, beginning with Pater in the seventies, that defined itself in opposition to ideas and dogmatic com-

mitments. Yeats, in his essay "Art and Ideas" (1913), draws a line from
Shelley and Keats through early Tennyson and the Pre-Raphaelites (who
preferred early Tennyson) to the poets of the nineties and the twentieth-
century poetry of Yeats himself. The opposing impulses that Tennyson
along with Browning and Arnold contained within themselves were po-
larized by the end of the century between, on the one hand, the extreme
aestheticism of Yeats and his friends, the poets of the nineties, who
sought to empty their poetry of content, and, on the other hand, the
socially responsible naturalism of Ibsen and Shaw. Yeats in his *Autobiography* (1938) writes that he and his friends could not escape the
antithetical Ibsen, because "we had the same enemies."[3] The enemies
were, of course, the middle-class Philistines—which suggests that both
sides were revolutionary and had in common a principle of progress opposed to that of the Philistines, a principle based on more complex criteria than the rise in national wealth and population. To this larger principle of progress, the nineteenth century gave the elusive name of
"culture."

   In the introduction to his important book *Culture and Society
1780–1950*, Raymond Williams lists five key words that either came into
common use or acquired new meanings at the turn of the nineteenth
century. From these words, changes in life and thought can be charted.
And of these words—*industry, democracy, class* (rather than *rank*), *art*
(as a specialized activity superior to all other human skills), and *culture*—the last presents the most important and complex cluster of concepts. Williams goes on in the rest of the book to investigate the development and ramifications of the idea of culture through studies of major
figures from Burke through the Victorians to Lawrence, Eliot, the Marxist critics and Orwell. He locates the idea of culture in the principle held
in common by such contrasting pairs as the late-eighteenth-century conservative Burke and the radical Cobbett; or the early-nineteenth-century
Tory Southey and the socialist Robert Owen. Both sides "attacked the
new [industrializing] England from their experience of the old England,"[4] and were concerned with what had been lost.

   Such reconciliation of opposites relates to John Stuart Mill's advice
to his contemporaries, in the essay on Coleridge, to "master the premises
and combine the methods" of Bentham and Coleridge. Bentham was a
radical, utterly irreverent of the past, who thought all laws and institutions ought to be subjected to the test of utility, "the greatest happiness
of the greatest number"; while the later Coleridge, the Coleridge of the
prose writings who exercised so much influence on the Victorians, was a
romantic conservative, who was mainly out to rehabilitate old institutions. By absorbing into his own inherited Benthamism the opposite Col-

eridgian view, Mill worked out for himself what was to be the characteristic Victorian synthesis—the absorption, that is, into a progressivist
philosophy of a new respect for the past and for those institutions and
values of the past that could not have been what the Benthamites thought
them, mere frauds, since they had engaged the best minds and hearts of
so many centuries.

When Mill goes on to say that the Germano-Coleridgian school has
made the largest contribution towards "the philosophy of human culture," he means that the school of Herder and Goethe, with its influence
on Michelet in France and Coleridge in England, has taught us to view
alien societies, whether past or present, as manifestations of national
character at a particular phase of development.[5] Societies are not,
in other words, to be judged by a fixed abstract standard, but are to
be understood as *characteristic* and therefore self-justifying—once
we understand how they came to be as they are and how their parts cohere to make an organism adapted to its geographical and historical
environment.[6]

I use the biological metaphor to make a point Mill does not make—
that the central idea of the nineteenth century is the organicist or evolutionary idea, launched in England by Burke's answer to the French Rev-
olutionists who wanted to wipe out the past and start over with an abstract blueprint for the perfect society. Burke's answer was to say that the
state is in some respects like a plant, that it is organized according to a
living principle of continuity that cannot be abrogated and that transforms separate persons into a people—into an entity greater than and
different from the sum of its parts. The state is an artificial creation, but
one which functions for man, who is a reasonable being, *like* a natural
organism—for "Art is man's nature."[7]

That paradox of Burke's—"Art is man's nature"—helps us understand the nineteenth-century concept of culture: the concept behind the
attempt of the Victorians to reconcile change with continuity and order.
The Latin *cultura* means cultivation of the soil; and the obvious emphasis, the emphasis one still finds in Arnold, is on education, on the things
man adds to nature. But Arnold is aware that culture is also an unconscious inevitable growth; and Carlyle insists that the principles that
really hold society together are unconscious.

In our own time, when sociologists, anthropologists and depth psy-
chologists have further expanded the concept of culture, the word is seldom used in serious discussions to mean belles lettres, but comprehends
every characterizing aspect of a people, their *whole* way of life. The most
trivial characteristics—the ones of which we are not conscious—may be
most fundamental, because indicative of that internal life of a people that

survives political change. It is internality, if not subconsciousness, that stands behind Coleridge's distinction between cultivation or culture and civilization: "a nation can never be a too cultivated, but may easily become an over-civilized, race"; or behind Mill's criticism of Bentham: "Man is never recognized by Bentham as a being capable of pursuing spiritual perfection as an end."[8] T. S. Eliot, however, has both internality and subconsciousness in mind in *Notes towards the Definition of Culture*. Since "culture cannot altogether be brought to consciousness," says Eliot, it cannot be dominated or directed by politics or education. "The culture of which we are wholly conscious is never the whole of culture: the effective culture is that which is directing the activities of those who are manipulating that which they *call* culture."[9] Like Burke, Eliot uses the concept of culture to oppose the engineered or totally manipulated society.

One has to understand that the word *culture* was from the beginning charged with a world-view and a battle cry. In a revolutionary age, the word was used to define a principle of continuity underlying political, economic and even social change. It was used in an industrial age, which measured progress by numbers, to ask about the *quality* of life—especially since quality seemed to be declining. Since the economy required specialization and dehumanization, the word *culture* was invoked as an argument for the harmonious development of all our human faculties. Since the dominating middle class viewed art as useless and therefore as a mere luxury product, the antithetical concept of culture came to include the idea that the art of a period is an index to its quality and that aesthetic judgments are therefore inextricably related to moral and social judgments. This was the lesson taught, as regards architecture and the visual arts, by Pugin, Ruskin and Morris; and, as regards literature, by Matthew Arnold. In "The Function of Criticism at the Present Time," Arnold writes: "For the creation of a master-work of literature, two powers must concur, the power of the man and the power of the moment, and the man is not enough without the moment; the creative power has, for its happy exercise, appointed elements, and those elements are not in its own control."[10] Style came to be regarded as organic to a society and therefore as an index to its real or subconscious character. Influenced by Freud, we have in our own time come to regard the quality of our sexuality as another index of cultural health, and have benefited in the 1980s from studies of Victorian sexuality as an element of Victorian culture.[11]

Because the Victorians' attack on their own age is so largely expressed through the concept of culture, the literature of the age is inextricably connected with its histories and social criticism. For the concept of culture was the product of the literary mind when it was turned upon the unprecedented conditions of the nineteenth century. Indeed the literary mind, with its memory of other world-views and of "the best [in Arnold's words] that is known and thought in the world," offered the one hope of escape, that was not a mere return to stale orthodoxy, from the latest shibboleths—"the greatest happiness of the greatest number" or "doing as you like with your own."

It took a mind stored with cultural memory to see, as Coleridge does, how unprecedentedly brutal was the economists' justification of depressions as self-regulating machinery to help "things find their level."

> But Persons are not *Things*—but Man does not find his level. Neither in body nor in soul does the Man find his level! . . . Be it that plenty has returned and that Trade has once more become brisk and stirring: go ask the overseer, and question the parish doctor, whether the workman's health and temperance with the staid and respectful Manners best taught by the inward dignity of conscious self-support, have found *their* level again!

Thinking of moral versus laissez-faire economic principles, Coleridge says: "formerly MEN WERE WORSE THAN THEIR PRINCIPLES, but . . . at present the PRINCIPLES ARE WORSE THAN THE MEN."[12] It took a mind stored with cultural memory to see, as Carlyle does in the powerful opening chapter of *Past and Present,* that England in the "hungry forties" lay under a Midas enchantment—dying of starvation with wealth all around. The enchantment was the paralyzing laissez-faire dogma that forbade tampering with the free market; so that men could not reach out and distribute the wealth they were producing. It required cultural memory to see in the case of the pauper Wragg, who strangled her unwanted baby on the bleak Mapperley Hills, to see in the case, as Arnold does in "The Function of Criticism," not so much the age-old story of poverty but, through the ugliness of the names and setting and the impersonal newspaper account, an unprecedentedly dismal cultural situation.

In "The Function of Criticism," Arnold means by "criticism" just such a turning of the literary mind upon public affairs. Not only has the literary mind access to a high and wide tradition by which to judge the current scene, but it has the "disinterestedness," the ability to play freely with ideas and possibilities, which is the peculiar reward of literary study. Because of this disinterestedness, the literary mind can give assent to opposite positions—as, according to Arnold, Burke did when he concluded his arguments against the French Revolution as follows:

"If a great change is to be made in human affairs, the minds of men will be fitted to it; the general opinions and feelings will draw that way. Every fear, every hope will forward it; and then they who persist in opposing this mighty current in human affairs, will appear rather to resist the decrees of Providence itself, than the mere designs of men. They will not be resolute and firm, but perverse and obstinate."[13]

Like Arnold, who though a liberal spent most of his career criticizing liberals, Burke paid allegiance to a principle of culture that can be served by a properly informed liberal or conservative position. The conservative Coleridge, for example, influenced the Christian Socialist and the Broad Church or liberal Anglican movements. And Arnold, in *Culture and Anarchy* (1869), connects the working-class movement of the sixties with Newman's Oxford or High Church movement which, in promoting thirty years earlier the dogmatic, Catholic character of Anglicanism, helped undermine the Protestant, liberal individualism of the middle class.

Perhaps the most important advantage of the literary mind is that its figurative way of reading events and using language enables it to deal at once with external and internal matters. This advantage accounts for a peculiar phenomenon of the age. I mean the so-called Victorian prophets or sages—prose writers like Carlyle, Newman, Arnold, Ruskin (I would add Pater and the discursive Morris; Shaw and Lawrence are in the same tradition) who, whether they wrote on history, or on political, social or economic subjects, on religion, literature or the visual arts, wrote under a governing principle of culture that connected any one of these subjects with all the others and with a demand for action, either personal or social. The most distinctive things about these discursive prose writings is that they ranked with the poetry and fiction of the age as literature.

In a brilliant introduction to his book *The Victorian Sage,* John Holloway shows why these discursive writings can be regarded as literature. Like the poet and novelist, the Victorian sage persuades not by logical argument but by projecting a coherent vision of life into which his argument fits. "The methods traced here persuade because they clarify, and clarify because they are organic to a view presented not by one thread of logical argument alone, but by the whole weave of a book." To judge the argument, "one must have a critic's sense of how the parts of a book unite in what is not a logical unity." The views of the Victorian sages cannot be judged by summaries; for "what gave their views life and meaning lay in the actual words of the original . . . to work by quickening the reader to a new capacity for experience is to work in the mode of the artist in words." Thus Holloway extends the term *Victorian sage* to cover novelists like Disraeli, George Eliot and Hardy, who deal with the same subjects as the discursive writers through "illustrative incidents in a story" analogous to the latter's "illustrative examples in an agrument."[14] Indeed, all the major poets and novelists dealt like the Victorian sages with the same cluster of subjects, subjects related to each other through a governing concept of culture.

Victorian writers dealt with the fragmentation of life in the nineteenth century, just because they carried in their heads an ideal of cultural unity. But the ideal in their heads was itself a result of fragmentation, of their being forced to internalize those values of the superseded agrarian, aristocratic and Christian society, the loss of which in the public domain produced the feeling of fragmentation. Thus the Victorian writers established what remains the special knack of modern intellectuals—the knack of inhabiting two or more cultures at the same time. We can appreciate in literary or historical discussion the virtues of noblemen and peasants, or of an age of faith, or of exotically primitive peoples, at the same time that we vote for more democracy and social welfare and, crowning irony, the industrialization of agrarian societies. That is how we arrive at the paradoxical position described by E. M. Forster. For we have appropriated to the realm of the spirit the aristocratic pursuit of distinction and the bold individualism of the laissez-faire principle, even though we have abolished the aristocracy from our political life and the laissez-faire principle from our economic life.

The Victorian writers have taught us that culture can and should be antithetical to the prevailing ideology—not so much to destroy the ideology (though that may at times be necessary) as to complete it. The rage of our brightest intellectuals (during the 1970s and 1980s) for anti-humanism and deconstruction of our culture has proved revivifying for our culture and, yes, for humanism too.

In teaching us that the mind must inhabit and judge from a much larger sphere than any ideology can supply, the Victorian writers have bequeathed us the crucial principle by which societies in our time might be differentiated. For now that in politics the democratic *principle* is universally acknowledged even if it is not universally in effect, and now that the distinction is dissolving between capitalist and communist economies (as capitalists move toward regulation and communists toward a free market), the crucial difference ought to be between open and closed societies—between societies that respect the autonomy of culture and those that use culture to close up all avenues of intellectual escape, to reinforce the dreary clichés of political and economic bosses.

I say *ought to,* because the concept of culture is hard to maintain after all we have been through in the first half of the twentieth century. Auschwitz might be read as a portent of the future; and if we read it so, what happens to our faith in the organically inevitable enlargement of consciousness? Besides, the organic metaphor, which derives everything from the soil, may be inappropriate to a time when man is taking off from Earth itself. More immediately discouraging is the spectacle of the open societies of the West, where the autonomy of culture has led to a binge of "consumerism" and a taste for intellectual pap—to a freely chosen intellectual sleep. Even more serious, the increasing use of drugs by people of all social classes, and especially by young people, poses a terrible question as to what in our culture produces the hopelessness? boredom? that makes people need such an escape.

Orwell's *Nineteen Eighty-Four* projects the nightmare future of a technologically advanced socialist society without culture—without the individuality, spirituality and intellectual freedom, without memory of the whole heritage of the past that originally produced the technology and socialism. To achieve total tyranny, to make consciousness identical with ideology, the party reduces the area of private life by discouraging sexual and family love, and reduces the range of consciousness by reducing available vocabulary and obliterating all memory of the past. The one glimmer of hope is in the hero, an obsolete man who still has some primitive instincts and some cultural memory. Similarly, to the extent that we can think optimistically about the future, our thoughts are necessarily based on the cluster of ideas connected with the word *culture*—ideas that give coherence to the main body of nineteenth- and twentieth-century literature.

Is Guido Saved? The Meaning of Browning's Conclusion to *The Ring and the Book*

IN regard to Browning's *The Ring and the Book,* there are only two points of interpretation on which the critics seriously divide. One is whether the poem is relativist, whether its moral judgments are to be understood as conditioned by the people who make them and the historical period in which they are made; or whether the poem is absolutist in that it renews and reinforces the received Christian concepts of good and evil. The other issue has to do with the final meaning of Guido's second monologue, with what we are to understand about the way Guido goes to his death. Are we to understand that Guido has finally seen the light and therefore is or will be in Christian terms saved; or are we to understand that Guido is irredeemably evil and therefore in Christian terms damned? The question cannot, in the manner of certain critics, be dodged or fudged. We must answer it one way or the other, for on our answer depends our understanding not only of Guido's character but of the poem's design and meaning. Our answer to this second question will also help us answer the first—as to whether *The Ring and the Book* is relativist or absolutist.

The crux is in the final lines of Guido's second monologue. After having railed against Christianity and against Pompilia, the wife he murdered, Guido, in the extreme moment when he sees the black-hooded Brotherhood of Death come to take him to execution, cries out desperately for help. He calls, in psychologically ascending order, upon the Granduke and the Pope, upon the Abate and the Cardinal who have attended him in the death cell, upon Christ, Maria, God, and in the final line he cries: "Pompilia, will you let them murder me?" (ll. 2427).[1] In *The Poetry of Experience,* I have seen in that cry Guido's salvation, the sign that he has arrived at true moral insight; for the cry carries Guido's acknowledgment of Pompilia's goodness and his own evil. Critics on the other side, however, see in the cry only the climactic example of Guido's cowardice. After all, it is not salvation but life that Guido cries for; and to gain a reprieve, he is ready to exploit even her whom he hates, since he knows she is the sort to forgive him and to stand well with the Christian God.

Such early critics as Henry Jones, Charles W. Hodell, and Arthur Symons saw promise of deliverance in Guido's final utterance. But in 1920, A. K. Cook, in his influential *Commentary upon The Ring and the Book,* saw Guido as like Iago beyond redemption, and he was followed in this view by W. C. DeVane in his even more influential *Browning Handbook.* Among later critics, Park Honan sees Guido as saved; while Richard Altick and James F. Loucks, in their book-length study of the poem, think him irredeemable because the devil incarnate. Our stand does depend on whether we see Guido as human and therefore capable of development, or whether we see him as belonging to another order of existence, as an Iago or devil figure.

For me, one of the strongest arguments in favor of redemption is that Guido's second monologue is superfluous if its only function is to elaborate what is sufficiently established without it—that Guido is utterly evil. Taking off from what Browning, speaking in his own voice, tells us in Book 1, Roma King, in *The Focusing Artifice* (1968), and Roy Gridley, in his essay "Browning's Two Guidos"[2] which is the best study along this line, explain the difference between Guido's two monologues. The first, called "Count Guido Franceschini," takes place in court where the public figure uses every trick of rhetoric, argument and flattery to deceive his judges and save his life. The second, called "Guido," takes place in the death cell where the human being speaks to his would-be confessors in order to understand himself. In Book 1, Browning alerts us to the difference between Guido's two monologues by saying that the first is play-acting and the second inadvertently confessional. Guido's second monologue, I would add, resembles Browning's great dramatic monologues elsewhere in that the self-understanding is inadvertent. The dying Bishop, in "The Bishop Orders His Tomb," prescribes to his sons the costly tomb he wants, but his words come back to him with the developing message that he is not going to get such a tomb. Similarly, even as Guido argues that he is better and stronger than Pompilia, his words come back to him with the slowly developing opposite message. In both monologues, the speaker talks to others as a way of talking to himself. As in a psychoanalysis, he talks out all the lies in order to arrive inadvertently at the truth. I shall argue for the fundamental sincerity of Guido's second monologue.[3]

The French psychoanalyst Jacques Lacan, who uses as an epigraph to his book *Speech and Language in Psychoanalysis* two lines from

Browning's "Parleying with Bernard de Mandeville," describes the psychoanalytic session as a verbal and dramatic performance that reminds me of a dramatic monologue. The quoted lines, "'Flesh composed of suns—/ How can such be?' exclaim the simple ones," refer to the literalists' expectation that the constellation Orion, because it is named after a man, ought to contain a real man rather than the symbolic outlines of a man. These literalists do not know how to read language symbolically, how to "Look through the sign," says Browning, "to the thing signified" (ll. 188–92). "Psychoanalysis," writes Lacan, "has only a single intermediary: the patient's Word. . . . I shall show that there is no Word without a reply, even if it meets no more than silence, provided that it has an auditor: this is the heart of its function in psychoanalysis." The analyst (like the reader of the dramatic monologue) analyzes "the subject's behavior [symbolically] in order to find in it what the subject is not saying." In learning to verbalize so-called free association and direct it to his auditor, the patient (like the speaker of the dramatic monologue) becomes "a skilled craftsman,"[4] who makes of his discourse something that can be construed by the analyst (or reader of the dramatic monologue) as saying something other than he is ostensibly saying.

To return to Roma King and Roy Gridley, they fail to draw the necessary conclusion from their own finely perceptive arguments. Having shown the human and developmental quality of Guido's second monologue, they fail to realize that if Guido can arrive at self-understanding, then he can go further toward salvation. A French critic, Bernard Brugière, formulates the question regarding Guido's last line, then stakes out the ideas by which an answer would have to be evolved. Does the last line, asks Brugière (and I translate from the French),

> signify a saving illumination which echoes that in the Pope's last line . . . ,
> thus underlining the structural and thematic parallels between the two
> monologues . . . ? Or does the last line signify (and this would certainly
> be more in accord with the reader's general impression) a supreme trick,
> or still another cry of abject fear aroused by the imminent danger to Guido's life? . . . This would contradict, however, Browning's usual conceptions of evil as expressed in the following lines from "A Bean-Stripe" in
> *Ferishtah's Fancies:*
>
> Of absolute and irretrievable
> And all-subduing black,—black's soul of black,
> Beyond white's power to disintensify,—
> Of that I saw no sample.

Brugière cites various poems to show that Browning believed not in hell but in purgatory—in an afterlife of continuing spiritual progress. "There is no doubt," he concludes, "that Guido, even he, will attain those 'other heights in other lives' [sic] of which Rabbi Ben Ezra speaks. In Browning's world, the worst is never a certainty"[5]—is always redeemable. Given Browning's often stated views of the afterlife, there should be no doubt of Guido's eventual salvation. The question remains, however, whether he turns toward salvation before his death.

So far we have been trying to understand Browning's intentions concerning Guido by examining the internal evidence, the evidence of *The Ring and the Book* and other Browning poems. Let us now turn to the external evidence, the evidence that comes to us through letters and biography. The most conspicuous piece of external evidence—the exchange of letters on *The Ring and the Book* with Julia Wedgwood—tells against my argument that Guido is saved. The high-minded Miss Wedgwood found the whole story of *The Ring and the Book* entirely too sordid for her taste. But Browning writes back to say he did not invent the story:

> The business has been, as I specify, to explain *fact*. . . . But remember, first that this is God's world, as he made it for reasons of his own, and that to change its conditions is not to account for them—as you will presently find me try to do. I was struck with the enormous wickedness and weakness of the main composition of the piece, and with the incidental evolution of good thereby,—good to the priest, to the poor girl, to the old Pope, who judges anon.

Although Browning says his purpose is to account for or justify the evil, he does not mention incidental good to Guido as part of the justification.

Browning says "anon," because Miss Wedgwood has read only the first two volumes (*The Ring and the Book* came out successively in four volumes during 1868–69). The next two will contain among others, Browning tells her, Guido's second monologue. "I see no possibility of good in Guido," Miss Wedgwood writes back. "He seems to me to retain nothing, not only of what God made, but of what . . . God can use. . . . But, oh, be merciful to us in Guido's last display! Shame and pain and humiliation need the irradiation of hope to be endurable as objects of contemplation." In a letter accompanying the third volume, Browning replies: "Guido 'hope?'—do you bid me turn him into that sort of thing? No, indeed! Come, I won't send you more, if you will but lift your finger!"

This reply is the strongest argument against me, and I must do what I can to try to diminish its force. First, this letter was written in pique, as the last quoted sentence indicates. Miss Wedgwood's charges may have touched old wounds, for Browning had always been accused of writing ugly poems that were morbidly concerned with perverse or wicked characters. Miss Wedgwood may also have recalled to Browning painful disagreements with his dead wife. Why don't you write, Miss Wedgwood admonished him, like "one who has been taught supremely to believe in goodness by the close neighborhood of a beautiful soul." "My wife," he replies in this same angry letter, "would have subscribed to every one of your bad opinions of the book: she never took the least interest in the story, so much as to wish to inspect the papers."

In repudiating Miss Wedgwood's word "hope," Browning may have been lashing out not against the idea of Guido's salvation, but against the sentimental deathbed conversion she had in mind. Guido's "wickedness does," he says, "or rather, by the end, *shall* rise to the limit conceivable," but the good to the other characters, he adds, "comes through—is evolved by—that prodigy of bad: hence its use.[6] Its use to the *other* characters. But if we are to go on to argue that Guido himself may be saved, then it can be in no such facile way as Miss Wedgwood probably had in mind. Guido is saved not through having miraculously abandoned his character, but rather through being what he is to the last intensity.

To argue this, I shall have to return to the poem. But before doing so, I should like to point out three other pieces of external evidence that to some degree negate the damaging evidence of the Wedgwood letters. Browning commented to William Allingham on Providence as the key to the poem's structure: "A builder will tell you sometimes of a house, 'there's twice as much work underground as above,' and so it is with my poem. Guido's not escaping better, man won't give him post-horses; the Pope, as Providence; Guido has time for confession." On the same day (Sunday, 27 December 1868), Browning showed Allingham the Old Yellow Book; "and translates to me," Allingham recalled, "the letter of the lawyer, de Archangelis, written on the day of the execution, saying, among other things, 'Guido is lamented for by all respectable people.'"[7] Did Browning have on his mind that day the probability of Guido's Christian death? The Pope says Guido's accomplices were planning to kill him, so his arrest was providential because it gave him time for confession. If it matters that Guido had time for confession, then his confession must have been efficacious.

Furthermore, the Secondary Source, a contemporary account of the execution which Browning later consulted in addition to the Old Yellow Book, says that Guido at least outwardly died as a good Christian; and Browning in Book 12 uses this information without casting doubt upon it. The Secondary Source is more than confirmed in an account Browning never saw, an account like that of the Old Yellow Book but more than twice its size, which Beatrice Corrigan discovered in 1940 in Cortona. The Cortona Codex contains many of the same documents as the Old Yellow Book, but even more that were hitherto unknown. Among the new documents is a description of Guido's death, which shows him as unrecognizably pious. When Guido learned he was to be executed, he said only,

> "Then because I defended and repaired my honour must I die in this manner?" And entering the chapel between his comforters he knelt down before the altar, where in less than an hour he became fortified and self-possessed, and was made so fit for death that he was able to give to all and each such an edifying example that since time immemorial no one can remember similar and comparable things.[8]

Guido paid for masses for himself, his wife and her parents. These items of external evidence are all the more important in that Browning made clear to Furnivall that the final judgment of Guido was his invention. He would not even have known from the Old Yellow Book how the court's sentence went, were it not for the three manuscript letters at the end mentioning the execution. Although the first two suggest that Guido died well, Browning apparently felt he had chosen his ending and found it confirmed by the Secondary Source's account, which "I obtained a long while afterwards," of the execution and Guido's Christian death. In answering Furnivall's question as to the meaning of Guido's last line, Browning wrote: "The fact is that the two ecclesiastics passed the night preceding his execution with Guido: and knowing as he did the innocence of his wife, what so likely as that, in his last utterance of despair, her name, with an appeal to it, should suggest itself?"[9] This third piece of external evidence confirms Guido's recognition of Pompilia's innocence and, by implication, his own culpability.

Since the external evidence more or less cancels itself out, my main argument must proceed through an analysis of the poem. I shall try to show that Browning has planted so many signposts pointing toward Guido's salvation that if the salvation doesn't come off, then the signposts lead to nothing and the poem must to that extent be an artistic failure.

In Book 1, Browning prepares us to see the difference between Guido's first and second monologues. In his first monologue, addressed to the judges, Guido is fighting for his life, and his speech is pure acting. In the second monologue, hope for life is gone; so Guido speaks truth.

> While life was graspable and gainable,
> And bird-like buzzed her wings round Guido's brow,
> Not much truth stiffened out the web of words

He wove to catch her: when away she flew
And death came, death's breath rivelled up the lies,
Left bare the metal thread, the fibre fine
Of truth, i' the spinning: the true words shone last.

(1. 1275–81)

Browning intends to distinguish, I think, between the spinning out of truth, the developing revelation of Guido's wickedness, and the true words, the cry to Pompilia, that *shone* last (Browning revised from "come" to "shone"). The honorific verb suggests an illumination, the truth that will save Guido.

Caponsacchi, Pompilia, the Pope and Guido himself reveal that Guido's motives were not merely worldly, that he did not mistreat and finally murder Pompilia simply to get her money or to save his honor, but that fundamentally he wanted, as Caponsacchi puts it, to "slay Pompilia body and soul" (6. 1798). Guido himself plotted to make Pompilia elope and have an affair with Caponsacchi. This does not mean that Guido is like Iago a motiveless malignity. It means that Guido is engaged in a struggle the true proportions of which elude him until the end. When he finally breaks through his own rationalizations to understand that he has been engaged in the cosmic struggle between good and evil, that he hates Pompilia simply because she is good, then he is on the way to salvation.

Don't kill Guido, says Caponsacchi to the judges, but let him find his proper level, his own hell, precisely by living. Let him not die

> so much as slide out of life,
> Pushed by the general horror and common hate
> Low, lower,—left o' the very ledge of things,
> I seem to see him catch convulsively
> One by one at all honest forms of life,

until "slowly and surely edged / Off all the table-land whence life up-springs" (6. 1911–22), he finds himself face to face and gappling with Judas, Judas who inhabits the bottommost circle of hell. Caponsacchi's prediction will be confirmed by Guido's own vision of what his life will be if he is saved from execution. We are to understand that the Pope's sentence is merciful; for he delivers Guido from the hell his life would be and gives him instead a chance for salvation through dying. We also see the moral superiority of Pompilia and the Pope who—unlike the heroic rather than saintly Caponsacchi—desire Guido's salvation.

Pompilia explains how the more she played the virtuous wife, the more she enraged Guido who wanted her to sin. Only when she became pregnant, and had another life than her own to protect, did she do what

Guido wanted by asking Caponsacchi to take her to Rome. She saved herself by the very weapon that threatened to destroy her: "So should I grasp the lightning and be saved!" (7. 1403). This paradox is at the heart of the poem's moral meaning. "Somehow, no one ever plucked," says Caponsacchi,

> A rag, even, from the body of the Lord,
> To wear and mock with, but, despite himself,
> He looked the greater and was the better.
>
> (6. 211–14)

To engage in moral action, even if it is to do the wrong thing, is in the long run a step toward salvation.

"I am saved through [Guido] / So as by fire," says Pompilia. "Nothing about me but drew somehow down / His hate upon me." But—and the statement is very important—"So he was made; he nowise made himself." The saintly Pompilia understands the full extent of Guido's wickedness. Yet she forgives him. "Let him make God amends," she says, suggesting that it is not for us to understand the ultimate sense in which Guido, even he, can be justified.

> We shall not meet in this world nor the next,
> But where will God be absent? In His face
> Is light, but in His shadow healing too:
> Let Guido touch the shadow and be healed!
>
> (7. 1702–5)

Surely here is a prediction, by one of saintly insight, that Guido will be saved through God's shadow side, through evil.

The most important prediction is the Pope's. The Pope is the most authoritative speaker in the poem. He delivers, Browning tells us in Book 1, "the ultimate / Judgment" (ll. 1220–21) that should determine ours. The pope is very old. This judgment of Guido will probably be the last and crowning event of his pontificate. Everyone therefore expects him to show mercy. It is with this expectation that Guido has appealed the verdict of the Roman court to the Pope. So the Pope is under tremendous pressure to spare Guido's life and give him time to repent; besides it is so civilized to show mercy, so "safe and graceful" (10. 2059). I *will* show mercy, the Pope decides, by sentencing Guido to death. For only the agony of impending death can bring on the crisis of self-understanding that can save him.

The Pope's judgment of Guido's motives is the harshest, for he allows no mitigating circumstances. Yet Guido is not the devil incarnate, for he is more saveable than his brother, the Abate Paul, who plotted the marriage and the murder. Beside

> This fox-faced horrible priest, his brother-brute
> The Abate,—why, mere wolfishness looks well,
> Guido stands honest in the red o' the flame,
> Beside this yellow that would pass for white,
> Twice Guido, all craft but no violence.
>
> (10. 880–84)

Guido's violence is at least human; it shows passion.

Thus his arrest was Guido's good fortune, for it gave him time for confession. Otherwise his accomplices in Pompilia's murder would have killed him for withholding the pay he had promised, and he would have gone, unconfessed, to hell: "Thither where, this same day, I see thee not, / Nor, through God's mercy, need, to-morrow, see" (10. 867–68). Were it not for this comparatively "irrelevant circumstance" of law, the Pope says later, we might see "Pompilia lost and Guido saved: how long? / For his whole life: how much is that whole life?" (10. 1423–26). Had Guido been "saved" physically, he would have been lost spiritually; so his arrest and condemnation should produce spiritual salvation.

All this leads to the epiphanic final passage. After having sentenced Guido and his four accomplices to death, the Pope says of Guido: "For the main criminal I have no hope / Except in such a suddenness of fate"—except in death. To explain how Guido might be saved, he recalls a night scene *suddenly* illuminated by a flash of lightning:

> I stood at Naples once, a night so dark
> I could have scarce conjectured there was earth
> Anywhere, sky or sea or world at all:
> But the night's black was burst through by a blaze—
> Thunder struck blow on blow, earth groaned and bore,
> Through her whole length of mountain visible:
> There lay the city thick and plain with spires,
> And, like a ghost disshrouded, white the sea,
> So may the truth be flashed out by one blow,
> And Guido see, one instant, and be saved.

Note that the illumination came through violence, a storm, just as in the story told by Pompilia the Christian virgin used lightning, the instrument of violence, to save herself (7. 1389–1403).

If the illuminating flash does not come to Guido, then, says the Pope, he goes directly to hell:

> Into that sad obscure sequestered state
> Where God unmakes but to remake the soul
> He else made first in vain; which must not be.

This hell is really purgatory, where God remakes the soul. But assignation to even so mild a hell "must not be." Therefore, I do what I can for Guido by sentencing him to death as the crowning Christian act of my life: "Enough, for I may die this very night: / And how should I dare die, this man let live?" (10. 2117–34). Surely such a passage, planted so conspicuously at the end of the Pope's monologue and just before Guido's second, has to be taken seriously as a sign of what's to come.

My argument rests mainly, however, on Guido's second monologue, which must be understood as showing a steady development toward illumination. Guido's second monologue is the greatest in the poem, because it is the most complex—it operates on so many different levels of consciousness. For every step forward toward illumination, Guido moves two steps backward. In fact, Guido moves toward illumination by seeming to move away from it, by revealing with increasing clarity to himself and his two auditors his wolf nature. For Guido, the way up is through the way down. In the agony of anticipating execution, he descends into a purgatorial hell. We see before our eyes what the purgatorial experience is like.

Guido begins in the vein of his first monologue by flattering the Cardinal and Abate; but when he realizes there is nothing to be accomplished, he abruptly turns insulting—and sincere. "Life!" he bursts out, "How I could spill this overplus of mine" (11. 143–44) to drench with sap the dried-up lives of old men like the Pope who are pushing him to his death. Guido is surprised by this new experience of speaking truth: "Lucidity of soul unlocks the lips: / I never had the words at will before." And there follows his first recognition that in speaking truth he is more like Pompilia:

> I'm my wife outright
> In this unmanly appetite for truth,
> This careless courage as to consequence,
> This instantaneous sight through things and through,
> This voluble rhetoric, if you please,—'t is she!

Here you have that Pompilia whom I slew,
Also the folly for which I slew her!

(11. 159–60, 170–76)

For the first time Guido admits—it is an admission from which he will retreat and to which he will return in the end—that he killed Pompilia because of her virtues.

It is because the preciousness of life bursts upon Guido that he starts his descent into hell by agonizing over his impending execution. He tells how strolling one beautiful May evening in Rome he first came on mannaia, the guillotine that will behead him:

Came on your fine axe in a frame, that falls
And so cuts off a man's head underneath,
Mannaia,—thus we made acquaintance first:
· · · · · · · · · · · · · · · · · · · ·
All of it painted red: red, in the midst,
Ran up two narrow tall beams barred across,
Since from the summit, some twelve feet to reach,
The iron plate with the sharp shearing edge
Had slammed, jerked, shot, slid,—I shall soon find which!—
And so lay quiet, fast in its fit place,
The wooden half-moon collar, now eclipsed
By the blade which blocked its curvature: apart,
The other half,—the under half-moon board
Which, helped by this, completes a neck's embrace,—
Joined to a sort of desk that wheels aside
Out of the way when done with,—down you kneel,
In you're pushed, over you the other drops,
Tight you're clipped, whiz, there's the blade cleaves
   its best,
Out trundles body, down flops head on floor,
And where's your soul gone? That, too, I shall find!

"There's no such lovely month in Rome as May," Guido sums up. And May's fertility was "One greenish-golden sea" glimpsed

right 'twixt those bars
Of the engine—I began acquaintance with,
Understood, hated, hurried from before,
To have it out of sight and cleanse my soul!
Here it is all again, conserved for use:
Twelve hours hence, I may know more, not hate worse.

(11. 184–86, 220–35, 250–58)

Guido's execution takes place in February, but Browning sets his vicari-
ous or hellish anticipation of it in May, not only to enhance the horror
by contrast, but also, I think, to establish the imagery of death and rebirth. After my death, says Guido, I shall not hate worse than I do now.
In other words, I am in hell right now; after death I shall be—and this
is important for Browning's scheme of salvation—the same person I
am now.

Let us have Gospel rather than Law, cries this erstwhile upholder of
Law. Isn't the duty of Peter's successor " 'To free the prisoner and forgive
his fault!' " As Christ teaches, "Respite me, save a soul." But the Pope, as
Guido claims to see it, is thrusting him into hell. The Pope, who ought
to be a shepherd, thrusts this "shuddering sheep, he calls a wolf, / Back
and back, down and down to where hell gapes!" (11. 328, 360, 405–6).

Guido often says one thing as a way of coming to understand that
he really means the opposite. Having called himself a sheep, he can a few
lines later throw off the disguise and declare himself a wolf: "There, let
my sheepskin-garb, a curse on't, go—/ Leave my teeth free if I must show
my shag!" (11. 443–44). The Pope is a thief who hates wolves as com-
petitors in plundering the sheep. Guido is throwing off the pretence of
adhering to the Christian world-view, but in doing so shows a thorough
understanding of that view: "if ever was such faith at all / . . . 'Tis dead
of age." We are all thieves, pleasure is our sole good, and we are out to
get all the pleasure and profit we can; law is the social contract by which
we protect ourselves against each other. The philosophy is Hobbesian
and Benthamite, but presented in a Christian perspective; so that Guido
is in effect saying with Milton's Satan: "Evil be thou my good." He shows
himself to be fundamentally Christian just because he portrays himself
as voicing not the right philosophy, but the devil's:

> Don't fidget, Cardinal!
> Abate, cross your breast and count your beads
> And exorcise the devil, for here he stands
> And stiffens in the bristly nape of neck,
> Daring you drive him hence!
>
> (11. 553–61)

Far from making Guido the devil incarnate, this self-portrayal is a station
on his way to self-understanding and therefore salvation.

Why repent, asks Guido, since repentance will not save my life? Not
repentance, but "truth shall save [my soul], since no lies assist!" Guido
is right, since truth is the acknowledgment of his and the world's *opera-
tive* philosophy. He admits he deserves no more mercy than he showed
Pietro, who,

> When I chased him here and there,
> Morsel by morsel cut away the life
> I loathed,—cried for just respite to confess
> And save his soul: much respite did I grant!
> Why grant me respite who deserve my doom?
>
> (11. 461, 471–75)

Guido's strict opportunism is belied by his preoccupation, revealed more than once, with the fact that he did not grant Pietro time to confess (e.g., 11. 1278–81).

The next big step comes with Guido's transforming vision of eyes. He envisions "All those eyes of all [deceived] husbands in all plays, / At stare like one expanded peacock-tail," and then envisions God's eye turned accusingly upon himself:

> When you cut earth away from under me,
> I shall be left alone with, pushed beneath
> Some such an apparitional dread orb
> As the eye of God, since such an eye there glares:
> I fancy it go filling up the void
> Above my mote-self it devours, or what
> Proves—wrath, immensity wreaks on nothingness.

Guido's description of a night fire as analogous to the purgatorial experience of God's eye is like the night lightning the Pope compares to the instant of illumination that could save Guido. "First a spark," says Guido,

> Tipped a bent, as a mere dew-globule might
> And stiff grass-stalk on the meadow,—this
> Grew fiercer, flamed out full, and proved the sun.

Guido realizes his arguments have so far been directed to man:

> What shall I say to God?
> This, if I find the tongue and keep the mind—
> "Do Thou wipe out the being of me, and smear
> This soul from off Thy white of things, I blot!
> I am one huge and sheer mistake,—whose fault?
> Not mine at least, who did not make myself."
> Someone declares my wife excused me so!

You can wipe me out, says Guido, but you cannot change me. I am "Unable to repent one particle / O' the past" (11. 913–46), because I cannot reject what I am.

Guido is wrong to throw the blame on God. But his self-recognition is, I think, sincere. Pompilia has offered just this justification for him, suggesting that if Guido is to be saved it will have to be through his own base nature. Guido covertly recognizes Pompilia's moral wisdom by citing her. His fundamental sincerity emerges when he proceeds to turn God's eye into Pompilia's. His hate began at their first encounter when, as a "thirteen-years'-old child, with milk for blood," she was led like a sacrificial victim to the marriage altar—mute, only her eyes spoke. "Struck dumb,"

> She eyes me with those frightened balls of black,
> As heifer—the old simile comes pat—
> Eyes tremblingly the altar and the priest.
>
> (11. 965, 976–79)

"I resent my wrong," he says of the terror he read in her eyes. And of her submissiveness in marriage, I "Resent the very obedience."

> There had been compensation in revolt—
> Revolt's to quell: but martyrdom rehearsed,
> But predetermined saintship.
>
> (11. 986, 1048–54)

Her obedience became threatening: "I see the same stone strength of white despair" (11. 1325). "A nullity in female shape," he calls her; yet says she may seem "the simple kid to others" but is a "lion" and "serpent" (11. 1113–25). His uncertainty whether she is weak or strong leads to the climactic passage in which, by acknowledging the strength in her gentleness, he connects her with God and points toward his final appeal to her:

> I advise—no one think to bear that look
> Of steady wrong, endured as steadily
> —Through what sustainment of deluding hope?
> . . . .
> This self-possession to the uttermost,
> How does it differ in aught, save degree,
> From the terrible patience of God?
>
> (11.1373–80)

Guido's disturbance over Pompilia's look is a sign of the conscience that makes him redeemable. His disturbance is like Stavrogin's, in Dostoevsky's *The Possessed,* over the mute child-victim Matryosha whom he rapes; Stavrogin, too, feels accused by Matryosha's look and finally her suicide. The more these two villains are aware of the passive Christlike qualities of their girl-victims, the more they want to abuse them; yet the awareness brings moral enlightenment.

Guido retreats from the above high point of perception to return to it in the end. Having blamed God, he now blames the Church for his murderousness; for in trying to make his fortune through toadying to cardinals, he has had to suppress his own nature to gratify theirs:

> "Suppression is the word!"
> My nature, when the outrage was too gross,
> Widened itself an outlet over-wide
> By way of answer, sought its own relief
> With more of fire and brimstone than you wished.
> All your own doing: preachers, blame yourselves!
>
> (11. 1514–19)

As in his social criticism, so here in his psychological self-analysis, there is an element of truth in what Guido says. His murderousness can be partly explained by the frustrations of poverty, ugliness, failure. But in the acknowledgment of his murderousness, he is moving toward moral self-judgment.

In describing the murder, he contradicts his hypocritical account in his first monologue. There is no talk here of Christian compunction on Christmas Eve, the night of the murder, nor does he pretend that he murdered only because he lost his head when the hated Violante opened the door. He admits that he went to Rome with the intention of murdering Pompilia. And he admits that she has conquered by staying alive long enough to tell her story:

> whom find I
> Here, still to fight with, but my pale frail wife?
> . . . .
> She too must shimmer through the gloom o' the grave,
> Come and confront me—not at judgment-seat
> Where I could twist her soul, as erst her flesh,
> And turn her truth into a lie,—but there,
> O' the death-bed, with God's hand between us both,

> Striking me dumb, and helping her to speak,
> Tell her own story her own way, and turn
> My plausibility to nothingness!

$$(\text{II. } 1676-89)$$

Guido's claim that he could twist her soul at the judgment-seat is belied by his portrayal of her potency as a shimmering figure in his own conscience.

Now his movement toward self-understanding takes an unexpected leap forward. For he realizes that if he had been pardoned, his future would hold nothing but failure. The public would side with his murdered wife. His brothers would quietly edge him out of his property. And his son—that Gaetano for whose sake he asked in his first monologue to be pardoned—his son would ruthlessly displace him just as Guido had displaced his own father. To suppress such rebellion, Guido, not being the fool his father was, would persecute his son as he persecuted his wife. Pardon would, as the Pope foresaw, make Guido even worse, mire him still deeper in the living hell Caponsacchi wanted for him.

Guido admits it is better for him to die, but he boasts that he wants to die by his own hand in the pagan manner, that he "never was at any time / A Christian" (II. 1916–17). He imagines a pagan afterlife where each soul becomes, through Ovidian metamorphosis, what it really is. "Let the weak soul," said Ovid, "end / In water," but

> The strong become a wolf forevermore!
> Change that Pompilia to a puny stream
> Fit to reflect the daisies on its bank!
> Let me turn wolf, be whole, and sate, for once.

Pompilia may in the Christian view be better, but he is justified in the pagan view as the stronger. Nevertheless, what follows is subtly Christian, what we would nowadays call Christian existentialist. Let me, says Guido, glut the wolf nature that has been suppressed by the humanity that is the other half of me. Let me grow worse, so that realizing my nature to the full I can grow better:

> Grow out of man,
> Glut the wolf-nature,—what remains but grow
> Into the man again, be man indeed
> And all man? Do I ring the changes right?
> Deformed, transformed, reformed, informed, conformed!

The honest [wolf] instinct, pent and crossed through life,
Let surge by death into a visible flow
Of rapture.

Guido foresees what will happen to him up to the instant of his conversion. He is describing the purgatorial experience of self-recognition; he
is in Browning's purgatorial hell during this monologue.

Self-recognition involves understanding Pompilia, for Guido continually measures himself against her. The question always is whether her
goodness is not a mere negative virtue, the product of weakness and
stupidity:

Again, how she is at me with those eyes!
Away with the empty stare! Be holy still,
And stupid ever!

He is all too aware of her potency, just as he fundamentally adheres to
the Christian judgment of her. Stay in your grave, he says, don't follow
me with

those detested eyes,
No, though they follow but to pray me pause
On the incline, earth's edge that's next to hell!
None of your abnegation of revenge!
Fly at me, tug while I tear again!
There's God, go tell Him, testify your worst!
Not she! There was no touch in her of hate;
And it would prove her hell, if I reached mine!
To know I suffered, would still sadden her,
Do what the angels might to make amends!

I, instead, he says bitterly, would rather forego heaven if to ascend I had
to take my foot off my prostrate foe:

I who, with outlet for escape to heaven,
Would tarry if such flight allowed my foe
To raise his head, relieved of that firm foot
Had pinned him to the fiery pavement else!
So am I made, "who did not make myself."

A man who can say this about himself is not lost. Guido sees that since
God made him, there must be a place in God's scheme even for him:

                                        Some use
There cannot but be for a mood like mine,
Implacable, persistent in revenge.

                                        (11. 2051–2107)

These lines about Pompilia and himself constitute his confession, as does
later on his rejection of the crucifix proffered to be kissed as if in recognition that he has confessed:

Cardinal, take away your crucifix!
Abate, leave my lips alone,—they bite!
Vainly you try to change what should not change,
And shall not.

                                        (11. 2221–24)

Having returned once more to a true perception of Pompilia, Guido
again retreats. He wishes he had had a wicked wife, like Lucrezia Borgia,
who would have been an accomplice in crime; and he resorts to desperate
stratagems to persuade the Cardinal to save his life. When he sees the
stratagems are useless, he reveals again his wolf-nature: "take / Your crucifix away, I tell you twice!" Peter denied Christ three times, so we may
expect a third denial from Guido before the moment of illumination.
     Now Guido takes his stand in unilluminated hell:

                              I have gone inside my soul
And shut its door behind me: 't is your torch
Makes the place dark: the darkness let alone
Grows tolerable twilight.

                                        (11. 2287–94)

He displays his wolf-nature with such brutal imagery that the Cardinal
fears violence to himself. This, Guido's lowest point except for the groveling final passage, continues with a spiteful speech declaring: you all
follow me in death. Miraculously, however, this speech modulates into
his noblest utterance:

You never know what life means till you die:
Even throughout life, 't is death that makes life live,
Gives it whatever its significance.
For see, on your own ground and argument,
Suppose life had no death to fear, how find
A possibility of nobleness
In man, prevented daring any more?

What's love, what's faith without a worst to dread?
Lack-lustre jewelry! but faith and love
With death behind them bidding do or die—
Put such a foil at back, the sparkle's born!
From out myself how the strange colours come!

In seeing the value of death and in himself, as death approaches, a strange sparkle, Guido bears out the Pope and shows signs of regeneration. Having taken his stand in hell, he now conceives himself in heaven:

Is there a new rule in another world?
Be sure I shall resign myself: as here
I recognize no law I could not see,
There, what I see, I shall acknowledge too:
On earth I never took the Pope for God,
In heaven I shall scarce take God for the Pope.
Unmanned, remanned: I hold it probable—
With something changeless at the heart of me
To know me by, some nucleus that's myself:
Accretions did it wrong? Away with them—
You soon shall see the use of fire!

(11. 2375–97)

The phrase "some nucleus that's myself" explains the scheme according to which Guido is saved. Even in heaven, he will still be Guido, the kind of person who believes in God only when he can see Him. He will, however, have been "remanned," the purgatorial fire will have burnt away the accretions obscuring the essential self that is, as are all essential selves, justified.

That will be in heaven. On earth, "All that was, is; . . . / Nor is it in me to unhate my hates." Guido has built his identity on a continuity of hate, a continuity that may be transformed in heaven. But here he goes on hating Pompilia. He rejects her "pale / Poison," which in his moments of true perception he took for "food"; he calls her a weak vine around his strong tree. Then suddenly he hears the Brotherhood of Death descending to take him to execution—and he panics. He repudiates the bravado and the Olympian insight into the necessity of death. He repudiates the whole development of his monologue as he regresses to a groveling cowardice we have not yet seen in him. Life is all that counts; he will do or say anything, anything—if only he can be allowed to live:

All was folly—I laughed and mocked!
Sirs, my first true word, all truth and no lie,

Is—save me notwithstanding! Life is all!
I was just stark mad,—let the madman live
Pressed by as many chains as you please pile!
Don't open! Hold me from them! I am yours,
I am the Granduke's—no, I am the Pope's!
Abate,—Cardinal,—Christ,—Maria,—God,—
Pompilia, will you let them murder me?

                                                    (11. 2399–2427)

It is true that he calls upon the Granduke, the Pope, the Abate, Cardinal,
Christ, Maria, God and Pompilia as part of this cowardly clutching after
straws. But the placement of Pompilia last transforms the final line into
a moment of self-recognition—recognition that he is the clinging vine
and she the strong tree, that her goodness goes with strength.

If we take this final passage as the last word, we might well think
Guido is not saved. But we should remember that in Browning's dramatic
monologues, the speaker often in the end repudiates his utterance only
to return more intensely than ever to the character he has been developing. Fra Lippo Lippi repudiates his unorthodox remarks only to display,
in describing the picture he will paint as amends, his inveterate love of
this world. So Guido's repudiation of his utterance should be understood
as his third denial of Christ, the denial that precedes the instant of illumination. The instant may be understood as occurring either in the last
line: "Pompilia, will you let them murder me?" or in the instant just
after. Twice Guido arrived at self-recognition through a true understanding of Pompilia and himself, and twice he was unable to break through
to conversion. Intellectual recognition is not enough. The Pope was right.
Only death, confronted as an inescapable agonizing reality, can provide
the emotional impetus for internal transformation. That may be why the
Cardinal finally summoned the Brotherhood of Death, who were waiting
for word of Guido's confession and absolution. Aware of the Pope's purpose, and seeing Guido retreat once more from a high point of perception
(the speech on the necessity of death and himself in heaven), the Cardinal
may as a last resort have summoned the Brotherhood of Death to provide
Guido with the necessary, the saving agony.

To see Guido as saved is to justify the poem's design—to understand
why Browning gave Guido two monologues and how the Pope's monologue leads into Guido's second. (Since Guido is saved by fulfilling his
own nature, his salvation does not violate the principle that in the dramatic monologue there are no conversions.) Once having understood the
advances as well as the retreats in Guido's second monologue, we can
surely expect him to return to at least his point of farthest advance. If

Guido is not saved, then *The Ring and the Book* is absolutist in that it simply illustrates Guido's absolute evil and consigns him to an orthodox hell. To see Guido as saved is to understand the sense in which the poem is relativist—in that all limited points of view, all selves, are justified as part of God's scheme. Through being what they are intensely enough, they lead back to God. The relative is the index to an absolute reality that cannot be *known* through human institutions and judgments, but can at certain intense moments be felt.

Browning and the
Question of Myth

THE history of criticism is largely the history of the changing questions we ask about works of art. The pre-eminence in our time of Yeats, Eliot and Joyce, and the connection of these writers with an artistic method and a mode of thought that Eliot, in reviewing Joyce's *Ulysses,* has himself called *mythical*—all this leads me to ask about Browning's use of myth. The question seems particularly relevant since Yeats and Browning had in common an intense admiration for Shelley. Now Yeats, we know, admired not Shelley the Godwinian radical, but Shelley the Platonist and mythmaker—the Shelley who, in the manner of Blake, used archetypal symbols.[1] The question is whether Browning—who did for a time admire Shelley the Godwinian radical—had affinities also with Shelley the mythmaker and (the two terms are inextricably connected) symbolist.

It is certainly the visionary whom Browning praises in the essay he wrote on Shelley in 1852. "I would rather consider Shelley's poetry as a sublime fragmentary essay towards a presentment of the correspondency of the universe to Deity, of the natural to the spiritual, and of the actual to the ideal, than I would isolate and separately appraise the worth of many detachable portions which might be acknowledged as utterly perfect in a lower moral point of view, under the mere conditions of art." Shelley's main excellence is "his simultaneous perception of Power and Love in the absolute, and of Beauty and Good in the concrete, while he throws, from his poet's station between both, swifter, subtler, and more numerous films for the connection of each with each, than have been thrown by any modern artificer of whom I have knowledge; proving how, as he says,—'The spirit of the worm within the sod / In love and worship blends itself with God.'"[2]

Those lines might have been written by Blake—a sign that Browning comes in this passage very close to Yeats's appreciation of Shelley in terms applicable to a mythmaking poet like Blake. Browning offers, in defining Shelley's main excellence, a good definition of the mythmaking poet—of the poet who does not merely make decorative allusions to an established literary mythology, but who actually *sees* the world as mythical, who sees man, nature, and God as intimately engaged in a natural-supernatural story.

To ask about Browning's use of myth is to ask two questions. The first is whether Browning believed in using—as Arnold did in *Sohrab and Rustum* and *Merope,* and Tennyson did in the *Idylls of the King*—the grand old enduring subjects that have come down to us in the literary tradition. The answer to the first question is no. Browning agreed with Miss Barrett, when she said in that often-quoted letter to him: "I am inclined to think that we want new *forms,* as well as thoughts. The old gods are dethroned. Why should we go back to the antique moulds, classical moulds, as they are so improperly called?"[3] Browning himself said as much and more when, at the end of his life, he dealt, in "Parleying with Gerard de Lairesse," with the question of how far the Greeks ought to be used as models for modern art. We have gone beyond the Greeks, he concluded, in religion and in moral and psychological insight. Modern poets should not, therefore, pour new wine into old bottles. They should no longer

> "Dream afresh old godlike shapes,
> Recapture ancient fable that escapes,
> Push back reality, repeople earth
> With vanished falseness, recognize no worth
> In fact new-born unless 'tis rendered back
> Pallid by fancy, as the western rack
> Of fading cloud bequeaths the lake some gleam
> Of its gone glory!"
>
> (Ll. 382–89)

We should not ignore reality in favor of old subjects from mythology. Nor should we render modern facts poetical by decorating them with outworn mythological allusions.

On the issue raised by Arnold in the preface to his *Poems of 1853*— the issue as to which subjects are better for modern poetry, the grand, enduring subjects or subjects drawn from modern life—Browning stood against Arnold and with the modern realists.[4] It is true that Browning himself almost always used subjects drawn from the past. But he used them as history rather than myth. This explains his taste for little-known characters and incidents out of the past. For such characters and incidents have clearly not come down to us through the literary tradition. We can believe in the factuality of characters and incidents whose existence is authenticated even though they are no longer remembered. The forgotten historical character is the very opposite of the mythical character whose historical existence is doubtful even though he is vividly 'remembered.'

The historical attitude suggests that the past was as confused and unglamorous as the present. The historical attitude is also interested in tracing change—in showing how different were the ideas and values of the past from ours, in showing that the past was itself in the process of change. Yet the historical change is apparent because we can measure it against a recognizably continuous human or psychological reality. This again is opposite to the mythical attitude, which idealizes the past in order to set it up as a permanent criterion of value. At the same time, the mythical attitude makes the people of the past seem different from us, larger, sometimes superhuman. It is the past as permanent criterion that Arnold had in mind in his preface. In his very use of the past, then, Browning disagreed with Arnold. And he disagreed, too, on that other important issue of the preface—Arnold's attack on internal drama, on the idea that modern poetry ought to treat, in Browning's phrase, "the incidents in the development of a soul."

On the issues raised by Arnold in his preface and elsewhere, Browning was mainly right. For it is surely a weakness in Arnold's critical position that, while he could see art as dependent on the power of both the man and the moment, he should have supposed that the masterwork of one historical moment could or should have the virtues of the masterwork of another historical moment. Browning, on the other hand, was wrong in not understanding the importance of an action or of some external mechanism for portraying an internal state. Browning's poems fail just to the extent that his characters describe and analyze their thoughts and emotions without any vividly apparent external reason for doing so. Browning was interested in talking about both history and psychology, and his problem as an artist was to find a means for doing so. Now a *mythos* or action, properly understood, is a way of accomplishing this end. For the kind of action we call mythical, just because it does not imitate a strictly external reality, is the kind that can speak with one voice of both internal and external reality. The problem is to use myth or the mythical method without archaizing—to use them in a distinctively modern way.

We have here a criterion for understanding the course of Browning's development and for assessing his work. For while he failed in *Paracelsus*

and *Sordello* to reconcile internal and external reality, the two are successfully brought together in the best dramatic monologues. In *Paracelsus,* Browning fails because he has pushed offstage just those historical
events that might have given outline and interest to his obscure historical
character. What we get through a long poem is a continuing high-pitched
reaction to we hardly know what; and we find ourselves longing for
those vulgar events that Browning was so proud to have excluded.

In his long labors over *Sordello,* however, Browning apparently
wrestled with the problem of reconciling internal and external reality. As
DeVane has shown in his *Browning Handbook, Sordello* was written in
four different periods, in each of which Browning took a quite different
view of his subject. In the first version, Browning treated his obscure
historical character in the manner of *Paracelsus*—he gave us the history
of a soul. In the second version, he made Sordello a man of action, a
warrior and lover, thus showing Sordello's impact on the world around
him. In the third version, he neglected Sordello himself and concentrated
on the historical events of the period. In the fourth version, he rounded
out his plot by making Sordello the champion of the masses and Salin-
guerra's son. The four Sordellos, which are imposed one upon the other,
never do add up to a single *Sordello.*

It is just the elements of the first three *Sordello*s that are brought
together in the best dramatic monologues. They are not brought together
by plot—if by plot we mean a complete action, the kind that ties all the
threads together and therefore seems to modern writers, especially novelists, who judge by the criteria of realism, to offer too neat a rationali-
zation of the material. But the three elements are nonetheless brought
together by an action—a direction of the speaker's energies outward. It
is because the speaker is not trying to tell the truth about himself, but is
trying to accomplish something or make an impression, that he actually
does reveal himself truly. This is the way characters reveal themselves in
drama.

As in drama, the speaker has outline because we see him not, as we
see Paracelsus, in a confiding relation; we see him rather in a conflicting
relation with another person. And we get, therefore, through the contrast, a sense of how he looks from the outside. The speaker also has
outline because his fundamental human energies are clothed in the predi-
lections peculiar to his age—as in "The Bishop Orders His Tomb," where
the Italian Renaissance bishop manifests his competitiveness and desire
for immortality by ordering for himself a more expensive tomb than his
rival's. A whole way of seeing, thinking and feeling is manifested through
that aim; so that we get through one action the man and the age, the
man as he looks to others and himself, the outer and the inner reality.

The action is, however, incomplete. That is the price Browning pays for using a realistic action; for the characteristically realistic action is the slice of life.

His best dramatic monologues entitle Browning to his rank among the two or three best Victorian poets. But is he also—as he certainly aimed to be—one of the great poets of English literature? In trying to answer, we have to admit that even in his best volume, *Men and Women,* Browning was tempted—in dramatic monologues like "Cleon" and "Bishop Blougram"—to slip back to the analytic, discursive style of the earlier, the *Paracelsus* period. And we know how, in the later dramatic monologues—in "Mr. Sludge," "Prince Hohenstiel-Schwangau," "Fifine"—he did slip back, without even the lyric fire of the *Paracelsus* period.

We have also to admit that even his very best dramatic monologues remain, after all, only splendid vignettes—"prismatic hues," as he himself called them. They do not add up to what Browning called "the pure white light,"[5] the total vision of life that the greatest poets give us, and that Browning from the start—from the time of *Sordello*—intended to give us. *The Ring and the Book,* of course, is Browning's climactic attempt to give us a total vision of life. He brings several dramatic monologues, several points of view together, in order to collapse the "prismatic hues" into "the pure white light"—in order to make explicit what is implicit in all the dramatic monologues, that the relative is an index to the absolute, that the relative is our way of apprehending the absolute.

This brings us to the second question about Browning's use of myth, the question that arises from our experience of Yeats, Eliot and Joyce. In reviewing *Ulysses* for the *Dial* of November 1923, Eliot argues that Joyce is not as people think a "prophet of chaos," but that he has given us the materials of modern disorder and shown us how to impose order upon them. He has done this by what Eliot calls "the mythical method." Eliot is referring to the continuous parallel between the trivial and apparently meaningless events of Joyce's novel and the events in the *Odyssey.*

> In using the myth, in manipulating a continuous parallel between contemporaneity and antiquity, Mr. Joyce is pursuing a method which others must pursue after him. . . . It is simply a way of controlling, of ordering, of giving a shape and a significance to the immense panorama of futility and anarchy which is contemporary history. It is a method already adumbrated by Mr. Yeats. . . . It is a method for which the horoscope is auspicious. Psychology . . . ethnology [i.e., anthropology], and *The Golden Bough* have concurred to make possible what was impossible

even a few years ago. Instead of narrative method, we may now use the
mythical method. It is, I seriously believe, a step toward making the modern world possible for art, toward . . . order and form.

With the mythical method, the modern writer can render the disordered
surface of modern life, while showing how nevertheless the mythical patterns inevitably reassert themselves at the unconscious roots of existence.
This is the method Eliot himself uses in *The Waste Land*.

Now the whole point of *The Ring and the Book* was to pull out of
a forgotten and sordid old Roman murder case the Christian scheme of
sin and redemption. Having himself, in an experience of illumination,
seen through to the *truth* of the case, Browning's artistic strategy for
conveying that truth was to restore *The Old Yellow Book* in which he
had found the documents of the case. He wanted to give us the experience of reading the raw documents, to give us the jumbled real-life surface of the case and yet make us see through the facts—the facts so peculiar to the place and time—an eternal pattern. This is something like
what Eliot says Joyce does.

Something, but not quite. For the case, as Browning renders it, does
not really present a surface of ambivalence; and the pattern is rather too
explicitly a moral pattern. We feel, as a result, that we are getting not
absolute truth, but Browning's notions about absolute truth. *The Ring
and the Book,* therefore, in spite of the many great things in it, does not
in the end quite come off. Browning is more convincing in the best dramatic monologues, where he gives us truth as simply a relative manifestation that points somehow to the absolute. How? Through the fundamental human energy of the speaker, that seems to lead back to an
unconscious ground of existence where all energies merge and are
justified.

It is out of this unconscious ground that myths, according to twentieth-century theory, arise.[6] And there remains, in *The Ring and the
Book,* a pattern which is in Eliot's sense mythical because underlying. I
mean the pattern of the Andromeda-Perseus myth and its Christian analogue, the myth of St. George and the dragon. We know that Browning's
imagination was dominated throughout his career by the image of the
beautiful Andromeda, chained naked to the rock, waiting helplessly for
the serpent to come out of the sea to devour her, but waiting also (though
she does not consciously know this) for Perseus to descend miraculously—to "come," as Browning puts it in *Pauline*, "in thunder from the
stars"—to rescue her. The combination of sexual and spiritual ramifications gives the image its strength and validity.

The Andromeda-St. George myth connected Browning's life and art, giving him, as only myths can, what Yeats called Unity of Being. In the greatest event of his life, he repeated the mythical pattern by rescuing Miss Barrett. And there is no doubt that he recognized the same mythical pattern when he read in *The Old Yellow Book* about Caponsacchi's rescue of Pompilia. He even changed the date of the rescue to make it fall on St. George's Day. It was because Browning was able to assimilate the murder case to the myth that *The Ring and the Book* is at once a very personal and a very impersonal poem.

There are many references throughout *The Ring and the Book* to the Andromeda-St. George myth, and it is used rather as the vegetation myth is used in *The Waste Land*. We are made to see a continuity between the pagan and Christian versions of the same myth. And all the characters seem inevitably to have some memory of the myth—though the debased characters remember it in a debased form; while the cynical characters, who see Caponsacchi's rescue as an abduction, turn the myth into its obverse, the myth of Helen and Paris.[7] Nevertheless, the references remain only references—mythological allusions to illustrate points that are really being made discursively.

The Ring and the Book is an important poem, because it moves in the right direction. It moves away from myth as overt subject matter; but it brings back the mythical pattern—not the particular events and characters of the Andromeda story, but the pattern—as inherent in the very structure in the mind, in what we would nowadays call the unconscious. *The Ring and the Book* does the same thing for the Christian pattern of sin and redemption—bringing Christian virtue alive again out of what Miss Barrett, in the letter I have quoted, calls "this low ground," and through circumstances, like Caponsacchi's abduction of Pompilia, which would seem the reverse of virtuous. The fact that Miss Barrett goes on, after inveighing against subjects drawn from classical mythology, to say that "Christianity is a worthy *myth*, and poetically acceptable" (1: 43), shows that she and Browning were against the classical mythology of the official literary tradition because it projects obsolete meanings we only pretend to believe in as a literary game. It is because Browning did not go far enough in his use of mythical pattern, did not allow the meaning of his poem to rest in the pattern, that he considered that myths could grow obsolete.

Browning's idea of progress would seem to prevent a complete reliance on mythical pattern. For Yeats, the symbols and myths are permanent and the ideas about them change. But for Browning, the myths change; myths are the progressively changing symbolic language for the same continuing idea. In "Parleying with Charles Avison," in *Parleyings with Certain People of Importance in Their Day* (1887), Browning takes off from the idea, expressed forty years earlier in a letter to Miss Barrett, that "'in Music, the Beau Idéal changes every thirty years'" (1: 523). Music, like Avison's, of a generation or two ago, seems obsolete; yet the thing music talks about remains the same, and it requires only a few technical adjustments to translate from an old to a new musical idiom. We need the ever-changing idioms to startle us over and over again into ever-new apprehensions of the old truth. For "Truths escape / Time's insufficient garniture: they fade, / They fall"—when the old garniture seems to turn into a lie. In the same way,

> Soon shall fade and fall
> Myth after myth—the husk-like lies I call
> New truth's corolla-safeguard.

> (Ll. 371–73, 378–80)

Certainly, the mythical method as practiced by Yeats, Eliot and Joyce depends on an idea of recurrence, on a cyclical rather than a linear view of history.[8] The idea of progress requires that you keep track of time; while the mythical method requires that you collapse time. Browning does collapse time whenever he writes about Andromeda, and it is significant that he always writes well on that subject. The Andromeda passage in his first poem, *Pauline* (ll. 656–67), is one of the finest passages he ever wrote. The passage is quite remarkably echoed by Hopkins's "Andromeda" sonnet.

I mention the similarity to suggest that Hopkins, in spite of the many nasty things he said about Browning (things that show a minute knowledge of the older poet's work), must to some extent have learned his music from Browning. Both poets are obscure because they are trying to use words in such a way as to overcome the analytic effect of language—the effect Browning has in mind when he talks about Sordello's failure to create a satisfactory poetic language,

> Because perceptions whole, like that he sought
> To clothe, reject so pure a work of thought
> As language: thought may take perception's place
> But hardly co-exist in any case,
> Being its mere presentment—of the whole
> By parts, the simultaneous and the sole
> By the successive and the many.

> (2:589–95)

The crowd, Browning goes on to say, which deals in ready-made thoughts, has merely to tack them together; and presumably the crowd

can be lucid. But for Sordello, thought and language are the things perception has been rent into. They are the diffusion and destruction of
perception; and it is the point of poetic language to give a sense of the
original perception behind the diffusion and destruction. Park Honan
sees in Browning's pessimism about the possibilities of language a sign
that he was experimenting in *Sordello* toward a new poetic style. J. Hillis
Miller sees Browning's language as approximating "whole perceptions"
because so "often close to the inarticulate noise which is the source of all
words." This can be true of Browning but, as Miller's examples show,
not at his best; it is sometimes true of Hopkins at his best, as in "The
Windhover."[9] Both Browning and Hopkins break up conventional syn-
tax and multiply associations with bewildering rapidity, in order to make
us feel that the things language has laid out in spatial and temporal
succession are really happening simultaneously—in order to restore the
instantaneous, orchestrated quality of the original perception. Both poets
are working for an effect characteristic of symbolism and the mythical
method.

In defending himself in a letter to Ruskin against Ruskin's charge of
obscurity, Browning explains that the poetry or effect of simultaneity lies
precisely in the jumps that the reader is forced to make for himself.

> I *know* that I don't make out my conception by my language, all poetry
> being a putting the infinite within the finite. You would have me paint it
> all plain out, which can't be; but by various artifices I try to make shift
> with touches and bits of outlines which *succeed* if they bear the concep-
> tion from me to you. You ought, I think, to keep pace with the thought
> tripping from ledge to ledge of my "glaciers," as you call them; not stand
> poking your alpenstock into the holes, and demonstrating that no foot
> could have stood there;—suppose it sprang over there? In *prose* you may
> criticise so—because that is the absolute representation of portions of
> truth, what chronicling is to history—but in asking for more *ultimates*
> you must accept less *mediates,* nor expect that a Druid stone-circle will
> be traced for you with as few breaks to the eye as the North Crescent and
> South Crescent that go together so cleverly in many a suburb.

And he says of a poem of his: "Is the jump too much there? The whole
is all but a simultaneous feeling with me."[10]

Browning sketches out what has come to be the dominant twentieth-
century theory about poetry—that it makes its effect through the association in the reader's mind of disparate elements, and that this process
of association leads to the recognition, in what has been presented successively, of static pattern. The recognition is often in the twentieth cen-

tury called "epiphany." It is the recognition of what Hopkins calls the "inscape" of the object in poetry.

The difference between Browning and Hopkins is that Hopkins dislocates language in order to make his *image* more palpable—to make us feel the force of the bird's soaring in "The Windhover," and the even greater force of its falling movement. The meaning emerges as paradox, and then only by implication—the implication that the active and passive life are equally intense, that Christ triumphed through failure. Browning, on the other hand, tries to achieve the effect of simultaneity through discursive thought itself. That is why Browning is hardly ever at his best where he is obscure; while Hopkins is often at his best where he is obscure. Hopkins goes farther than Browning in symbolizing and mythmaking.

Yet if you can get certain knotty passages of Browning sufficiently well in mind to leap playfully from idea to idea with the swiftness and freedom of Browning's mind, you actually start a process of association that turns the discursive thought into poetry. Swinburne gives the best description of the pleasure to be derived from the discursive Browning. In comparing Browning with a really obscure poet like Chapman, Swinburne denies that Browning is obscure at all. For obscurity is the product of a confused and chaotic intellect; whereas

> if there is any great quality more perceptible than another in Mr. Browning's intellect it is his decisive and incisive faculty of thought, his sureness and intensity of perception, his rapid and trenchant resolution of aim. . . . He is something too much the reverse of obscure; he is too brilliant and subtle for the ready reader of a ready writer to follow with any certainty the track of an intelligence which moves with such incessant rapidity, or even to realize with what spider-like swiftness and sagacity his building spirit leaps and lightens to and fro and backward and forward as it lives along the animated line of its labour, springs from thread to thread and darts from centre to circumference of the glittering and quivering web of living thought woven from the inexhaustible stores of his perception and kindled from the inexhaustible fire of his imagination. . . . It is hopeless to enjoy the charm or to apprehend the gist of his writings except with a mind thoroughly alert, an attention awake at all points.[11]

To return then to our two questions about Browning and myth, we might say that Browning defined his realism precisely through opposition to myths as overt subject matter. He was, however, feeling his way, through realism and psychology, to a twentieth-century psychological use of myth. In rejecting myth in "Parleying with Gerard de Lairesse," Browning asks whether he would do better to tell two stories—to repeat the old myth through realistically apprehended modern circumstances, repeat the myth of Dryope plucking the lotus blossoms through the story of an English girl plucking "fruit not fabulous" but "Apple of English homesteads." "Advantage would it prove or detriment / If I saw double?" (ll. 118–26).

It is through just such double vision that twentieth-century writers have returned to myth. Browning's phrase recalls Blake's distinction between single vision, which is Newton's way of seeing facts as just facts, and double vision, which is the capacity to read facts symbolically.[12] "Oh, we can fancy too!" Browning continues,

> but somehow fact
> Has got to—say, not so much push aside
> Fancy, as to declare its place supplied
> By fact unseen but no less fact the same,
> Which mind bids sense accept.
>
> (Ll. 149–53)

We have here the modern distinction, derived from Coleridge, between neoclassical fancy and romantic or modern imagination. The neoclassicist went on using the old myths, not because he believed in them, but because they were decorative and poetical. The neoclassical painter Lairesse could, in the walk described in his book on painting, maintain the old mythical view because he was blind. But the modern artist insists on the truth of his mythical vision—his perception of "the links," in Browning's words, that "bind / Our earth to heaven" (ll. 145–47)—because it evolves out of direct perception of the facts. The modern artist creates his own myths and symbols by bringing to the sensuous apprehension of reality the whole mind or imagination.

This is the essence of modern symbolist theory. Not only "Lairesse" and "Avison," but the whole *Parleyings* can best be understood as Browning's verse essay on symbolism. In "Bernard de Mandeville," we are told to read the opposition between good and evil as symbolic of the absolute design of things, and not to take evil as in itself a substantial reality. If in a ground plan we were told that *A* is the house, we would be foolish to ask where's the roof to *A*. But

> Why so very much
> More foolish than our mortal purblind way
> Of seeking in the symbol no mere point
> To guide our gaze through what were else inane,
> But things—their solid selves?
>
> (Ll. 184–88)

"A myth may teach," says Browning: "Only, who better would expound it thus / Must be Euripides not Aeschylus" (ll. 204–6). Euripides did not, like Aeschylus, take myth literally, but understood it as symbolic, as a way of talking about life. Euripides was, in other words, a realist and therefore a symbolist.

Browning then makes a myth. In the morning of creation, only man was sullen because he could not, like the plants and animals, enjoy the sun unconsciously. Man yearned to understand the sun, both in its visible aspect and as an all-informing principle of energy. Man yearned, in other words, to make contact through his mind with the "outside mind" behind the sun, and so love the sun consciously through his understanding. Finally, "Prometheus helped him" by offering "an artifice," a magnifying glass,

> whereby he drew
> Sun's rays into a focus,—plain and true,
> The very Sun in little: made fire burn
> And henceforth do Man service—glass-conglobed
> Though to a pin-point circle—all the same
> Comprising the Sun's self, but Sun disrobed
> Of that else-unconceived essential flame
> Borne by no naked sight.
>
> (Ll. 301–9)

Prometheus is conceived as having taught man to draw down through a magnifying glass a symbolic representation of the sun, which could be looked at, understood, and used to start a fire, as the sun itself could not. From the symbol we can "infer immensity," but only the symbol can engage our affection: "In little, light, warmth, life, are blessed— / Which, in the large, who sees to bless?" (ll. 317–19). The whole crucial passage recalls Coleridge's dictum that a true symbol "always partakes of the Reality which it renders intelligible." [13]

In "Daniel Bartoli," Browning rejects a kind of symbolism quite different from the modern—the kind set forth in Bartoli's *Dei Simboli Trasportati al Morale,* where the seventeenth-century Jesuit historian does two things Browning does not like. Bartoli repeats implausible legends, and uses them to teach moral lessons; whereas for Browning "historical fact had," as DeVane puts it, "a righteousness of its own" (*Browning's Parleyings,* 53). Bartoli is represented as telling an absurdly miraculous legend of a female saint, in order that Browning may, by way of contrast, tell a story from a memoir, in which a real girl, acting in plausible circumstances, shows herself to be a saint in a far more important sense than Bartoli's Saint Scholastica.

In "Christopher Smart," Browning draws from the case of the poet who once and once only wrote a great poem,—and then when he was in the madhouse—the essential doctrine of symbolist poetry: that poetry is, as Yeats put it, a revelation and should make the effect of a revelation. Smart achieves his effect not by giving an exhaustive catalogue of details like modern naturalists, nor by concerning himself like the aesthetes with appearances only. Smart uses his *selected* details as symbols—making them stand for the rest and imbuing them with ideas and moral meaning. He does not, on the other hand, like the scientists and their followers, start with abstract laws that when applied to nature must inevitably devalue it. Smart's ideas are inseparable from the palpaby rendered objects that embody them. He gives in his "Song to David" the truth about nature, because he gives "her lovelinesses infinite / In little" (ll. 144–45).

In "George Bubb Dodington," Browning shows that this second-rate Machiavellian failed in politics because he operated by rational laws of calculated self-interest that we all understand too well. But the great Machiavellian—Browning has Disraeli in mind, the whole parleying is an attack upon him—is the great charlatan who, like the artist, knows how to turn himself and his work into a symbol. He does this by wrapping himself in mystery, operating by motives we cannot understand.

> No animal—much less our lordly Man—
> Obeys its like . . .
>   Who would use
> Man for his pleasure needs must introduce
> The element that awes Man. Once for all,
> His nature owns a Supernatural.
>
>   (Ll. 134–35, 188–91)

In "Francis Furini"—the parleying that makes the most complete statement of symbolist doctrine—Browning is doing something more important than just defending his son's nude paintings. Browning defends the nude in painting by showing that the nude figure is more symbolic than the clothed figure, and symbolic precisely of soul. The artist agonizes

>   to adumbrate, trace in dust
> That marvel which we dream the firmament
> Copies in star-device when fancies stray
> Outlining, orb by orb, Andromeda—
> God's best of beauteous and magnificent
> Revealed to earth—the naked female form.
>
>   (Ll. 138–43)

The artists who see most clearly God's purpose—to dispense "all gifts / To soul through sense"—are those who "bid us love alone / The type untampered with [i.e., the archetype], the naked star!" (ll. 233–47). In *The Nude: A Study in Ideal Form* (1956), Kenneth Clark concludes:

> The Greeks perfected the nude in order that man might feel like a god, and in a sense this is still its function, for although we no longer suppose that God is like a beautiful man, we still feel close to divinity in those flashes of self-identification when, through our own bodies, we seem to be aware of a universal order.[14]

In symbolism, there is no high or low; symbolism demonstrates that we can know the so-called high only by knowing the so-called low. There you have the error of the Darwinians—and it is no digression for Browning to associate them with the prudish enemies of the nude—who think that their knowledge of man's low origin negates his spirituality. Once we see that the large subject of "Furini" is symbolism, then the attack on the Darwinians has even more cogency, and Browning's deprecation of man's cognitive faculties has more philosophical justification than De-Vane in his book on the *Parleyings* makes out. We can see how Browning's relativism leads to symbolism when, in criticizing in a letter of 1881 the Darwinian idea that evolution is ungoverned by intelligence, Browning says that "time and space" are "purely conceptions of our own, wholly inapplicable to intelligence of another kind."[15]

The Darwinians do not realize, Browning implies in "Furini," that their theory is itself, by its hierarchical arrangement of nature, an anthropomorphizing symbol system based on intuition of a perfection from which all nature can be scaled downward. The Darwinians, who take an abstract view of nature, looking downward from the top, see only what is lacking. An artist like Furini, instead, who takes his stand within nature, can through loving penetration of a particular living thing uncover "Marvel at hiding under marvel, pluck / Veil after veil from Nature" (ll. 395–96), and thus see the living thing as pointing upward, as symbolizing the whole perfect scheme.

The pre-eminence that the Darwinians themselves give man derives not from man's power or even from his knowledge. For the proportions of nature are so incommensurate with our cognitive faculties that we can never know nature as it is in itself:

> . . . what *is* minuteness—yonder vault
> Speckled with suns, or this the millionth—thing,

> . . . that on some insect's wing
> Helps to make out in dyes the mimic star?
>
> (Ll. 293–96)

The thing that gives us pre-eminence is our moral sense, our intuition of perfection; and all the individual knows for sure is his consciousness of himself as having that sense. The individual finds in and through his self-consciousness anthropomorphizing images—"thus blend / I, and all things perceived, in one Effect" (ll. 361–62)—which, by some mysterious law, he understands as corresponding to the external world. What the individual knows, in other words—and here Browning comes close to Blake's "Where man is not, nature is barren"[16]—is *imagined* nature.

Like Andromeda, the individual clings to his "rock-spit of self-knowledge" (l. 410), with the sea of ignorance surging round. Art teaches him about spirit by directing his gaze precisely toward the body, toward

> Those incommensurably marvellous
> Contrivances which furnish forth the house
> Where soul has sway! Though Master keep aloof,
> Signs of His presence multiply from roof
> To basement of the building. . . .
>   He's away, no doubt,
> But what if, all at once, you come upon
> A startling proof—not that the Master gone
> Was present lately—but that something—whence
> Light comes—has pushed Him into residence?
>
> (Ll. 533–43)

Suddenly, in an epiphany, the physical details light up from within, manifesting the invisible in the visible, turning into a symbol.

Browning is trying to say what Yeats says more pithily—that "Man can embody truth but he cannot know it."[17] The passage even concludes with Yeats's favorite circular symbol of the serpent with its tail in its mouth.

> "Was such the symbol's meaning,—old, uncouth—
> That circle of the serpent, tail in mouth?
> Only by looking low, ere looking high,
> Comes penetration of the mystery."
>
> (Ll. 544–47)

In the *Parleyings*—which is the most complete statement of his maturest thought—Browning answers the problems of his time by suggesting that we change the nature of the questions we put to the universe, that we turn upon all aspects of life double rather than single vision. Had Browning been able to realize such doctrine in his art, had he been able to make his fragmentary glimpses of life symbolic of the whole, of an absolute vision, he would have broken through to the modern mythical method. He would have broken through to a final clarity of vision and style and been one of the great poets of English literature. As it is, he is a poet of enduring interest—partly because his very faults show that he was turning analytic thought against itself, that he understood what had to be done.

I would like to conclude, however, by mentioning a few poems in which Browning does use, and with great success, the modern mythical method. The first is the famous "Childe Roland," where the meaning is not extractable but is simply *in* the pattern of movement. Although the poem dramatizes a reference in a well-known play to a well-known figure, it hardly deals with one of Arnold's grand, enduring subjects. Browning has made in the poem his own private myth.

The second is a major work. Yet it is undeservedly overlooked in courses on, and discussions of, Browning. I refer to *Balaustion's Adventure,* in which the Greek girl Balaustion retells Euripides' *Alcestis* as translated by Browning. Balaustion is fresh, gentle, sweet, compassionate. She has what Browning thought of as the very best qualities of nineteenth-century sensibility; so that, in filtering Euripides' play through her, Browning makes us feel how modern in its sensibility the play is, and how modern Euripides is. He makes us understand why, in *The Ring and the Book,* the Pope says that Euripides was a Christian before the advent of the Christian era. For without giving the *Alcestis* a Christian construction—and it is a good thing that Balaustion herself is a contemporary of Euripides—Browning makes us feel, through his rendition, that any person has a Christian heart who understands that love is a greater force than death.

Published in 1871, *Balaustion's Adventure* was written directly after *The Ring and the Book.* I certainly agree with DeVane, in the *Browning Handbook,* that *Balaustion's Adventure* ought to be considered as closing—which is to say as within—Browning's best period. It is actually more successful than *The Ring and the Book* in achieving what it sets out to do. If I hesitate to rank it above or even with *The Ring and the Book,* it is only because the poem is after all mainly Euripides. Yet I am not sure this matters. We probably ought to understand the poem as we understand Ezra Pound's translations—as a creative appropriation of ancient material, a way of giving an ancient poet a historical consciousness he himself could not have had. Eliot said of Pound that he "is much more modern, in my opinion, when he deals with Italy and Provence, than when he deals with modern life."[18] This way of being modern is what Eliot means by the mythical method.

Eliot means something quite different from that use of established classical mythology so expertly traced by Douglas Bush in *Mythology and the Romantic Tradition.* Bush is mainly right when he says that "Browning was not a poet of mythological imagination; the few moments in which he seems to deserve that name only emphasize his normal character as a novelist in verse." I demur, however, when Bush gives as evidence the fact that in Browning's Greek poems "the Greece he presents is a mixture of the completely real and the completely unreal. Whatever solid properties can be seen or touched are Greek; the psychological motives he evolves are usually not Greek."[19] The modern mythical method challenges and re-establishes mythical pattern precisely through realism and through psychology in the modern sense; though the poem will indeed be novelistic where mythical pattern is not re-established. That is the difference between the novelistic *Ring and the Book,* where the re-establishment of mythical pattern is only incidental, and the Greek *Balaustion,* where it is central.

The Ring and the Book and *Balaustion* employ the mythical method from opposite sides. For we start in *Balaustion* with the myth or pattern, and the narrator undertakes to make it real—to describe for us, as she says, the human expressions beneath the masks of the mythical characters. The myth of Alcestis is another version of the Andromeda-Perseus myth; Heracles, who brings back Alcestis from the dead, is even a descendant of Perseus. The thing Balaustion does is to draw out, through her comments on Euripides' tragicomedy, the underlying tragicomic pattern—the pattern of impasse and miracle—that is at the heart of Browning's view of the world and of his Christian faith.

Heracles' entrance into the play is beautifully interpreted by Balaustion. Left to themselves, human motives and the logic of events have led to an impasse; Alcestis must die and there is no help for it. But then, suddenly, there breaks upon the scene "that great interrupting voice" (l. 1032). There is certainly a Christian analogue in the fact that the appearance of the god is heralded (a touch not really in Euripides) by his voice. "Sudden into the midst of sorrow," says Balaustion,

leapt
Along with the gay cheer of that great voice,
Hope, joy, salvation: Herakles was here!
Himself, o' the threshold, sent his voice on first

To herald all that human and divine
I' the weary happy face of him,—half God,
Half man, which made the god-part God the more.

(Ll. 1045–51)

It is because Heracles was a man that we can see as miraculous his will-
ingness to labor for men for no reason other than his love—that he can,
in other words, symbolize Divinity.

The movement is assimilated to the pattern of death and rebirth in
the vegetation cycle. When Heracles goes gaily off to bring back Alcestis
from the dead, Balaustion comments:

I think this is the authentic sign and seal
Of Godship, that it ever waxes glad,
And more glad, until gladness blossoms, bursts
Into a rage to suffer for mankind,
And recommence at sorrow:

just as, Balaustion continues, the flower is willing, at the height of its
bloom, to drop its seed—

once more die into the ground,
Taste cold and darkness and oblivion there:
And thence rise, tree-like grow through pain to joy,
More joy and most joy,—do man good again.

(Ll. 1918–29)

The same cyclical pattern governs the moral and spiritual life of each
individual. After Alcestis's husband Admetus has said everything except
the truth—that he ought not to have allowed Alcestis to die for him—
after Admetus has told all the lies: after, in Balaustion's metaphor, "the
last of bubbles broke" leaving the surface "placid," then "up swam / To
the surface the drowned truth, in dreadful change" (ll. 2047–50). The
metaphor describes perfectly the psychological movement of the best
dramatic monologues—where it is after the speaker has told all his lies
that inadvertently, and as if of its own accord, the truth rises to the surface. Only here we see how the deepest psychology leads back to a mythical pattern that is itself imbedded in the very order of things.

We see in the tragicomic pattern of impasse and miracle the meaning
behind the Andromeda myth. The miracle in the *Alcestis* is, as Browning
interprets it, the transformation of Admetus's consciousness. It is when
Admetus—who feared death as the worst of evils—suddenly *sees* "how
dear is death, / How loveable the dead are" (ll. 1952–53), that Alcestis

is restored to him as the external sign of the internal transformation. The same thing happens in "Childe Roland," where a transformation of consciousness makes the dark tower appear and turns all the facts that spell defeat into victory. The logic of events leads to winter; *spring* is the miracle. Transformation of consciousness is the way through the impasse logic leads to! This is Browning's understanding of the Incarnation, the descent of Divinity into human life.

Such collapsing of diverse events into a single pattern is at the heart of the mythical method. An interest in *Balaustion* might lead to revaluation of certain other neglected poems—of, for example, that strange and difficult late lyric, "Numpholeptos." "Numpholeptos" is like "Andrea del Sarto"—in its Tennysonian echoes (echoes here of "Tithonus"), in its sustained contrast between images of silver and gold, and in the speaker's final choice of continued enslavement to the lady against whom he has said so much. The comparison helps us see that the lady of "Numpholeptos" is another kind of Lucrezia, one who torments by being all too idealistic and sexlessly pure. The comparison helps us see that the case here is still psychological. But the psychology is in "Numpholeptos" projected through a peculiarly modern penetration of mythical figures, the nymph and nymph-enraptured lover, who are themselves seen as emerging out of natural phenomena—the cold radiance of the moon, and the white light that is refracted through the dust of earth into warm hues that, like the man of the poem, go forth only to return and die into their origin in the white light.

An interest in *Balaustion* might suggest that Browning did, after all, go farther than I have indicated toward projecting a total vision of life. *Balaustion* should certainly make us pay attention to the beautiful little lyric on spring with which Browning, in "Parleying with Gerard de Lairesse," concludes his argument against the use of classical mythology. This is, he says, the modern poet's way of making rhyme about, say, the miracle of spring which "the Greek Bard sadly greets: / 'Spring for the tree and herb—no Spring for us!'" The modern lyric, through a precise rendition of spring flowers, suggests all that the myths tell us about death and rebirth.

> Dance, yellows and whites and reds,—
> Lead your gay orgy, leaves, stalks, heads
> Astir with the wind in the tulip-beds!
>
> There's sunshine; scarcely a wind at all
> Disturbs starved grass and daisies small
> On a certain mound by a churchyard wall.

Daisies and grass be my heart's bedfellows
On the mound wind spares and sunshine mellows:
Dance you, reds and whites and yellows!

(Ll. 423–34)

Christianity, Browning implies, makes such realism possible by confirming our deepest intuition that the vegetation cycle is, indeed, symbolic of our fate after death.

"Numpholeptos" and the lyric on spring work from opposite directions—the first from the archetype to the human situation or seen fact, the second from the seen fact to the "fact unseen but no less fact the same." They both, however, employ double vision, and thus show how realism and psychology lead to the distinctively modern recovery of symbol and myth.

A New Look at
E. M. Forster

T HE successful filmings of *A Passage to India* (1984) and *A Room with a View* (1986) have produced a Forster revival. Aside from the still incomplete Abinger edition of Forster's works begun in 1972, the 1986 list of his books in print is notably longer than the list for 1979–80, with the best known books easily available in cheap editions.

Another source of renewed interest has been the public acknowledgment, since Forster's death in 1970, of his homosexuality. P. N. Furbank's *E. M. Forster: A Life* (1977) is explicit on the subject as earlier books on Forster were not. Forster's semi-autobiographical homosexual novel *Maurice*, which he wrote in 1913–14 but dared not publish, appeared in 1971. *Maurice* is a surprisingly poor novel—surprising when we consider that he wrote it between such successes as *Howards End* and *A Passage to India*. Nevertheless *Maurice* is in 1986 being filmed by the producers of *A Room with a View*, who are apparently betting on a continuing large audience for Forster.

In 1972 there appeared a collection of stories, *The Life to Come*, eight of which (including the title story) are about homosexuality and were thus hitherto unpublished. Forster wrote many such "indecent" stories, as he called them, for his own delectation, showing them to only a very few intimate friends and destroying many. One possible reason that Forster stopped writing novels was the "weariness," as he noted in his diary for 16 June 1911, "of the only subject that I both can and may treat—the love of men for women & vice versa." "I should have been a more famous writer," he noted on 31 December 1964, "if I had written or rather published more, but sex has prevented the latter." [1]

Explicit awareness of Forster's homosexuality does not seriously change our interpretations of his fiction. But it does help us understand why, in his fiction, proper heterosexual relations are always pallid, while erotic force is generated by the heroine's unconscious attraction to dark-complexioned, usually lower-class, men—to Italians at first, but finally, in Adela's unconscious attraction to Aziz in *Passage to India,* to an Indian.

For many years Forster loved a tall, handsome Indian Moslem, Masood, clearly the model for Aziz. Forster first knew Masood in England—he tutored him when Masood was preparing for Oxford—then saw him again in India after Masood had married (*Passage to India* is dedicated to him). Masood apparently did not respond to Forster sexually. Forster had sexual relations in Alexandria with an Egyptian tramcar conductor, and later in India with a Hindu barber. But he does not seem to have been very active sexually; he apparently spent most of his life in a state of frustration. As a Cambridge undergraduate Forster experienced with another student, H. O. Meredith, a passionate friendship which did not go beyond kisses and embraces (*A Room with a View* is dedicated to H. O. M.). This initiation into homoeroticism is the main subject of Forster's posthumously published novel *Maurice,* in which Clive is modeled on Meredith.

To those of us who have admired Forster, all five of the novels published during his lifetime exhibit his special charm and are therefore indispensable. Yet future readers who are not specialists in English literature may remember him for only one novel, *A Passage to India.* Despite the revival of interest in *A Room with a View* through its filming, Forster's last novel, published in 1924, increasingly detaches itself from the rest of his work as incommensurably major.

Wilfred Stone, in *The Cave and the Mountain: A Study of E. M. Forster* (1966), shows the advantage of such critical hindsight—an advantage over Lionel Trilling who, in his brilliant introductory study of 1943, rated *Howards End* highest—in that Stone treats all Forster's works in order to show *Passage to India* as a culmination. In this big, thoroughly researched book Stone makes us realize how unpredictable and incalculable was the leap of imagination that produced *Passage to India.* Forster published his first four novels quickly between 1905 and 1910, but waited fourteen years to publish *Passage to India,* which he began during his first visit to India in 1912–13 and wrote with difficulty and lack of confidence, having suspected after *Howards End* (1910) that he would write no more novels. Stone describes the years after 1910 as a spiritual passage eastward—accomplished through Forster's residence in Egypt (especially Alexandria) about which he wrote three nonfiction books, and finally in India where he returned in 1921. Although Forster made hesitant stabs at the novel during his two visits to India, he couldn't really write it until his return to England in 1922.

Stone helps us understand why Forster wrote no fiction after *Passage* to *India*; for he shows how in *Passage to India* Forster answers all the questions posed in the earlier work, and indeed enlarges the questions themselves. Given Forster's starting point in turn-of-the-century liberal-ism and aestheticism, he says in *Passage to India* all he had to say and all perhaps that there is to say. Afterward he wisely preferred writing criticism and biography to writing inferior fiction.

Actually, Forster wrote two masterpieces—his last novel and his first, *Where Angels Fear to Tread* (1905). *Angels* is on a much smaller scale than *Passage to India*; it is a perfect little comedy of manners. Such success at first try shows that Forster's talent is essentially comic; and criticism, which is better suited to talk about the ideas and symbols in the novels, has never done justice to their lightness and charm. Except for George Eliot in her lighter moments, Forster is the only English nov-elist in whom one can discern another Jane Austen. The question is why Forster was not content to go on writing comedy.

The answer is that no writer of integrity, standing this side of the romantic and relativistic nineteenth century, can write for long like Jane Austen. To write like her, a novelist has to believe in his society, believe that its norms represent some ultimate truth and that the job of comedy is to correct deviations from the norms. Forster's characters have, in-stead, to be judged and to work out their destinies through shifting and inadequate standards. That is why Forster takes a comparative attitude toward cultures, and why his more enlightened characters work out their destinies between cultures. The lack of valid standards leads to a com-plex irony that criticizes not only English middle-class values, but the alternatives as well, and the very characters who seek the alternatives. The lack of standards leads also to concern with a mystical reality behind the shifting social surfaces. Hence the romantic emphasis on nature and imaginative apprehension, that assorts so oddly with the witty notation of manners. Hence Forster's attempt to combine comedy with prophecy or vision.

The characteristic combinations of Forster's art are most complex in *Passage to India*, which compares three cultures—West European Chris-tian, Indian Moslem, and Indian Hindu—as decreasingly inadequate representations of the unmeaning echo in the Marabar Caves and Mrs. Moore's imaginative apprehension of the echo. The European culture stands for will and order; the Moslem for emotion and erotic love; the Hindu for a disorder and impassivity that comes closest to representing a comprehensiveness that dissolves distinctions and manifests itself as nothingness. Thus the *metaphysical* adequacy of Hinduism, especially for the modern scientific view of the world, the fact that Hinduism op-erates way beyond good and evil, order and disorder, exclusiveness and inclusiveness, makes it for all *practical* purposes the most inadequate of the three cultures. Neither Forster nor his hero, Fielding, can finally accept it—though they see that it takes into account more of reality than "poor talkative little Christianity" with its attempt to draw an ethical and rationalistic pattern from the most recent history of only one species, man, in the vast round of animate and inanimate nature.

A far simpler book, *Where Angels Fear to Tread* compares only two cultures—England, standing for will and order, and Italy, standing for emotion and erotic love. By reference to comic stereotypes, Forster quickly sketches in the manners of Sawston, upper-middle-class English suburbia, and throws them into comic juxtaposition with the manners of San Gimignano (here called Monteriano), the almost perfectly preserved thirteenth-century town near Siena. Haughty old Mrs. Herriton of Sawston sends her aesthetical son, Philip, out to rescue Lilia, the giddy widow of her dead son, from an impending marriage to "Italian nobility" (Mrs. Herriton snorts at the "fatuous vulgarity" of that phrase in the telegram from Italy). Our laughter proceeds from recollection of other comedies about snobs; so that we know how to respond when Philip on arriving learns, to his "personal disgust and pain," that what Lilia has in fact married is of all things the son of a dentist! "A dentist! A dentist at Monteriano. A dentist in fairyland! False teeth and laughing gas and the tilting chair at a place which knew the Etruscan League, and the Pax Romana, and Alaric himself . . ."[2]

Yet this is another order of snobbery that takes us beyond the external comedy of national and class distinctions. For Philip, unlike his mother and his sister, Harriet, has the tourist's attitude and rejects Gino as betraying Philip's ideal of Italy. The thing, however, that ties all the Herritons and Lilia and Caroline Abbott, the sensitive spinster who chaperoned Lilia in Italy, is what Forster in his essay "Notes on the English Character" has called the "undeveloped heart."[3] Forster transforms the traditional comedy of manners to dramatize the conflict between English middle-class manners of the undeveloped heart and Italian manners of authenticity. The Italian manners belong to no class (Gino does not behave like an Italian bourgeois); they have been idealized out of the observable natural courtesy of guides and servants.

We see the manners of the undeveloped heart in the ludicrous contrast between Monteriano and the picture of Harriet squeezing out her sponges, as, after Lilia's death, she prepares dutifully and with distaste to accompany Philip on a second mission to the lovely old Tuscan town—this time to rescue Lilia's baby from the Italian cad, Gino. Philip and Caroline are better, but even they violate Italy by refusing to see it as it is, by using it as a romantic escape from the social grooves. (Lilia married Gino to escape, then learned to her sorrow that Italy has its own social grooves.) There are in this and the other novels three grades of Englishmen—the Philistines, who never see beyond middle-class values, the tourists or sensitives who try to break away but can't quite, and the authentic people who either are or become what they ought to be.

By the standards of authenticity, the Herritons are vulgar in the compact they make to keep secret the existence of Lilia's son and in their purpose, once the secret is out, to procure the baby just to preserve their good name. Even the heroine, Caroline Abbott, is vulgar in attempting to buy the baby in order to assuage her conscience for having encouraged Lilia to marry Gino (she did so to satisfy vicariously her own unacknowledged attraction to him). Gino, for all his coarsely avowed fortune hunting (coarseness reveals, vulgarity conceals—says Forster in *Longest Journey*), never for a moment considers their offers. We can never be sure about Gino's motives, but his actions are somehow right—though without moral pretension.

Gino is authentic because he is like Italy itself a vital and attractive mixture of "Beauty, evil, charm, vulgarity, mystery" (112). Caroline, who is sure Gino is not fit to bring up the baby, learns from him "the horrible truth, that wicked people are capable of love." Gino's relation to his son is justified by his grasp of a biological mystery Miss Abbott cannot understand—the sense that through his son "physical and spiritual life may stream out of him for ever" (136–37).

Gino is an erotic force, the only *man* in the book, since Philip is an aesthetical eunuch. Gino—who is irresistibly attractive to Lilia, Caroline and Philip, even when they disapprove of him—stands a little way beyond good and evil, pointing toward the romantic erotic force of Dr. Aziz in *Passage to India* and the meaningless erotic force of the caves.

Forster has worked throughout his career, notably in the short stories, to evoke such a force. The first story he ever wrote, "The Story of a Panic" (1902), is about a beautiful, destructive manifestation of Pan at Ravello which brings to fruition, as we now realize, a homoerotic relation between the fourteen-year-old boy Eustace and a Southern Italian fisher lad. The relation may recall Forster's idyllic friendship at about eight with a garden-boy named Ansell: "the two," Furbank writes in his biography, "enjoyed lying in each other's arms, screaming and tickling." [4] "Ansell" is the title of a story (in *The Life to Come*) written shortly after "Story of a Panic," about a twenty-three-year-old Cambridge student who meets again the garden-boy Ansell with whom he had an idyllic friendship at the age of fourteen; Ansell rescues him from bookishness, returning him to nature. Ansell is also the name of Rickie Elliot's philosophical Cambridge friend in *The Longest Journey*. The garden-boy theme comes to a climax in *Maurice* when, as in a wish-fulfilling dream, Clive's gamekeeper enters through Maurice's bedroom window to give him at last the sexual satisfaction he has not yet enjoyed.

In the novels, erotic force is generated only by Gino and Dr. Aziz. The sensitive English people, capable of venturing a few steps beyond the moral categories, can apprehend such erotic force; but since even they must tamper, must impose their moralizing and transcendentalizing wills, the experience turns destructive. In transcendentalizing Italy and Gino, Philip and Caroline practice a destructiveness that differs only in subtlety from the destructiveness of Harriet, who finally kidnaps the baby which gets killed in an accident.

In the final scene, where we learn that Caroline loves Gino but will do nothing about it and that Philip thinks he loves Caroline but is relieved, after her confession about Gino, that he need do nothing about it, in this scene we understand why Forster had to go beyond comedy of manners. For the failure here is too psychological, and too intimately determined not only by place and class but by the historical moment, to be capable of any solution at all, let alone a solution expressed as a shift to "good" manners or well-balanced behavior. As in *Passage to India*, the contrast is not only between English character and that of another country, but between the distinctively modern and the traditional in character. *Where Angels Fear to Tread* brings comedy up against its limits in the hopelessness of the modern condition, but never itself advances into prophecy or the poetical.

Forster's subsequent concern with comedy and prophecy explains the distinction he makes, in *Aspects of the Novel* (1927), between "flat" and "round" characters. Flat characters are the characters out of old-fashioned comedy who, like the female Herritons, are solidly entrenched in a social order and display one or two leading traits deriving from their position in that order. But the sensitive characters, who question the code, find their identities in an inner life at odds with the social order and "continually threaten to achieve roundness." To the extent that they do achieve roundness, our view of them becomes psychological and empathic rather than comic. "The prophetic aspect," writes Forster, "demands . . . suspension of the sense of humour."[5] The two principal influences on Forster were Jane Austen and Proust. From Jane Austen, Forster said, he learned "the possibilities of domestic humor," and from Proust, "ways of looking at character . . . the modern subconscious way."[6]

Although Stone does not give sufficient credit to *Where Angels Fear to Tread* (he does not recognize its purely comic achievement because he gives more attention to Philip and his problems, treats him as "rounder," than the novel warrants), he is acute on the limitations of the three subsequent novels. In one of his many perceptive summations, Stone says that "Forster's fiction is essentially an experiment in self-confidence. One after another his main characters, like so many groundhogs, poke their heads out of their sanctuaries to see whether it is safe to emerge further."[7] The sanctuaries are the ivory towers of pure speculation and sensibility that Forster inhabited among his intellectual friends in Cambridge and later Bloomsbury. If we add the notion that Forster was also finding out how far it was safe to emerge from the sanctuary of comedy, we have a good key to the subsequent novels. In *The Longest Journey* (1907), his most purely poetical and least successful novel, he emerges very far from comedy—attempting an internal drama of failed idealism, a kind of *Alastor,* for which like Shelley himself he has not found an adequate machinery of events. He retreats in *A Room with a View* (1908), writing what he himself calls his "nicest" book, a sentimental comedy that slyly evades the modern condition (one reason perhaps for the film's success). He emerges again in *Howards End* (1910), where, in taking his first really serious look at English society, he writes his most intelligent novel except for *Passage to India.* But even *Howard's End* conducts us back to a sanctuary.

In emerging from Cambridge, the antihero of *Longest Journey,* lame, sensitive, self-accusing Rickie Elliot, moves into social reality by marrying Agnes and taking a job teaching at the snobbish Sawston Public School where her odious brother Herbert is a master. Although the general tone is that of an ironical realism that sees around moral questions, all Rickie's antagonists, his wife, brother-in-law and brutal father, show up as melodramatically villainous. Forster is clearly paying off old personal scores—which is to say that he is uncertain about his distance from Rickie. Rickie comes out, therefore, as more of a sap than the author can have intended.

Forster fails also in his characterization of Rickie's antiself, his illegitimate half-brother, Stephen Wonham. Stephen is intended to be a hero and a natural man. But his naturalness is never a significant force, because it is not displayed as an erotic force. Compared to Gino, Stephen is curiously emasculate and 'pure'—a muscular Peter Pan. If erotic force were a reality in this novel, we would be able to understand why for Rickie the acknowledgment of Stephen as his brother is a shattering initiation into reality. We would understand that it is the erotic revelation about his mother, and not simply preference for her over his father, that causes Rickie to faint when he learns that Stephen is the bastard not, as he had automatically assumed, of his hated father but of his beloved mother. We would understand why Rickie's aunt takes him when she breaks the news of his relation to Stephen, to the center of the Cadbury Rings, a double circle of ancient earthworks—which is, unlike the dell at Cambridge where Rickie liked to retreat, an enclosure at the heart of reality, a kind of womb of England. Stone connects the symbolism of enclosures, throughout Forster's work, with the caves in *Passage to India* and with the symbolism of Hindu temples from which *The Cave and the Mountain* derives its title (300–304).

Partly this is a Shelleyan story, exalting idealism and Platonic friendship over the possessiveness of sexual love (hence the title, deriving from Shelley's *Epipsychidion,* his hymn to Platonic love). Partly it is a Laurentian novel manqué, exalting nature and the life force without explicitly exalting sexuality. The conflict between the Cambridge ivory tower and the social reality of Sawston is supposed to be subsumed in Wiltshire— the county which is, we are told, the quintessence of English landscape— and in an authentically English type that emerges from this landscape. Stephen seems at times to be this authentic type, but at other times he falls short because of his brutality. He certainly falls short of his father, an educated farmer who emerges as unequivocally authentic—but in a passage too short to make much impression. This part of the novel is not successful.

The successful story is the *Bildungsroman,* the story of how Rickie, the young writer, discovers his true self and his true vocation by finally recognizing his brother. But in abandoning Agnes, whom he had idealized, for Stephen, Rickie can only swing from one overblown ideal to another. Rickie transcendentalizes Stephen (Forster himself sometimes participates in the process and is sometimes ironical about it), when he thinks of his alliance with him as a decision for "trusting the earth."

Because Rickie has never *seen* Stephen as he is in himself, he is extravagantly disillusioned when Stephen gets dead drunk, thus breaking a promise not to drink for a few days. In dying to save Stephen's life, Rickie finally makes contact with reality because he sacrifices his life for a failed ideal—for Stephen lying drunk in the path of an oncoming train. Although there are no heroics in Rickie's *action,* he dies with the old overblown nonsense on his lips when he whispers that he ought to have bewared of "the earth," meaning Stephen.[8] It is just such ironical qualification of even intense moments that marks Forster at his best. And, indeed, there is in this novel so much finely ironical intelligence coupled with tender intimacy as to endear it, in spite of its faults, to Forster's admirers—especially since it is a seedbed of his subsequent work and "always his favorite among his novels. It was the one he had written most easily and with most rapture" (Furbank, 149).

In *A Room with a View,* the contrast is again between Sawston and

Italy (Part One, the Italian part, was written at the same time as *Where Angels Fear to Tread*); but Italy in this novel is not a serious cultural alternative. It is a pastoral setting where Englishmen on holiday can find their heart's desire, aided by Italians who are the shepherds and nymphs of pastoral masquerading as guides and other attendants upon tourists.

For Lucy Honeychurch, the heroine, there is no question of cultural migration; her problem is whether she dares marry an Englishman, one notch below her on the middle-class scale, whose father is an outspokenly atheistical socialist. Old Mr. Emerson offends because his manners are all too good—benevolently democratic, free of affectation and snobbery. It is clear from the start that the Emersons pose no real threat to Sawston and that when Lucy, after the inevitable wrong engagement to a coxcomb, finally follows her own heart and good sense and marries George Emerson, the social order will be strengthened. The only distinctively modern element in the book is the psychological treatment of Lucy's puritanically repressed cousin and chaperone, who is vicariously involved in Lucy's relation with George. But Charlotte's story is treated lightly so as not to destroy the novel's gossamer workmanship. As a piece of finely wrought flimflam *A Room with a View* is successful (it is Forster's most charming novel), and might be considered Forster's holiday before he undertakes his most earnest novel, *Howards End.*

In *Howards End,* Forster finally writes about metropolitan intellectuals, people like his Bloomsbury friends, who are liberals, aesthetes, 'tourists.' I say finally though Forster has written all along about this position, which is his own (he might be called the novelist of the tourist mentality; a reader of guidebooks, he himself wrote a guide to Alexandria). Up till now, however, the real loyalties of his characters have been to class and country, even if they showed a tourist's appreciation of Italy. The upper-middle-class Schlegel sisters of *Howards End,* instead, feel classless and therefore alienated from society. It is a sign of their alienation that they are half-foreign—daughters of a German idealist who left his country when he felt it had abandoned its own best principles.

The Schlegel sisters are gently satirized for moving in that "aura of self-congratulation" which Lionel Trilling finds characteristic of liberal intellectuals.[9] They take a tourist's attitude toward England in their desire to "connect" with it—a desire no one committed to some social niche would feel. Helen Schlegel is thrilled by the rich business family, the Wilcoxes, because they challenge her stand on public issues when they call "Equality . . . nonsense, Votes for Women nonsense, Socialism nonsense, Art and Literature . . . nonsense."[10] Margaret Schlegel delights in the gaucheries of the low-middle-class clerk Leonard Bast, because she is moved by his attempt to improve himself through self-education and culture. Later, the sisters switch allegiances. Margaret marries the Wilcox father; and Helen, out of class guilt, gives herself to Leonard and has a child by him to atone for the economic injury Mr. Wilcox has done him. But since these connections with such impossible men are not accounted for by erotic infatuation (eros is not a reality in this book), they can only be taken allegorically.

Allegorically the connections represent attempts to put together an original cultural unity represented by the first Mrs. Wilcox and the farmhouse, Howards End, that has come down to her through her family. (All the other houses in the book are rented.) The elderly Ruth Wilcox is Forster's first draft of his greatest portrayal, the elderly Mrs. Moore of *Passage to India.* Until now, Forster's authentic characters have been men who exert force through vitality. With Ruth Wilcox, he portrays authenticity through negative qualities—passivity and stillness. She is the most memorable character in *Howards End,* for she carries her own atmosphere with her; she is not just another character, she is another order of existence altogether. Although failing in health, she seems stronger than her modern-minded husband and children, because she is rooted in Howards End which is in turn rooted in the landscape. This rootedness makes her, though she is not clever like the Schlegels' intellectual friends, thoroughly cultured, an aristocrat.

> She seemed to belong not to the young people and their motor, but to the house, and to the tree that overshadowed it. One knew that she worshipped the past, and that the instinctive wisdom the past can alone bestow had descended upon her—that wisdom to which we give the clumsy name of aristocracy. High-born she might not be. But assuredly she cared about her ancestors, and let them help her. (22)

Mrs. Wilcox, on her deathbed, leaves Howards End to Margaret in an unsigned note that the Wilcoxes destroy. This raises the book's central question. Like Wiltshire in *Longest Journey,* Howards End is traditional England. And the question is: Who shall inherit England—the Philistine guardians of her material wealth, who are governed by self-interest; or the disinterested guardians of her culture, who transcend the clash of class interests by an appeal to principles, to the best that has been thought and said? I borrow terms from Matthew Arnold to show that *Howards End* dramatizes Arnold's idea of culture. When Margaret says "Only connect!"—the phrase is the book's epigraph—"only connect the prose and the passion" (186–87), she is aspiring toward that Unity of Being for which Arnold, in "To a Friend," praises Sophocles whom "Business could not make dull, nor passion wild; / Who saw life steadily, and saw it whole." But Forster's idea of culture derives also from the larger romantic tradition that sees culture as reaching perfection, both in society and the individual, at that point where it coincides with nature, where culture shows forth as man's equivalent for nature.

It is allegorically right that Margaret, who has tried to breach the modern gap between business and passion, should eventually acquire Howards End by marrying Mr. Wilcox. Yet the tableau at the end is less encouraging than Forster seems to realize. Howards End is inhabited by Margaret and Helen, with Helen's illegitimate baby boy. The eldest Wilcox son is in prison for having helped bring on Leonard Bast's death by beating him up; Mr. Wilcox is a broken man dependent on Margaret for guidance, because he has had no inner ballast with which to withstand catastrophe. The implication is that if England is to have culture, it must be in the hands of women. Nor is Forster being ironical about the ending; for his hopes are apparently on Helen's son, who will inherit Howards End. But what chance has Helen's son, raised in such a household, not to turn out like the Schlegel brother, Tibby, a cultivated dishrag of a man?

For all its fascinating play of ideas, *Howards End* can be criticized for the dead stretches when characters and events are merely at the service of the ideas, and for the inept scenes dealing with Leonard Bast and his sluttish wife. Forster admitted he knew nothing about the home life of such people (*Paris Review,* 33). He cannot do lower-class characters unless they are exotic enough to be turned into symbols of natural force—like his Italian guides, or the naked Untouchable who moves the fan in the courtroom in *Passage to India*. But the main objection is Stone's when he criticizes Forster's evasiveness in making women his experimenters in excursion, and in presenting finally "a moral failure as a triumph" (266). The idea of culture as feminine is imbedded in Anglo-Saxon, as it is not in Latin, countries. But the idea is also a peculiarity of Forster and of his homosexual Cambridge friend G. Lowes Dickinson, about whom Forster wrote a biography. It is the spinsterish fastidiousness of Forster's comedy that reminds us of Jane Austen; but the old-maid quality can, when it shows forth seriously, mar his work.

To understand Forster's intellectual milieu, one has to understand Dickinson, the Cambridge don who most influenced Forster. Dickinson was a latter-day Shelley, a Shelley gone sedentary and soft, but still it was through Dickinson's sentimental Hellenism, his Platonic mysticism distrustful of religious creeds, his opposition to imperialism and war, his exaltation of friendship, that Forster imbibed the spirit of idealism that provides one pole in the dialectic of his novels. One has also to understand the Cambridge "set," Tennyson's society of the Apostles, to which

Forster and Dickinson belonged. In Tennyson's time, the Apostles avoided the opposing dogmas of Christian orthodoxy and utilitarianism through a romantic position that yielded religious intensity without theology. In Forster's time, the Apostles opposed to the latest dogmas a frankly aesthetic attitude and an extravagant faith in the sanctity of the individual. It was from these Apostles, regathered in London, that the original Bloomsbury Group drew most of its members. For Bloomsbury (of which Forster was a fringe member), all creeds, especially political creeds, were suspect; ideas in action were crude. All that mattered was the refinement of individual sensibility through art and personal relations.

Both Stone and Frederick Crews, in his book on Forster, trace the nineteenth-century background to Forster's intellectual position—showing how as great-grandson of the Evangelical and utilitarian M.P. Henry Thornton of Clapham, Forster made the characteristic century-long migration of English liberal intellectuals from Clapham to Bloomsbury. Clapham, center of the upper-middle-class intellectual elite of the early nineteenth century, believed, as I have explained above in "The Victorian Idea of Culture," in reform, moral action and laissez-faire economics. Their descendants, as represented by Bloomsbury and *The Independent Review* of which Dickinson was a founder, cared only for a laissez-faire of the spirit and to achieve that—says Crews in his revealing chapter on Forster's liberalism—were ready to accept "collectivist legislation" as "positively necessary to prevent society from exercising a tyranny of fortune and opinion over the individual." In this, says Crews, they were following the evolution of English liberalism out of the later John Stuart Mill.[11] They were also, I would add, in their suspicion of action and their respect only for a liberalism of ideas, following Matthew Arnold. They were certainly following Arnold in treating politics as a branch of culture. In the liberalism of *The Independent Review,* we saw, says Forster, "avenues opening into literature, philosophy, human relationships. . . . Can you imagine decency touched with poetry?"[12]

But the paeans to the individual really covered up secret misgivings that the individual was soon to count for nothing. "The people I respect most," writes Forster in *Two Cheers for Democracy,* "behave as if they were immortal and as if society was eternal. Both assumptions are false: both of them must be accepted as true if we are to go on eating and working and loving, and are to keep open a few breathing holes for the human spirit."[13] Crews sees this "combination of pessimism and idealism" as characteristic of Forster's novels. The combination is especially characteristic of *Passage to India,* and accounts for its continuing relevance.

To appreciate Forster's achievement in *Passage to India,* we have to roll up into this last novel not only his earlier writings, but the whole liberal tradition with all the questions it has bequeathed us. What advance does *Passage to India* make over the earlier novels? Although "disenchantingly realistic" in its historical notation, as the Indian scholar G. K. Das points out,[14] *Passage to India* is set into a universe so much larger as to change our perspective toward human affairs and therefore the meaning of the questions raised, though they are ostensibly the same. We have seen how from the start Forster sets his comedies in a natural world beyond good and evil. India showed him, however, that even his natural settings were too domestic and pretty, and led to the false expectation of an answer to moral questions since such questions occurred in a world that at least aesthetically made sense.

India, we are told in *Passage to India,* is not beautiful. It is not romantic, for it is a "muddle" not a "mystery." Mystery promises an answer, and romanticism is concerned with the adumbrations of order to be found in beauty and mystery. India, in its social and historical muddle and in its formless landscape, is developed as a powerful symbol of unknowable reality.

The perspective of *Passage to India* is established in sentences like this: "It matters so little to the majority of living beings what the minority, that calls itself human, desires or decides." Not only are human affairs seen in the perspective of the whole animal world, but all of life is seen as an almost imperceptible instant in the vast and timeless story of inanimate nature.

> The high places of Dravidia have been land since land began, and have seen on the one side the sinking of a continent that joined them to Africa, and on the other the upheaval of the Himalayas from a sea. They are older than anything in the world. No water has ever covered them, and the sun who has watched them for countless aeons may still discern in their outlines forms that were his before our globe was torn from his bosom. If flesh of the sun's flesh is to be touched anywhere, it is here, among the incredible antiquity of these hills. . . . To call them "uncanny" suggests ghosts, and they are older than all spirit.[15]

Here are to be found the Marabar Caves, so featureless, so alike and yet so unlike anything else in the world that they cannot be talked about.

Approaching the Marabar on the picnic arranged by Dr. Aziz, the English hark back nostalgically to Grasmere with its recollections of Wordsworth and his so different view of nature. "'Ah, dearest Grasmere!' Its little lakes and mountains were beloved by them all. Romantic

yet manageable, it sprang from a kindlier planet" (138). Even the cultured skepticism that unites Fielding and Adela Quested seems too romantic and manageable to be adequate to the reality projected in this
novel.

> When they agreed, "I want to go on living a bit," or "I don't believe in
> God," the words were followed by a curious backwash as though the uni-
> verse had displaced itself to fill up a tiny void, or as though they had seen
> their own gestures from an immense height—dwarfs talking, shaking
> hands and assuring each other that they stood on the same footing of in-
> sight. (264)

It is in these vast interstellar spaces that the old Forster themes are
played out—the comedy of manners, the romantic belief in experience
and personal relations, the liberal search for a just political order. The
morally annihilating effect of so much space-time is projected through
the echo in the cave that throws Mrs. Moore into a panic. The echo, she
recalls,

> had managed to murmur, "Pathos, piety, courage—they exist, but are
> identical, and so is filth. Everything exists, nothing has value." If one had
> spoken vileness in that place, or quoted lofty poetry, the comment would
> have been the same—"ouboum." . . . suddenly, at the edge of her mind,
> Religion appeared, poor little talkative Christianity, and she knew that all
> its divine words from "Let there be Light" to "It is finished" only
> amounted to "boum." (149–50)

In the comic misunderstandings that lead, at Fielding's tea party in
chapter 7, to the organizing of the fatal picnic, we see how comedy of
manners turns into something else. The picnic gets organized because
Adela has made the mistake of taking literally Dr. Aziz's invitation to
visit him. Dr. Aziz, thinking with horror of his wretched bungalow, suggests that the party come as his guests, instead, to the Marabar Caves. It
then turns out comically that Aziz has himself never been there; and
when he tries to get Professor Godbole to explain why the caves are
extraordinary, the Brahman can only say what they are not. Listening to
the friendly dialogue, Adela did not realize "that the comparatively
simple mind of the Mohammedan was encountering Ancient Night"
(76). Suddenly, the comic muddle turns symbolic.

Comedy returns with the entrance of Ronny, the priggish official
who is Mrs. Moore's son and the man Adela has come to India to marry.
Ronny's bad manners in disapproving of Adela's company unnerves Aziz,

who responds with an aggressive overfamiliarity that confirms Anglo-Indian prejudices. "What should have upset his [Aziz's] precious nerves? . . . Well, it's nothing I've said," says Ronny with sublime obtuseness. "I never even spoke to him." The party breaks up, the good manners of the salutations contrasting with the bad feeling. But then, Adela's merely polite remark to Godbole, "It's a shame we never heard you sing," brings back the symbolism of Ancient Night. For Godbole begins to sing, a tuneless song about a milkmaiden who repeatedly asks the god Krishna to come, but the god refuses. "But He comes in some other song, I hope?" asks Mrs. Moore, hoping for a rationale. "He neglects to come," is the reply (78–80).

In "Negation in *A Passage to India*," Gillian Beer shows that the novel is built on negative statements. Using the language of the latest theoretical criticism, she says it is "a book *about* gaps, fissures, absences, and exclusions: about bridge parties that don't bridge, about caves broached by man-made entrances, about absent witnesses who do not witness." But negation, in Forster's interpretation of Hinduism, is finally positive. "Absence," writes Beer, "is a condition of God . . . , as Godbole explains, . . . 'absence implies presence, absence is not non-existence.'" "In the *Bhagavad-Gita* it is said that God may be defined only by negatives." [16]

All the values of the novel are in this scene, which points toward the central episode of the cave. We see how Aziz gets involved in the relation of Adela and Ronny; so that Adela, who wanders into a cave thinking of Ronny's lack of attractiveness, has given back to her by the cave her own sense of Aziz's attractiveness when she imagines he has followed her inside to attack her. In the ensuing scandal and trial, Aziz seems again to have confirmed the worst Anglo-Indian prejudices. Most important, we see already in this scene the breakdown of amity through the upsurge of fundamental feelings.

Part 1, "Mosque," to which the scene belongs, is about the attempt to breach the gap between India and England through the friendship of enlightened individuals—notably the friendship of Aziz with Fielding and Mrs. Moore. Part 2, "Caves," is about the breakdown of this Apollonian hope before irrational forces. All the relations of part 1 dissolve. Mrs. Moore, who after her experience in the cave loses interest in people and moral issues, makes no move to help Aziz, but starts back to England, dying on the way. Adela and Ronny break up; she returns to England. Aziz, after the case has been dismissed, becomes suspicious of Fielding's motives in dissuading him from suing Adela; he suspects Fielding of intending to marry her. Fielding returns to England.

Part 3, "Temple," attempts a new synthesis. It takes place in a Hindu principality, where Godbole is now Minister of Education and Aziz, out of disgust with British India, has taken a post as court physician. The section opens with a long, masterful description of the festival celebrating the birth of Krishna. The festival reminds us of Christmas, showing the universality of the myth. But the differences are even more important. "They did not one thing which the non-Hindu would feel dramatically correct; this approaching triumph of India was a muddle (as we call it), a frustration of reason and form" (284–85).

Part 3 has puzzled many critics; some have even judged it a letdown, whereas the book moves most boldly forward in part 3. For to the book's central question, the conflict between reality and justice, Forster is offering the Hindu answer—the mythical view of life. One remembers Yeats's remark that his mythical system helped him "to hold in a single thought reality and justice." [17] Through myth, Forster tells us, "the human spirit had tried by a desperate contortion to ravish the unknown, flinging down science and history in the struggle, yes, beauty herself" (288). Myth, with its muddle, comes as close as expression can to rendering accessible the formlessness of reality. Myth is the human equivalent to the natural reality of the caves.

The festival is curiously efficacious. For there, in an atmosphere "thick with religion and rain" (298), Aziz and Fielding are reconciled and Aziz's bond with Mrs. Moore is renewed through her children, Ralph and Stella (Aziz learns that Fielding has married Stella, not Adela). In the same way, Mrs. Moore becomes a potent force in the novel after she breaks through, in the experience of the cave, to a mentality like Godbole's, to the mythical mentality. Because she refuses to take a stand based on the distinction between good and evil, she does not assail people from outside but takes them over from inside. She becomes part of the echo that haunts Adela's mind, causing her finally to withdraw charges against Aziz; she becomes a goddess to the Hindu mob, who imagine she was killed because she wanted to save an Indian; she retains her hold on Aziz's affection, though she has done less than Fielding and Adela to save him. Because of Mrs. Moore, Fielding gets married; and Aziz's reconciliation with Fielding begins with his sympathy for Ralph Moore, who is like his mother "Oriental" in spirit.

But we do not, as in part 1, make the mistake of supposing that success in one sphere can change matters in another. Although at the end Fielding and Aziz are horseback-riding together, we see that they have moved apart politically. Fielding now finds things to be said for British imperialism; while Aziz is frantically anti-British.

> "We shall get rid of you, yes, we shall drive every blasted Englishman
> into the sea, and then"—he rode against him furiously—"and then," he
> concluded, half kissing him, "you and I shall be friends."
> "Why can't we be friends now?" said the other, holding him affection-
> ately. "It's what I want. It's what you want."
> But the horses didn't want it—they swerved apart; the earth didn't
> want it, sending up rocks through which riders must pass single file . . .
> (322)

Personal settlements do not change political and natural reality.

Yet I cannot agree with Frederick Crews that the conclusion is entirely negative and hopeless. There is at the end the fortifying pleasure of
seeing all things in their due place, of understanding the validity of things
because we understand the limits of their validity. Nor is the vision of
reality entirely nihilistic. Although we cannot read Forster's symbolism
by reference to Hindu theology, for he takes what he wants from Hinduism, the lesson of the caves is not, as Crews thinks, *anti*-Hindu. Mrs.
Moore emerges from the caves as in effect a positive, beneficent force.
The very void projected by the echo is a spiritual presence. It is in just
such *"espaces infinis"* as filled Pascal with awe that the modern sensibility finds spirit. "Where there is nothing, where there is nothing—" says
Yeats, "there is God!" [18]

Stone catches perfectly the mood of part 3 when he speaks of its
"mud-bespattered hilarity" (the festival is full of horseplay; the English
party take a redemptive spill in the river when they row out to view the
festival).

> To say that "God so loved the world that he took monkey's flesh upon
> him" suggests a new mood of spiritual gusto. . . . Redemption is of the
> earth, earthy, and of the water, watery; it is full of filth and disorder, yet
> Forster mixes in it with joy. It almost seems that prophecy and a sense of
> humor may not, after all, be utterly incompatible. (303)

One might go farther and say that the two necessarily go together
when the vision is complete. For one is reminded of Thomas Mann's
observations, in "Freud and the Future," that the mythical view is the
complete, mature view and is characteristically "blithe." But this does
not make *Passage to India* itself a myth; for to offer myth as a solution
is to take a critical stance outside myth—a critical stance appropriate to
a great novel, a novel already established as a twentieth-century English
classic.

The Importance of Trilling's *The Liberal Imagination*

L IONEL Trilling occupied a special and pre-eminent place even among his brilliant generation of American critics. The other big names—Ransom, Tate, Blackmur, Brooks, Warren—were all New Critics; and while Trilling maintained good relations with the New Critics—he was an advisory editor of their main organ the *Kenyon Review*—he remained outside that significant movement of the forties and fifties. Trilling's work was different from but not incongruent with that of the New Critics; they complemented each other.

The New Critics were formalists. They followed Eliot in insisting that the poet was not a thinker, that he used ready-made ideas as grist for his mill, and that a poem's success depended not on its content but on patterns of words and images that constituted its form, a form that might qualify or even contradict its overt content. Trilling instead believed in the over-riding importance of content, and refused to distinguish between the intelligence of the artist and that of other great men. He thought that the artist, particularly the novelist, displayed the most complex form of intelligence because he went farther than other thinkers in combining the general with the particular, thought with feeling, and in bringing forth ideas from a mass of contradictory details. "Literature," he says in his preface to *The Liberal Imagination*, "is the human activity that takes the fullest and most precise account of variousness, possibility, complexity, and difficulty."[1] He begins his great essay "Freud and Literature" by saying: "The Freudian psychology is the only systematic account of the human mind which, in point of subtlety and complexity, of interest and tragic power, deserves to stand beside the chaotic mass of psychological insights which literature has accumulated through the centuries" (34). In contrast to the New Critics who made a sharp distinction between creative and noncreative forms of writing, Trilling saw a continuum along which a great work of psychology or history or criticism would display more intelligence and imagination than a poor poem or novel. I agree with him and so would many other critics of my generation, especially those theorists who refuse to "privilege" so-called creative writing.

Certainly Trilling's best essays are, like the best critical essays of Edmund Wilson and Matthew Arnold, more than mere commentaries on literature; they are literary works in themselves. All three wrote distinguished prose; and a critical work like a poem survives, in Auden's phrase, "in the valley of its saying." The volume of talk about Trilling since his death in 1975 suggests that he has a better chance of surviving than his contemporaries in criticism. Since 1975 there have appeared a twelve-volume uniform edition of his *Works,* four books so far,[2] and many essays on his work, also many controversial recollections of him in a spate of articles and books dealing with the New York intellectuals. Trilling always commanded a wider audience than the New Critics, an audience which included many people whose main interest was not literature. The reason for the wider audience is the same as the reason for the distinction of style—that Trilling always wrote as a man addressing other men about the urgency of human affairs, literature being an important part of what had urgently to be considered. The New Critics instead wrote as literary technicians addressing other literary technicians. Yet their work could hardly be spared, since some of them possessed powers of analysis and taste beyond Trilling's.

Trilling did not share the New Critics' interest in form and in the close analysis of texts. He thought, I suspect, that the microscopic analysis of language could be distorting, could get the proportions wrong. That is because Trilling was mainly interested in prose, both fictional and nonfictional; while the New Critics wrote mainly about short poems. Trilling's fine analysis in *The Liberal Imagination* of Wordsworth's "Immortality Ode"—which finally laid to rest the notion that the "Ode" is Wordsworth's dirge for his departing poetic power—is the exception that proves the rule since he never repeated that kind of close reading, though he proved he could do it very well if he wanted to.

The most important difference between Trilling and the New Critics is that the latter were for a time naively ahistorical in thinking that poems of different historical periods could be read as though they had a simultaneous existence. They refused to admit to themselves how many historical assumptions they were making in reading poems of the past; and though they admired Coleridge's criticism, they did not draw the obvious conclusion that their ideas about poetry were largely romantic, Hegelian and Freudian. Trilling's criticism instead is saturated with the sense of history and politics.

Insofar as the New Critics had any politics, it was the politics of Southern Agrarianism which was so backward-looking as to be inoperative. Like their master, T. S. Eliot, the New Critics, who were mainly Southerners, used as a political model the imagined social harmony that existed before the civil wars in England and America. They could not, however, express such politics in the voting booth. The only choices they could make to express such politics were religious and literary. They could join the Anglican or Roman Catholic churches; they could cultivate a taste for seventeenth-century poetry, excluding the poetry of the revolutionary dissenting Milton. In effect, therefore, the New Critics were apolitical. Trilling instead was a New York Jewish intellectual who during 1932–33 had, in his own words, "a tenuous relation with the Communist Party through some of its so-called fringe activities," then broke with it and became antagonistic.[3] He thus belonged to the mainstream of American political thought and had, in embracing and then breaking with Marxism, passed through the most significant political crisis of his generation. He therefore addressed his criticism to liberals in an attempt to examine liberal assumptions and to modify and define American liberal thought. But his aim, as he makes clear in the preface to *The Liberal Imagination,* was to salvage liberalism, "to recall liberalism to its first essential imagination of variousness and possibility" (xv).

How then did Trilling's criticism complement that of the New Critics? In matters of literary taste, Trilling and the New Critics had the same enemies. They fought against the importation into criticism of a simpleminded democratic egalitarianism that overestimated writers who dealt in either crude or vaguely grandiose terms with poor, inarticulate people, while condemning as conservative and aristocratic writers who portrayed with precision and wit affluent, intelligent, highly articulate people. Thus Henry James became a rallying point for Trilling and the New Critics; and they agreed in their support of such twentieth-century writers as Eliot and Joyce. They apparently disagreed about romantic and Victorian writers whom Trilling, almost alone with Jacques Barzun, supported at a time when nineteenth-century literature lay under a dark cloud of condemnation and neglect. Yet the New Critics, despite their theoretical condemnation of romanticism, did some of their best work on nineteenth-century poems (Brooks on poems of Wordsworth, Keats and Tennyson; Warren on *The Ancient Mariner*); while Trilling was able to argue for nineteenth-century literature in terms acceptable to the New Critics and their disciples of the next generation.

The principal link between Trilling and the New Critics was the conservative drift of their criticism. At a time when, as Trilling put it in his preface to *The Liberal Imagination,* liberalism was "not only the dominant but even the sole intellectual tradition," when there were "no conservative or reactionary ideas in general circulation" (ix), Trilling and the New Critics forced American liberals to test their facile assumptions against a respectable body of conservative thought. The New Critics did this necessary and salutary work from outside the liberal camp; Trilling did it from within. The forties and fifties were, if you had the New Critics in mind, the decades of the New Conservatism; but they were, if you had in mind Trilling and his friends on *Partisan Review* and *Commentary,* the decades of the New Liberalism.

Trilling's most important book, *The Liberal Imagination* (1950), derived power from its firm participation in the political crisis of the forties and thus influenced the literary and political thought of the fifties. His first collection of essays, essays published during the forties, *The Liberal Imagination* took Trilling out of the class of critics who merely explain other men's work and put him in the class of men of letters, men whose work is literature in its own right. The book has literary quality because Trilling uses criticism to work out a personal crisis, his own and that of a relatively few metropolitan intellectuals whom he addresses with the pronoun "we"—a "we" that offended certain readers who did not recognize in themselves the assumptions and experience of this small group. As always in literature, it is the personal story that has most universal significance; for *The Liberal Imagination* has been translated into several languages and has been enormously influential both here and abroad— Trilling rates especially high in Britain.

The crisis behind *The Liberal Imagination* is that of the young man raised in a liberal or even left-wing ambiance who, inevitably in the thirties, flirted with or joined the Communist Party, became disillusioned, and moved in a conservative direction. I myself, raised in the same ambiance a generation later, remarked when I first read *The Liberal Imagination:* "Here is a liberal who suddenly discovered that there is an intelligent case to be made for the conservative side and that discovery brought about his intellectual awakening." I had had a similar awakening during my sophomore year in college, the year of Pearl Harbor, when I took a course on T. S. Eliot and discovered, to my surprise and enlightenment, that there was an intelligent case to be made for the conservative side. Many liberals experienced that kind of intellectual awakening during the war, when we came to distrust the democratic idealist mentality that feared power and had therefore feared to use it to stop Hitler in time to prevent the war. When, after the defeat of Hitler, Stalin loomed as the adversary, we realized that the United States had better use power to stop him in time to prevent World War III. Whereas we had thought Communism was the inevitable goal of the liberal direction, we came to realize that liberals and conservatives within the democracies had more in common with each other than with the radical totalitarian right or left. Those who hung onto the old democratic idealism and during the Cold War years identified the zigzags of Soviet foreign policy with their own "progressive" aims were called Stalinists by their opponents. *The Liberal Imagination* is directed against the unreconstructed liberalism that got reflected as Stalinism.

But *The Liberal Imagination* is a book of literary criticism, and it is in terms of literary taste that the issues are fought out. In the first two essays, on Theodore Dreiser and Sherwood Anderson, respectively, and in the fourth, on Henry James's *The Princess Casamassima,* the issue is the need to change our literary preferences from Dreiser and Anderson to James for reasons that are not purely literary. *The Liberal Imagination* makes literary judgment auspicious, deriving it from a whole range of moral and political choices and from a distinctive view of reality. At the time Trilling wrote, James stood condemned by liberals as what the sixties—the decade that undid so much of the careful critical work of the fifties—was to call "elitist." That is because James believed in the efficacy of mind and will to shape and transform reality and thus raise life to its "richest and noblest expression." But "the chronic American belief," says Trilling in "Reality in America," his essay on Dreiser, is "that there exists an opposition between reality and mind and that one must enlist oneself in the party of reality." And "reality," he continues, "is always material reality, hard, resistant, unformed, impenetrable, and unpleasant" (10, 13).

Feeling when pitted against a reality unmediated by the refinements and discriminations of society, of class and manners, produces a literature that is at once too tough and too tender and always too abstract. "When feeling is understood as an answer, a therapeutic," says Trilling in his essay on Anderson, it makes "the world abstract and empty. Love and passion, when considered as they are by Anderson as a means of attack upon the order of the respectable world, can contrive a world which is actually without love and passion." "Is it strange," Trilling asks,

> that, with all Anderson's expressed affection for them, we ourselves can never love the people he writes about? But of course we do not love people for their essence or their souls, but for . . . certain specific relationships with things and other people, and for a dependable continuity of existence: we love them for being there. (28, 31)

It is social context that gives the characters of fiction solidity. Lack of social context has political significance in that it suggests the author's disrespect for society.

Social context and the tragic sense—these are Trilling's criteria for a proper stance in literature and politics. They fall under the heading of "moral realism"—the ability to sustain moral contradictions and to base a moral and political position on the realities of money, power, class and on the evil, aggressive impulses in man. Moral realism implies an author's ability to see the moral contradictions in his characters and still love them. Once again James is the touchstone. In his brilliant essay on James's political novel *The Princess Casamassima*, Trilling quotes as a contrast to the simple humanitarian optimism of America James's remark: "But I have the imagination of disaster—and see life as ferocious and sinister." Trilling adds: "Nowadays we know that such an imagination is one of the keys to truth" (60). We know this if we have read and been convinced by Trilling; for such a tragic imagination leads to the rejection of the quest for purity and simple solutions in literature and politics.

In "Freud and Literature," Trilling criticizes Freud for speaking of art with contempt as a "substitute gratification" and an "illusion in contrast to reality." Nevertheless Freud's contributions to literature outweigh his errors; for Freud makes poetry indigenous to the constitution of the mind, showing in a scientific age how we still think in images. Freud also brings back the old tragic sense with his theories of the repetition compulsion (the need to repeat painful experiences) and the desire for death. Thus Freud like James counteracts the simple humanitarian optimism of received liberalism. Freud and James make us liberals in a new sense—liberals who work for social change while recognizing that social change cannot abolish human suffering, though suffering may take new forms.

Trilling moved in a conservative direction because, like Arnold, he was correcting the dominant liberal stance. In a predominantly conservative milieu, he would no doubt have moved in the opposite direction. That is why Trilling—though he is a major influence on the neoconservatives of the seventies and eighties—was not himself and would not have become (as Mrs. Trilling confirms) a neoconservative. For Trilling observes Arnold's distinction between the realm of political action and the realm of a free, disinterested play with ideas. He would therefore have seen in neoconservatism an ideologizing of his complex thinking. Trilling's thinking was above all critical, ready to qualify, even turn against itself as Burke—in the great passage Arnold quotes and Trilling admired (quoted above, 86)—turns against himself when, having inveighed against the French Revolution, he welcomes the social change that must inevitably follow intellectual change. In an uncollected essay, "T. S. Eliot and Politics" (1940), Trilling recommends Eliot's *The Idea of a Christian Society* to the "*attention*" of his liberal readers though certainly not to their "allegiance." He quotes Arnold: "it must be apt to study and praise elements that for the fulness of spiritual perfection are wanted, even though they belong to a power which in the practical sphere may be maleficent."[4]

Trilling also follows Arnold in practicing the finest discriminations of judgment. Even his beloved Freud comes in for heavy criticism before he is praised. In the typical plot of his essays, Trilling sets forth a positive position and then says all that can be said against it before returning to the advancement of his original position. The reader waits in suspense to see how he will make his way back to the original position, and is finally dazzled by the number of ideas, books, men, and events that have been covered on the way. In an age of overspecialization, Trilling's essays are clarifying and synthesizing because they bring together so many disparate subjects and contradictory directions in small compass. Only Henry James is spared negative criticism, perhaps because he was already so beleaguered by others.

The issue of James's *The Princess Casamassima*—art versus moral and political action—is the main issue of *The Liberal Imagination*. Hyacinth Robinson, the revolutionary bookbinder who has pledged to commit an assassination for his anarchist cell, undergoes a change of heart when he goes to Venice and receives the full impact of great art. Hyacinth comes to realize that "his view of human misery is matched by a view of the world 'raised to the richest and noblest expression'" that "the monuments of art and learning and taste have been reared upon coercive power," and that in his readiness "to fight for art," he would unlike his revolutionary friends make "some reconciliation with established coercive power." Hyacinth also realizes that the principle of democratic egalitarianism cannot be imported into the realm of art, that you cannot cut a Tintoretto into pieces and distribute it among the people. It is odd that Trilling does not himself cite this last passage, since this is a lesson he and Arnold are always teaching. "Hyacinth recognizes," says Trilling making one of his favorite points, "that civilization has a price, and a high one" (83). In the end Hyacinth, unable to yield his loyalty either to his revolutionary obligation to assassinate or his obligation to art and civilization, commits suicide. For Trilling, however, there is no dilemma. He is always on the side of art, even against his beloved Freud.

When Trilling points out that it is the artistic Hyacinth and not the politician Muniment who has been chosen to perform the assassination, he is suggesting that it is the artist who comes closest to reality, including political reality. He also suggests, in discussing Hyacinth's change of heart in Venice, that you cannot have a proper political position until you have tested your politics against the complexities of art. The question Trilling does not raise is whether so much complexity and fine discrimination block political *action*. Hyacinth's suicide implies that art and politics can be fruitfully combined only in the realm of speculation.

In "Art and Neurosis," Trilling again takes his stand on the side of art. He disputes the popular idea, derived from Freud and spectacularly advanced by Edmund Wilson in *The Wound and the Bow* (1941), that the artist's neurosis is responsible for his art. "Anyone might be injured as Henry James was," Trilling argues, ". . . and yet not have his literary power." "What is surely not neurotic, what indeed suggests nothing but health," is the artist's "power of using his neuroticism. He shapes his fantasies, he gives them"—this is important in Trilling's line of criticism—"social form and reference." Art, he concludes, is "a gift." "Its essence is irreducible" (173–4, 179). Once again Trilling takes issue with people on his own side—in this case Freudians—to move them in a conservative direction. He is displaying what Arnold called disinterestedness, the free play of the mind, the critical spirit.

Trilling's critical spirit is even more relativistic, because more historical, than Arnold's. Arnold is sometimes ahistorical, as in his desire to make Aristotelian criteria apply to nineteenth-century literature. But Trilling's greatest passages, the passages that call forth all the resources of his style, combine literature and history, setting the changing literary phenomenon in its changing historical context. Consider for example this passage from "*The Princess Casamassima*," in which Trilling fits James's novel into the class of nineteenth-century novels about the young man from the provinces who makes good in the city:

> From the late years of the eighteenth century through the early years of the twentieth, the social structure of the West was peculiarly fitted—one might say designed—for changes in fortune that were magical and romantic. The upper-class ethos was strong enough to make it remarkable that a young man should cross the borders, yet weak enough to permit the crossing in exceptional cases. A shiftless boy from Geneva, a starveling and a lackey, becomes the admiration of the French aristocracy and is permitted by Europe to manipulate its assumptions in every department of life: Jean-Jacques Rousseau is the father of all the Young Men from the Provinces, including the one from Corsica. (64)

Or consider this passage from "Manners, Morals, and the Novel," the essay which is to my mind the best in the volume. The passage leads

to Trilling's definition of manners as "a culture's hum and buzz of implication. . . . It is that part of a culture which is made up of half-uttered or
unuttered or unutterable expressions of value."

> As we read the great formulated monuments of the past, we notice that
> we are reading them without the accompaniment of something that al-
> ways goes along with the formulated monuments of the present. The
> voice of multifarious intention and activity is stilled, all the buzz of impli-
> cation which always surrounds us in the present, coming to us from what
> never gets fully stated, coming in the tone of greetings and the tone of
> quarrels, in slang and humor and popular songs, in the way children play,
> in the gesture the waiter makes when he puts down the plate, in the na-
> ture of the very food we prefer.
>   Some of the charm of the past consists of the quiet—the great distract-
> ing buzz of implication has stopped and we are left only with what has
> been fully phrased and precisely stated. And part of the melancholy of the
> past comes from our knowledge that the huge, unrecorded hum of impli-
> cation was once there and left no trace—we feel that because it is evanes-
> cent it is especially human. We feel, too, that the truth of the great pre-
> served monuments of the past does not fully appear without it. From
> letters and diaries, from the remote, unconscious corners of the great
> works themselves, we try to guess what the sound of the multifarious im-
> plication was and what it meant. (205–6)

This is opposite to the kind of criticism represented by Northrop Frye,
who treats literature as an autonomous system working out in ahistorical
cycles its own internal logic; and to deconstructionist criticism which
treats language and literature as referring only to themselves.

"Manners, Morals, and the Novel" exemplifies the moral realism
that Trilling demands in politics and literature, and finds best expressed
in the novel of manners which draws its moral conclusions from a hard-
eyed scrutiny of money and class. "The novel is born," he observes
acutely, "with the appearance of money as a social element"—which is
to say that "the novel is born in response to snobbery," to "pride in status
without pride in function." Even in the most spiritual of novelists, Dostoevsky, every situation, "no matter how spiritual, starts with a point of
social pride and a certain number of rubles. The great novelists knew that
manners indicate the largest intentions of men's souls as well as the small-
est." The novel is a "quest for reality, the field of its research being always
the social world, the material of its analysis being always manners as the
indication of the direction of man's soul." We have come full circle from
Dreiser and Anderson, from the egalitarian American notion that the soul
is too grand to be spoken of in social terms and that manners are trivial.

"It would seem that Americans have a kind of resistance to looking closely at society. They appear to believe that to touch accurately on the matter of class, to take full note of snobbery, is somehow to demean themselves" (209, 211–14).

Having described the novel of manners, Trilling in characteristic fashion reverses direction and announces its conspicuous absence in America. "Henry James was alone in knowing that to scale the moral and aesthetic heights in the novel one had to use the ladder of social observation" (212). Trilling cites James's famous passage on the insufficiency of historical and class differences in America for the display of a variety of manners. The result is that we are increasingly in our fiction substituting abstraction and ideology for manners. "In the degree that we speak in praise of the 'individual' we have contrived that our literature should have no individuals in it" (216); for individuals, we infer, are defined by the local attachments to place, family and class that produce distinctions of manners.

Trilling draws the political conclusion that the tendency to abstraction in our fiction parallels a tendency in our society that has been produced by liberalism, yet threatens liberalism and the freedom of the individual. Of the social directions forward or backward, "we all know," says Trilling in the end, which "we want." With that characteristic "we," Trilling places himself among the advanced liberals who are the targets of his criticism.

> But it is not enough to want it, not even enough to work for it—we must want it and work for it with intelligence. Which means that we must be aware of the dangers which lie in our most generous wishes. Some paradox of our natures leads us, when once we have made our fellow men the objects of our enlightened interest, to go on to make them the objects of our pity, then of our wisdom, ultimately of our coercion. (221)

Trilling is here summarizing the political point of the whole volume. For he is showing how liberals, when they lack moral realism and indulge in self-aggrandizing abstractions, can turn into Stalinists.

Certain entries in Trilling's notebooks (excerpts from which Diana Trilling published in *Partisan Review*, 1984–85) show the intellectual development that led to *The Liberal Imagination*.

June 13 (1936)

Am no longer certain that the future will be a certain—Marxian—way. No longer measure all things by linear Marxian yardstick.

(1945)

At the Harvard Club. . . . Money & snobbery—together—are the basis of the novel & one sees the signs of both here. And with money & snobbery, the "mustache" on which all good novels depend—eccentricities—meaningful ones—of manner: and here one gets them more than in most places.

(1945)

In three–four decades, the liberal progressive has not produced a single writer that it itself respects and reads with interest. A list of the writers of our time shows that liberal-progressivism was a matter of contempt or indifference to every writer of large mind—Proust, Joyce, Lawrence, Eliot, Mann (early), Kafka, Yeats, Gide, Shaw. . . . Thus the enormous breach between the journalism of liberalism—the "serious" writers—and the important works of the imagination of our time.

(1946–47)

The modern feeling that spirit should find its expression *immediately* in the world of necessity and that all that falls short of the full expression of spirit is repulsive. . . . They have, one might say, no irony—for irony, perhaps, is the awareness with acceptance of the breach between spirit and the world of necessity—institutions, etc. . . . They do not understand the *tragic* choice. They want the reign of spirit immediately.[5]

The other major essays, "The Sense of the Past," "Art and Fortune," and "The Meaning of a Literary Idea," argue, like the essays already discussed, the importance of history, social observation and ideas. In "Art and Fortune," Trilling takes up the question whether the novel is dead now that the class differences with which it deals are disappearing, if indeed they ever existed in America. He predicts that ideological groups may in future replace social classes as a source of differing manners. His prediction has not, however, come true; besides, it contradicts the implication of "Manners, Morals, and the Novel" that ideologies are too abstract to produce the distinctions of manners that could delineate genuine individuals. The distinctions of manners in his own novel *The Middle of the Journey* (1947) stem mainly from class differences, though Emily Caldwell's bohemian affectations mark her as belonging ideologically to the hedonist 1920s, whereas the other middle-class characters belong ideologically to the leftist 1930s. Their developing ideological differences are not reflected in differences of manners. In "Art and Fortune" Trilling neglects to wonder whether ethnic and racial differences, which in America are more important than class differences, have not produced an American-style novel of manners.

Trilling's literary and political approval of the novel of manners explains the steadily growing appreciation of Jane Austen which he expressed in subsequent volumes. In his last full year at Columbia he taught a course devoted entirely to Jane Austen; and his last published work is an unfinished essay on her which appeared posthumously in the *Times Literary Supplement* of 5 March 1976. The passage I quoted from the end of "Manners, Morals, and the Novel" recalls a lecture I heard Trilling give at the University of Virginia shortly before his death. He spoke about the will and how he considered himself a nineteenth-century person because he still believed in the efficacy of the will at a time when few other intellectuals did. He got onto the subject of structuralism; and concluded by saying that thirty years ago he had fought against Stalinism and that he would, if he were young, fight structuralism today as another system antithetical to will and individual freedom.[6] The linkage shows the beautiful consistency of Trilling's thought and also what his criticism is all about—that he criticizes liberalism in order to preserve the liberal principle. The linkage also indicates the enduring benefit of Trilling's criticism. For in every generation there appears some deterministic system that seeks to negate the will and individual freedom; and as long as there are people around who look to literature as a refuge against such attack, Trilling's criticism will be there to help them draw from literature the necessary protection.

The New Nature Poetry

WHAT has happened to nature poetry? Ask this question of your up-to-date kind of poetry reader, and you will get a stare of blank amazement. There isn't any, he will mutter, although he will soon concede that there *is* Robert Frost. If he admires Frost, he will probably assure you that Frost is no mere nature poet, the implication being that nature poetry can no longer have serious relevance. He will have behind him the authority of critical opinion, of even Joseph Warren Beach, who, in *The Concept of Nature in Nineteenth-Century English Poetry* (1936), the most thorough study of the subject, says that the very name and concept of nature have virtually disappeared from twentieth-century poetry. Frost himself is not a nature poet, says Beach, since he writes not about nature but about this, that and the other thing in the country.

Beach has in mind the philosophical and protoreligious concept of nature that flourished in the eighteenth century and was already on its way out in the nineteenth. The religion of nature derived from Newton's demonstration that everything from the fall of an apple to the movement of planets is governed by a single law. To people whose Christianity was waning, a nature so orderly seemed to offer new evidence of God's existence and a new source of religious emotion. But the religion of nature was threatened, first, by early-nineteenth-century geology, which found in the rocks evidence of catastrophes that had wiped out whole species, and finally by Darwin's theory that the evolution of species is governed by a mindless force called natural selection. Under these assaults, nature poetry declined. Swinburne tried to be optimistic about post-Darwinian nature, and Hardy was definitely pessimistic about it. But both were being anthropomorphic still, at a time when the exciting new concept, the only one that could inspire conviction, was that of the mindlessness of nature, its nonhuman otherness—a concept *attempting* at least to transcend optimism and pessimism.

Now it is just this sense of nature that a number of twentieth-century American and British poets render superbly; so that far from being extinct, nature poetry has enjoyed a revival. It is better than it has been in a long time. I would like, through a few examples from these poets, to call attention to the existence and relevance of this new nature poetry. But why, if this poetry is so good, should it be necessary to point out its existence? Because, I think, the term *nature poetry* has fallen into such disrepute that no one wants to apply it to poems he likes; and because critics who are looking for the eighteenth-century concept of nature will not find it in poems that are precisely trying to rescue nature, as it is in itself, from the outmoded concept.

Take as an example of the new sense of nature Wallace Stevens's "The Snow Man," which contrasts the inevitably anthropomorphic human apprehension of a winter landscape with the landscape as it might be apprehended by the mindless "mind" of a snow man. "One must have a mind of winter / . . . And have been cold a long time"

                    not to think
Of any misery in the sound of the wind,
In the sound of a few leaves,

Which is the sound of the land
Full of the same wind
That is blowing in the same bare place

For the listener, who listens in the snow,
And, nothing himself, beholds
Nothing that is not there and the nothing that is.[1]

Or take Marianne Moore's poem about the sea, which she calls "A Grave" to suggest, as I understand it, the unmeaning nullity of the sea. She tells us in the opening lines that she will render the sea not from the human point of view, but as it is in itself:

Man looking into the sea,
taking the view from those who have as much right to it as
      you have to it yourself,
it is human nature to stand in the middle of a thing,
but you cannot stand in the middle of this;
the sea has nothing to give but a well excavated grave.

And the poem ends:

> The wrinkles progress among themselves in a phalanx—beautiful under
>   networks of foam,
> and fade breathlessly while the sea rustles in and out of the seaweed;
> the birds swim through the air at top speed, emitting catcalls as
>   heretofore—
> the tortoise-shell scourges about the feet of the cliffs, in motion beneath
>   them;
> and the ocean, under the pulsation of lighthouses and noise of bell-buoys,
> advances as usual, looking as if it were not that ocean in which dropped
>   things are bound to sink—
> in which if they turn and twist, it is neither with volition nor
>   consciousness.[2]

One might almost suppose for a moment that the ocean has volition and consciousness, but this is a delusion.

In the middle of the last century, Ruskin coined the phrase "pathetic fallacy," which defines among other things the modern reaction against the eighteenth- and nineteenth-century style of nature poetry. The pathetic fallacy is the false description that occurs when, under the pressure of strong emotion, the poet projects human feelings into natural objects (Kingsley's "cruel, crawling foam"). Ruskin considers the pathetic fallacy justified as long as the distortion is psychologically valid, appropriate to the observer's emotion. Such poetry, in which the emotions are "strong enough to vanquish, partly, the intellect, and make it believe what they choose," can be good poetry of the second order. But in poetry of the first order, like Dante's, "the intellect also rises, till it is strong enough to assert its rule against, or together with, the utmost efforts of the passions; and the whole man stands in an iron glow, white hot, perhaps, but still strong, and in no wise evaporating." Poetry of the first order retains the "plain and leafy fact" of the primrose, "whatever and how many soever the associations and passions may be that crowd around it."[3] Not only does Ruskin anticipate Eliot's attack on the "dissociation of sensibility" from thought, but he sets forth the program of the best twentieth-century nature poetry, which defines itself precisely by opposing, or seeming to oppose, the pathetic fallacy (one cannot perhaps get round it), and thus extending the range of nineteenth-century projectiveness. For to feel in nature an unalterably alien, even an unfeeling, existence is to carry empathy several steps farther than did the nineteenth-century poets who felt in nature a life different from but compatible with ours.

That is the point of the Stevens and Marianne Moore lines I have quoted. It is the point of Frost's poem "The Need of Being Versed in

Country Things," about a burnt-down farmhouse. The birds fly in and
out of the abandoned barn, "Their murmur more like the sigh we sigh /
From too much dwelling on what has been," but their sympathetic response is illusory. "Yet for them the lilac renewed its leaf," we are told,

> For them there was really nothing sad.
> But though they rejoiced in the nest they kept,
> One had to be versed in country things
> Not to believe the phoebes wept[4]

—not to commit the pathetic fallacy. The strategy of the last two lines is
like the strategy of Marianne Moore's last two lines; only Frost lets us
down so much more gently. In both poems, the inclination to commit the
pathetic fallacy is a sign that the object is loved, as is Stevens's projection
into the snow man. But in Stevens and Marianne Moore, the difference
between man and nature is wider, more irreconcilable, more dangerous
than in Frost. In Frost the life of man weaves so inextricably in and out
of nature that it comes as a surprise to the speaker to discover that they
are not identical. And the difference poses no real threat. The perception
of it is simply salutary. This makes Frost less radically twentieth-century
in his sense of nature than Stevens and Marianne Moore.

The difference in Frost often defines itself against such domestic consid-
erations as that of utility and ownership. In "Going for Water," the
speaker gains an insight into water not as something to be used or owned
but as it is in itself; and in "The Wood-Pile," the speaker realizes that the
precisely cut and measured cord of firewood, unaccountably abandoned
"far from a useful fireplace," has another *use:* "To warm the frozen
swamp as best it could / With the slow smokeless burning of decay."
There is a suggestion of danger in the famous "Stopping by Woods on a
Snowy Evening," where the speaker, who has interrupted his journey
homeward and trespassed on another's property to watch the woods fill
up with snow, pulls himself away reluctantly:

> The woods are lovely, dark and deep,
> But I have promises to keep,
> And miles to go before I sleep,
> And miles to go before I sleep.

The momentary insight into the nonhuman otherness of nature is salutary, but to prolong it is to seek unconsciousness, individual extinction,

before your time. In "Come In," the speaker, who comes at evening to
the edge of a dark wood, hears thrush music inside,

> Almost like a call to come in
> To the dark and lament.
>
> But no, I was out for stars:
> I would not come in.
> I meant not even if asked,
> And I hadn't been.

To consider nature purposively dangerous is also to commit the pathetic
fallacy. Besides, nature in Frost never is so dangerous that his speakers
cannot protect themselves against it. In *The Poetry of Robert Frost*
(1963), Reuben Brower speaks of the dramatic or ironical clash in these
two poems between "the social [or realistic] and the visionary voices,"
a distinction deliberately blurred in Wordsworth. Brower speaks of
"Frost's awareness of the temptingly mysterious view of the natural
world and his reluctant commitment to a sterner, more realistic view."
Frost's "integrity," he argues convincingly, is that "of the ironist," and
this gives his poetry the twentieth-century character "of entertaining an
illusion in the act of breaking it." [5] True, but the vision or illusion is a
kind of "reality" that Frost manages to keep in abeyance.

Frost takes into account nature's destructiveness, but his examples
of it are seldom very frightening. The whispering scythe of "Mowing"
must in performing its useful labor cut down the pale orchises and scare
a bright green snake. Before they "can mount again," the leaves of "In
Hardwood Groves" must "go down into the dark decayed." But the
scythe is whispering in effect that all is well; while toward the natural
cycle, the theme that gave birth to tragedy and religion, Frost takes a
merely commonsense attitude: "However it is in some other world / I
know that this is the way in ours." In "Storm Fear," the speaker, waking
to hear the wind and snow seem to challenge him to come out and fight,
is glad not to accept the challenge and wonders in despair whether he
and his family will have the strength to save themselves in the morning.
But even in this poem, we know that the despair is a passing mood, that
in the morning they will have the strength.

Death itself is adumbrated as a sleep in two perfect poems, "After
Apple-Picking" and "An Old Man's Winter Night." In both poems, the
man falls asleep when his work is almost but not quite finished, his sleep
corresponds to the sleep of nature in winter, and the natural process
takes over his unfinished work. Forgetting what he came to do in a room-
ful of barrels, the old man of the latter poem consigns to the moon his
snow upon the roof, his icicles, and sleeps.

One aged man—one man—can't keep a house,
A farm, a countryside, or if he can,
It's thus he does it of a winter night.

This shows harmony with nature—except that the old man's "clomping" in and out of the room makes an almost supernatural disturbance, scaring the cellar and the outer night; while the lamp he carries keeps him from seeing out-of-doors, it lights only himself with his own thoughts. The noise and the thoughts suggest the slightest disharmony with nature.

In "After Apple-Picking," it is also thoughts of the day's and season's apple picking, of the unpicked apples and of "magnified apples" better than any on the boughs, that will "trouble" the speaker's oncoming sleep, "whatever sleep it is." Is it a night's or winter's dream of the day's or autumn's activity; and is such a troubled slumber natural or supernatural?

The woodchuck could say whether it's like his
Long sleep, as I describe its coming on,
Or just some human sleep.

"Just," of course, from the woodchuck's point of view; for the speculation reminds me at least of Keats's fancy that our next life will be a spiritual repetition of this one "in a finer tone."

It is not to quarrel with these poems—who could be anything but grateful for perfection?—to say that they are idyls. The narratives about people, like "A Servant to Servants," are sometimes tragic. But there is in the nature poems (including Darwinian poems, like "On a Bird Singing in Its Sleep" and "Acceptance") a harmony even in the disharmony; they leave out the agony of dying. Here as elsewhere Frost's acceptances are won without anguish—partly because the danger is not dangerous enough, partly because of Frost's personal strength, which is always at least equal to the danger.

The Darwinian origin of Frost's great poem "Design" would be less obvious were we not alerted by Richard Poirier in *Robert Frost* (1977) to the poem's derivation from the following passage in William James's *Pragmatism*, a book Frost was reading when he composed the poem's first draft. James writes that Darwin demolished the old notion of design in nature by showing

the power of chance-happenings to bring forth "fit" results if only they have time to add themselves together. . . . He also emphasized the number of adaptations which, if designed, would argue an evil rather than a good designer. *Here,* all depends upon the point of view. To the grub under the bark the exquisite fitness of the woodpecker's organism to extract him would certainly argue a diabolical designer.[6]

But such an argument would be illusory. That is where Frost's poem takes off. What, the poem asks, brought together all those whitenesses—the white spider on the white flower, "holding up a moth / Like a white piece of rigid satin cloth." "What," the last lines ask, "but design of darkness to appall?—/ If design govern in a thing so small." What, in other words, but diabolical design (whitenesses make a dark design)—if there is such a thing as design, especially in matters so "unimportant"? The first draft, called "In White," ends: "Design, design! Do I use the word aright?" Frost's revision makes the ending even more enigmatic. Frost's last lines, when he is at his best, always deepen the enigma.

Even here Frost seems unflinching in his comprehension of nature's cruelty. One feels that the comprehension has strengthened him, as compared to Hardy's debilitating despair over the Darwinian spectacle. Hardy's "In a Wood" presents a speaker who, "City-opprest," takes refuge, in the Wordsworthian manner, in a wood, seeking in "Nature a soft release / From men's unrest." He finds, instead, a relentless struggle for existence—"Combatants all! . . . Ivy-spun halters choke / Elms"—and he flees back to the world of men, where "now and then are found / Life-loyalties,"[7] values, however illusory.

Frost's darkest nature poem is "Desert Places," where the snow and the dark wood are unambiguously desolate: "Snow falling and night falling, fast, oh, fast / . . . The woods around it have it—it is theirs."

> The loneliness includes me unawares.
>
> And lonely as it is that loneliness
> Will be more lonely ere it will be less—
> A blanker whiteness of benighted snow
> With no expression, nothing to express.
>
> They cannot scare me with their empty spaces
> Between stars—on stars where no human race is.
> I have it in me so much nearer home
> To scare myself with my own desert places.

But here, where Frost sees nature as a void and takes into account the implications of science, he turns into a kind of consolation that perception of an internal void which would be for another poet the most terrifying perception of all. "Loneliness . . . will be less" together with "scare myself" suggest that the scare is the illusory thing, almost a game (scaring one's self and others) of spooks.

Such resistance comes of sheer biological vitality, a self-preserving common sense, which Reginald Cook calls Frost's *sabiduría*—a Spanish word meaning "the wisdom of a people welling up in any one of its articulate members."[8] It is *sabiduría* that keeps Frost at the edge of the "dark wood," keeps him from following his insights through to their logical implications, from risking the destructiveness of abstract thought. "The world's one globe," he says in "Build Soil,"

> human society
> Another softer globe that slightly flattened
> Rests on the world, and clinging slowly rolls.
> We have our own round shape to keep unbroken.
> The world's size has no more to do with us
> Than has the universe's.

He is able to shrug off those conflicts between man and nature, thought and reality, head and heart, science and religion, which since the romantic period have torn other poets apart.

The result is a poetry that delivers us from the poignancy of the historical moment to place us in contact with a survival-making eternal folk wisdom. We can live by Frost's poetry as we could not by Yeats's or Pound's. Yet his poetry, although it must rank high in our affections, is not likely to be the favorite poetry of the most serious readers, just because Frost does not call into play all our faculties; he does not make poetry of our ideas, which in modern times have mainly to do with our sense of the age. The poets who have since the romantic period made the greatest impact are precisely those poets who have made us most aware of the historical moment, having themselves not merely known about but felt the conflicts of their age.

That is the difference between Wordsworth's nature poetry and Frost's. To talk about nature in Wordsworth's way was at the turn of the nineteenth century to be at the forefront of thought, to take into account the science, philosophy and psychology of the age, its religious skepticism, the French Revolution, the problem of the modern analytic intellect as the destroyer of feeling. If nature was orderly and the self an association of external impressions, then a life in the country would insure you the most favorable impressions. It would afford evidence of God's existence, an alternative or supplement to revolution and political reform for man's improvement, and an object that could still inspire feelings, even supernatural apprehensions. The deliberate return to nature went with the deliberate cultivation of the feelings as the necessary antidote to the conditions of modern life. No nineteenth-century reader could share in one of Wordsworth's epiphanies—one of his revelations through visible nature of "the life of things"—without a very poignant awareness of victory over the age. That is what John Stuart Mill meant when he called Wordsworth "the poet of unpoetical [distinctively modern] natures"; it is what Matthew Arnold meant when he said that in "this iron time" Wordsworth taught us to feel again.[9]

Now Frost's sense of nature as manageable is very like Wordsworth's, as is his method of conveying that sense. For Frost, too, gives us little dramatic actions that culminate in epiphanies. But Frost's are timid epiphanies, for they deliberately stop short of, where they do not explicitly repudiate, philosophical implications; and they do not arise, as they often do in Wordsworth, from an impasse in thought, thought grounded in the age. Frost's moments of awareness are accidents that could happen to anyone in any age. The sign of this is that they do not change the speaker, who simply goes back to his business; whereas Wordsworth's speakers undergo a measure of conversion. That is why his poems can be read in sequence as an evolution from eighteenth-century doubt through romantic transcendentalism to Christian orthodoxy.

In the sheer power to render nature, Frost may well be our best nature poet since Wordsworth. Yet it is because Frost's rendition of nature is so like Wordsworth's that he does not play in our time the role Wordsworth played in his, that he leads us away from rather than to the center of the preoccupations of the time. For Frost cannot embrace the transcendentalism that his way of seeing nature suggests; but neither does he have the so much wilder sense of nature that our latest nature philosophy requires. Our nature philosophy has been made not only by Darwin but by Freud and Frazer. It connects not only man's body but his mind and culture to the primeval ooze; and that sense of nature is difficult to convey in poems about the cultivated countryside of England or New England.

Dylan Thomas manages miraculously to revive, through the usual settings, Wordsworth's pantheistic vision—perhaps because Thomas was from Wales and more primitive than his contemporaries, but also because he was sophisticated and took into account Darwin, Freud, Frazer, along with the modern interest in theology and paradox. He connects our most metaphysical ideas with, in the poem of that title, "The force that through the green fuse drives the flower." And when, in "A Refusal to Mourn," he speaks of dying as entering

> again the round
> Zion of the water bead
> And the synagogue of the ear of corn,

he is at once more biological and more theological than Wordsworth, and therefore modern. But the paradox at the end, "After the first death, there is no other,"[10] is the same as Wordsworth's in "A Slumber Did My Spirit Seal"—that the girl achieves immortality through her very mortality in nature.

It is usually, however, about the tropics or the sea, the primeval sources of life, or about the lower forms of life, that modernist poets are apt to write when they do in our age what Wordsworth did in his—when they convey in their sense of nature their sense of the age. Wallace Stevens is fond of seascapes, Florida settings and tropical birds. Marianne Moore goes farther afield with her tropical lizards, her fish and mollusks, her frigate pelican, her small Sahara field mouse, her mongoose and cobra. Theodore Roethke writes about roots in a root cellar where "Even the dirt kept breathing a small breath" ("Root Cellar"), and the minute "lives on a leaf" include "bacterial creepers" ("The Minimal").[11]

One of the reasons the new nature poetry is not recognizable as such is that it is so often about animals rather than landscapes. The poet is less likely to commit the pathetic fallacy with animals, for they have a consciousness of their own. Then animals do for the landscape what the older kind of nature poet had to do himself—they bring it to life. They are the landscape crystallized into movement and consciousness; so that Marianne Moore begins "The Plumet Basilisk" by distinguishing this Costa Rican lizard from the landscape we take him for at first:

> In blazing driftwood
> the green keeps showing at the same place;
> as, intermittently, the fire-opal shows blue and green.

The new nature poetry deals often with the line between nonliving and living unconsciousness—as its way of evoking "the life of things." For the new nature poetry is really about that concept by which living unconsciousness has come to be understood as a form of consciousness and, paradoxically, the most vital form of it.

Nature poetry, which must always be about the living principle in nature, declined as it became more and more difficult to assert that principle, especially after Darwin seemed to remove mind from even the higher forms of life. The new concept of the unconscious, instead, has extended mind to the very borderline between animate and inanimate nature. For it has connected the substratum of our minds with the minds of the very lowest reaches of animal life, thus reanimating all of nature and making nature poetry possible again. We have already seen how, by emphasizing the deadness of the dynamic and life-giving sea, Marianne Moore makes us feel how nearly alive the sea is, thus enhancing our sense of what it is to be alive.

She starts higher up the scale in

The Fish

wade
through black jade.
   Of the crow-blue mussel-shells, one keeps
   adjusting the ash-heaps;
      opening and shutting itself like

an
injured fan

to move down, through the equivocally living mussel-shells, to barnacles stirred into life, and only thus distinguished from the sea, by "submerged shafts of the / sun," moving

       themselves with spotlight swiftness
  into the crevices—
    in and out, illuminating

the
turquoise sea
  of bodies

to the unalive erosive action of the sea against the cliff. This inorganic process is more dynamic than the jellyfish, crabs and toadstools that "slide" under its impetus "each on the other." Yet the emphasis in the end on its deadness and lack of reproductive capacity reminds us of the mysterious point where inorganic turns into organic process. The "chasm-side" of the cliff is

dead.
Repeated
  evidence has proved that it can live
  on what can not revive
    its youth. The sea grows old in it.

D. H. Lawrence's rank as a poet is still unsettled. But Lawrence had the genius to see the way things were tending and, in his animal poems,

set the style for the new nature poetry. In "Fish," he is interested in the
strangeness of a life that not only inhabits an element different from ours,
but that is one with this element and therefore without knowledge and
without self, an emblem of perfect unconsciousness.

> As the waters roll
> Roll you.
> The waters wash,
> You wash in oneness
> And never emerge.
>
> Never know,
> Never grasp.
>
> Your life a sluice of sensation along your sides,
> . . . .
> Even snakes lie together.
>
> But oh, fish, that rock in water,
> You lie only with the waters;
> One touch.

Near the end, he evokes the horror and beauty of this utterly alien life:

> I have waited with a long rod
> And suddenly pulled a gold-and-greenish, lucent fish from below,
> And had him fly like a halo round my head,
> Lunging in the air on the line.
>
> Unhooked his gorping, water-honey mouth,
> And seen his horror-tilted eye,
> His red-gold, water-precious, mirror-flat bright eye;
> And felt him beat in my hand, with his mucous, leaping life-throb,

then, perhaps too didactically, makes explicit the moral of many recent
animal poems:

> And my heart accused itself
> Thinking: *I am not the measure of creation.*
> *This is beyond me, this fish.*
> *His God stands outside my God.*

This is the moral of Lawrence's best known animal poem, "Snake," in
which the golden-brown snake, who contains within himself the tropical
heat and volcanic energy of a Sicilian July, seems, as he retreats into his

black hole, "a king in exile," the alien god of our submerged unconscious and libidinal life.[12]

In his stunning poem, "Pike," Ted Hughes makes even more apparent than Lawrence his resistance to the pathetic fallacy; for Hughes intensifies both the nonhumanness and the gorgeousness of his fish.

> Pike, three inches long, perfect
> Pike in all parts, green tigering the gold.
> Killers from the egg: the malevolent aged grin.
> They dance on the surface among the flies.
>
> Or move, stunned by their own grandeur,
> Over a bed of emerald, silhouette
> Of submarine delicacy and horror.
> A hundred feet long in their world.
>
> In ponds, under the heat-struck lily pads—
> Gloom of their stillness:
> Logged on last year's black leaves, watching upwards.
> Or hung in an amber cavern of weeds
>
> The jaws' hooked clamp and fangs
> Not to be changed at this date;
> A life subdued to its instrument;
> The gills kneading quietly, and the pectorals.
>
> Three we kept behind glass,
> . . . .
> Suddenly there were two. Finally one.
>
> With a sag belly and the grin it was born with.

In the end, Hughes takes just the leap Frost does not take in "Design." For the pike are turned into an idea of menace—of a slow, waiting time outside our sense of time, of a terror outside the reality framed by our petty human contrivances. The scene shifts to an ancient pond of legendary depth that held "Pike too immense to stir, so immense and old," the poet

>   silently cast and fished
> With the hair frozen on my head
> For what might move, for what eye might move.
> The still splashes on the dark pond,
>
> Owls hushing the floating woods
> Frail on my ear against the dream
> Darkness beneath night's darkness had freed,
> That rose slowly towards me, watching.

In Hughes's "Ghost Crabs," this same terror, represented by giant crabs that "emerge / An invisible disgorging of the sea's cold," is shut out by our toys, "the world of possessions"; but the crabs are called "God's only toys." [13] Lawrence and Hughes exaggerate to the point where nature is seen as supernatural because we cannot keep it in abeyance—the exaggeration resembles Frost's trick of locating nature just a step beyond utility and our vision into the "dark wood."

Theodore Roethke, instead, longs for the preconscious existence of nature. In "Snake," he would "be that thing" the snake is, "The pure, sensuous form." But in the late "Meditation at Oyster River," he would regress even farther, to formlessness. He longs to dissolve the configuration of self, and be one with the free-running river tides that flow into the bay.

> Over the low, barnacled, elephant-colored rocks,
> Come the first tide-ripples, moving, almost without sound, toward me,
> Running along the narrow furrows of the shore, the rows of dead clam
>   shells;
> Then a runnel behind me, creeping closer,
> Alive with tiny striped fish, and young crabs climbing in and out of the
>   water.

The poet, using Lawrence's verb "rock," wants for himself the prelapsarian existence of Lawrence's fish:

> Now, in this waning of light,
> I rock with the motion of morning;
> In the cradle of all that is,
> I'm lulled into half sleep
> By the lapping of water,
> Cries of the sandpiper.
> Water's my will, and my way,
> And the spirit runs, intermittently,
> In and out of the small waves;

water itself, in the final image of dissolution and salvation, is dissolved into light:

> In the first of the moon,
> All's a scattering,
> A shining.

Lawrence concludes "Fish" by saying:

In the beginning
Jesus was called The Fish . . .
And in the end.

Lawrence thus establishes the dialectic by which, in dealing with the evolution out of, and the regression back to, formlessness, the new nature
poetry takes us over from water to animals to gods.

Light is the vivifying principle in Wallace Stevens's "Tattoo," where the
light, crawling "like a spider" over the landscape and under your eyelids,
brings both your eyes and the landscape to life:

> There are filaments of your eyes
> On the surface of the water
> And in the edges of the snow.

Along with the sense of nature's otherness goes the sense that it cannot
be known in itself, that we can know only our own perception of it—
not only our individual perception but also (and this is where the new
nature poetry goes beyond that of the nineteenth century and of Frost
with his "dark wood") the perception our civilization, our style of art,
gives us. Thus Stevens gives "Thirteen Ways of Looking at a Blackbird,"
and tells us how the round jar he placed on a hill in Tennessee gave a
shape to nature, "made the slovenly wilderness / Surround that hill." The
jar made nature *see*able.

There is a dispute as to whether Stevens in "Anecdote of the Jar" is
praising art or nature. I would say both, on the evidence of his other
poems. Art is not the same as nature, but our perception of even natural
beauty depends on an aesthetic—an aesthetic which, like consciousness
itself, is a crystallization of the landscape but with an even more inexplicable difference. The rendition of nature through an art style calls
attention to the fact that nature can be known only through an aesthetic.
In "The Idea of Order at Key West," we hear the sea because we hear the
girl's song:

> It may be that in all her phrases stirred
> The grinding water and the gasping wind;
> But it was she and not the sea we heard.

> For she was the maker of the song she sang.

Thus the rendition of nature through an art style enhances our sense of
nature's otherness and unknowability. It is no accident that Stevens and

Marianne Moore are concerned not only with nature but also with styles of art and civilization—that they are known even for a certain preciosity. For there seems to be a direct proportion between our sense of nature as wild and nonhuman, and our appreciation of just the artificial surface, the distinctively aesthetic quality of art and civilization. It is because, in words of Valéry that express Stevens's thought, "The real, in its pure state, stops the heart . . .[that] the universe cannot for one instant endure to be only what it is," that we need, according to Stevens, a saving fiction.[14]

Marianne Moore, who can render the sea naturalistically, gives us in "The Steeple-Jack" the same sense of its dynamics when she renders it in the static style of Dürer: "water etched / with waves as formal as the scales / on a fish." To render the jerboa, or Sahara field mouse, she starts "The Jerboa" with an almost suffocating evocation of the highly artificial and excessively opulent beauty of the oppressive civilization of the Pharaohs; and she does this largely by cataloguing the multitude (the section is called "Too Much") of African animals they tamed, carved, worshiped: took as models for and forced into their art style. After tightening the spring for fifteen such stanzas, she releases it in two stanzas where she evokes by contrast the happiness, beauty, freedom of the jerboa, who "lives without water," in the midst of nothingness, and without reference to men: "but one would not be he / who has nothing but plenty."

In "The Plumet Basilisk," she no sooner brings the lizard to life from the "blazing driftwood" we take him for at first, than she says: "In Costa Rica the true Chinese lizard face / is found, of the amphibious falling dragon, the living fire- / work"—reminding us that the lizard was the dragon of art and mythology, even a god. Alarmed, he "dives to the stream-bed, hiding as the chieftain with gold / body hid in / Guatavita Lake"—a reference, the notes tell us, to the yearly ceremony in which the king, "powdered with gold-dust as symbolic of the sun," plunged into the lake. Recalling Frazer, we may infer that the king renewed his vitality or godhead by returning to the source of it, just as the lizard at this moment returns to his underwater "basilica." "The plumet portrays," we are told later on, "mythology's wish / to be interchangeably man and fish." And the basilisk is rendered in its relation to other lizards—and to the whole of evolution, from water, through the Reptilian Age (the birds toddle in and out among sea lizards' tails "laid criss-cross, alligator-style"), to the dragons carved over the door of the bourse in Copenhagen. The basilisk's retreat in the end from the observer is a return in consciousness to the legendary past of treasures guarded by dragons ("Thinking himself hid among the yet unfound jade axe- / heads") and a physical return to the water ("his basilisk cocoon"). The regression is the climactic manifestation of his vitality:

> he is alive there
>   in his basilisk cocoon beneath
> the one of living green; his quicksilver ferocity
>   quenched in the rustle of his fall into the sheath
> which is the shattering sudden splash that marks his
>   temporary loss.

There is a similar regression in Richard Wilbur's "The Death of a Toad," where the toad who has been caught in a power mower pours his "rare original heartsblood" back into the earth, lying "still as if he would return to stone," dying

> Toward misted and ebullient seas
> And cooling shores, toward lost Amphibia's emperies.[15]

We not only retrace the course of evolution back to inanimate nature, but we are reminded of antique statues ("the gutters of the banked and staring eyes," "the wide and antique eyes") and the death of gods. In Richard Eberhart's "The Groundhog," the speaker sees in the decaying corpse of a groundhog dead "In June, amid the golden fields," first the ferocity of the natural process, of the sun's "immense energy," and finally the pathos of the whole history of civilization which the speaker has recapitulated in his successive responses to the fact of death:

> I stood there in the whirling summer,
> My hand capped a withered heart,
> And thought of China and of Greece,
> Of Alexander in his tent;
> Of Montaigne in his tower,
> Of Saint Theresa in her wild lament.[16]

The associations in these two poems are a bit literary, a bit forced, but they illustrate all the better the climate of ideas behind the new nature poetry. They also show how animals operate in that poetry to connect inanimate nature with civilization through our current ideas about the vitality of the unconscious life and the origins of culture in the worship of animals, the contemplation of the vegetation cycle, and the killing of gods to renew the fertility of the soil.

The same psychological and anthropological knowledge can be applied to landscape. In a remarkable poem called "The Mountain," W. S. Merwin evokes the divinity of a mountain through the dispassionate accents of a modern, scientifically minded speaker who inhabits the lower slopes. "Only on the rarest occasions," the poem begins, "can one trace the rising / Slopes high enough to call them contours."

> Then
> It is with almost a shock that one recognizes
> What supposedly one had known always:
> That it is, in fact, a mountain; not merely
> This restrictive sense of nothing level, of never
> Being able to go anywhere
> But up or down, until it seems probable
> Sometimes that the slope, to be so elusive
> And yet so inescapable, must be nothing
> But ourselves: that we have grown with one
> Foot shorter than the other, and would deform
> The levellest habitat to our misshapen
> Condition, as is said of certain hill creatures.

No one has seen the summit, although the attempt was at one time "a kind of holy maelstrom, Mecca / For fanatics and madmen," and there have been recent expeditions with "expensive equipment."

> Very few
> Who set out at all seriously have
> Come back. At a relatively slight distance
> Above us, apparently the whole aspect and condition
> Of the mountain changes completely; there is ceaseless wind
> With a noise like thunder and the beating of wings.

Of those who came back, some were deaf, some blind, all "dazzled, as by a great light," those who perhaps went farthest lost the use of language and the sense of time—all of which seems "from earliest / Antiquity to have excited speculation."

> One legend has it that a remote king-priest figure
> Once gained the summit, spent some—to him non-sequent
> But to them significant—time there, and returned
> "Shining," bearing ciphers of the arcane (which,
> Translated into the common parlance, proved
> To be a list of tribal taboos) like clastic
> Specimens, and behaved with a glacial violence

Later construed as wisdom. This, though
Charming, does not, in the light of current endeavour,
Seem possible, even though so long ago. Yet
To corroborate this story, in the torrent
Gold has been found which even at this
Late date appears to have been powdered by hand,
And (further to confuse inquiry) several
Pediments besides, each with four sockets shaped
As though to receive the hoof of a giant statue
Of some two-toed ungulate. Legend being
What it is, there are those who still insist
He will come down again some day from the mountain.

As there are those

—and here the tension between the accumulating conviction and the skeptical language is resolved through a transformation of the discussion into psychological terms (myth is what happens whenever mind meets nature)—

                            who say it will fall on us. It
Will fall. And those who say it has already
Fallen. It has already fallen. Have we not
Seen it fall in shadow, evening after evening,
Across everything we can touch; do we not build
Our houses out of the great hard monoliths
That have crashed down from far above us? Shadows
Are not without substance, remind and predict;
And we know we live between greater commotions
Than any we can describe. But, most important:
Since this, though we know so little of it, is
All we know, is it not whatever it makes us
Believe of it—even the old woman
Who laughs, pointing, and says that the clouds across
Its face are wings of seraphim? Even the young
Man who, standing on it, declares it is not
There at all. He stands with one leg habitually
Bent, to keep from falling, as though he had grown
That way, as is said of certain hill creatures.[17]

The mountain is divine in the same sense as Marianne Moore's cobra in "Snakes, Mongooses." Whatever we think the mountain is, its irreducible otherness remains; and the cobra's perfect singleness of line, as it stands up from the snake-charmer's basket, annihilates distinctions, showing "that when intelligence in its pure form / has embarked on a

train of thought which is unproductive, / it will come back"—back to
the otherness of reality. These intuitions of reality are like Frost's "dark
wood," except that they involve, too, a distinct sense of the past, and
therefore of the present. Since they stimulate us to apply all we know of
current ideas, they bring out into the open what must be, I suppose, the
ultimate subject of nature poetry—the divinity in nature.

The history of nature poetry is in a sense recapitulated in Wallace
Stevens's lovely meditation "Sunday Morning." The consistent water imagery suggests that the modern cosmopolitan lady ought, to make the
poem properly meditative-descriptive, to be looking out over water as
she lounges late of a sunny Sunday morning, aware that she is not after
all in church. Certain tropical accouterments, "coffee and oranges,"

> And the green freedom of a cockatoo
> Upon a rug mingle to dissipate
> The holy hush of ancient sacrifice

but remind her, too, of sacrifices more ancient still than Christ's:

> The pungent oranges and bright, green wings
> Seem things in some procession of the dead,
> Winding across wide water, without sound.

"Why should she give her bounty to the dead?" she asks. "Divinity must
live within herself: / Passions of rain, or moods in falling snow." Thus
she comes past the rejection of Christianity to the transcendentalism of
romantic nature poetry with its moments of private insight. She remembers the alienation of religion from nature with sky-gods like Jove, and
how Christianity brought God back to earth again—although it bequeathed the uneasy question whether earth was to be brought to heaven
or heaven to earth. Nature is her paradise; no, better than paradise. For
death makes the difference, "is the mother of beauty," gives the outlet to
imagination, the savor to life.

Awareness of death leads to a vision of *communal* nature worship,
with this difference from ancient rites—that in the new religion of earth
the sun would be worshiped not as a god, but for itself:

> Supple and turbulent, a ring of men
> Shall chant in orgy on a summer morn
> Their boisterous devotion to the sun,
> Not as a god, but as a god might be,
> Naked among them, like a savage source.

It is when we see nature as a source of both life and death that appreciation turns into worship. The natural cycle is the source of all religions:

> They shall know well the heavenly fellowship
> Of men that perish and of summer morn.
> And whence they came and whither they shall go
> The dew upon their feet shall manifest.

In the final section, Stevens not only completes his poem by returning us to the water and answering the question he raised about Christianity, he also completes his history of nature poetry.

> She hears, upon that water without sound,
> A voice that cries, "The tomb in Palestine
> Is not the porch of spirits lingering.
> It is the grave of Jesus, where he lay."

In terms of its own supernatural claims, Christianity is dead; but after all that has been said in the poem we must understand, too, that as the worship of the dead god, of the natural cycle, Christianity is part of an inherent religion that always has lived and always will live. The poem ends with one of the very best passages of modern American nature poetry, a passage which, deriving its poignancy from the strength of its resistance to the pathetic fallacy, expresses perfectly the sense in which, with what we now know about the unconscious life of man and nature, we can feel that the world both is and is not God-abandoned.

> We live in an old chaos of the sun,
> Or old dependency of day and night,
> Or island solitude, unsponsored, free,
> Of that wide water, inescapable.
> Deer walk upon our mountains, and the quail
> Whistle about us their spontaneous cries;
> Sweet berries ripen in the wilderness;
> And, in the isolation of the sky,
> At evening, casual flocks of pigeons make
> Ambiguous undulations as they sink,
> Downward to darkness, on extended wings.

Those "ambiguous undulations" are the point where nature poetry comes full circle from the rejection of the old religion of nature to the discovery of an inevitably re-emerging religion of nature at the source of things.

Mailer's New Style

NORMAN Mailer is a most irritating author to write about. His public image is entirely too powerful and unattractive; and his ideas, as stated in his essays, are often nonsensical (his mystique of the apocalyptic orgasm or of the spiritual significance of cancer) and sometimes intolerable (his glorification of Hip criminality). The result is that people have not taken his recent novels seriously enough. Since his image is by now better known than his novels, people like the Sunday *Times* reviewer of *Why Are We in Vietnam?* are apt to write him off as belonging more to the history of publicity than to the history of literature. And the success of his political writings since the novels—*Miami and the Siege of Chicago* and *Armies of the Night* (1968)—has only made people say he is better as journalist than novelist.[1]

Yet if we forget the public image and read through his first five novels (I will treat elsewhere his last three novels, *The Executioner's Song* [1979], *Ancient Evenings* [1983] and *Tough Guys Don't Dance* [1984]), we find that Mailer's ideas are fruitful for his fiction and that he has as much artistic integrity as anyone writing today. First of all he has refused to capitalize on the spectacular success of his first novel, *The Naked and the Dead* (1948). Having at twenty-five triumphed in the received realistic style of American social-consciousness fiction, Mailer has been working ever since at finding a new style. It was not until 1965, the year *An American Dream* came out in book form, and 1967, the year of *Why Are We in Vietnam?* that he finally broke through to a style new enough to offend many of the reviewers.

"The realistic literature," said Mailer in a paper of 1965, "had never caught up with the rate of change in American life, indeed it had fallen further and further behind, and the novel gave up any desire to be a creation equal to the phenomenon of the country itself; it settled for being a metaphor." Novelists were "no longer writing about the beast but, as in the case of Hemingway (if we are to take the best of this), about the paw of the beast, or in Faulkner about the dreams of the beast."[2]

Mailer's whole attempt in his second novel, *Barbary Shore* (1951), is to turn fiction into metaphor, indeed into an allegory of the beast's political dreams. To achieve allegory, Mailer abandons scope. Whereas *The Naked and the Dead* portrays the Pacific campaign of World War II and the American society behind it, *Barbary Shore* takes place in a Brooklyn rooming house and involves only five adults and a child. The concentration produces an atmosphere of intensity that helps us accept the characters as personifications of political alternatives in the McCarthy era. The liberal hero, Lovett, whose war-induced amnesia makes him forget his old socialist sympathies, comes out in the end with a Trotskyite position; though Lovett seems to see, in the Trotskyite McLeod's failure with his wife, the failure of Communism to take sex seriously, to make an erotic appeal to the masses.

The Trotskyism didn't last long, as we see by Mailer's next novel *The Deer Park* (1955), where the morally sensitive hero is failed by Eitel, his model of political and artistic integrity, as the hero of *Barbary Shore* is not failed by his Communist model, McLeod. The hero of *The Deer Park* drifts in the end into that state of thorough disaffection which Mailer, in his famous essay of the period, "The White Negro," calls Hip. But the main subject of *Barbary Shore* accounts for the subsequent novels; for the subject—as Norman Podhoretz suggests in his introduction to the paperback edition—is the effect on modern life of the failure of the Russian Revolution to turn into a world revolution. Because the human spirit failed to take the necessary next stop in its evolution, it is dying of stagnation.[3] Mailer's vision of general disease and madness becomes ever more comprehensive and strident with each novel.

Although *Barbary Shore* is Mailer's faultiest novel, it is the seedbed of his new style. *The Deer Park,* instead, which is almost flawless, is Mailer's lightest novel. In *The Deer Park,* Mailer returns to realism, but uses the restriction of scope learned in *Barbary Shore* to give to his satirical depiction of the small Hollywood world a haunting suggestiveness that makes it vaguely applicable to all America. There are, however, two things in *The Deer Park* that point toward Mailer's remarkable breakthrough ten years later. One is the development, toward the end, of the pimp Marion Faye, with his illusionless honesty and courage, as a Hip answer to the self-deceptions of the liberal artist Eitel. "Mailer," writes Diana Trilling,

has a predilection for last-minute heroes; just as Croft's sudden triumph
at the end of *The Naked and the Dead* suggests the changes in feeling
that Mailer was experiencing in the course of composing his first novel,
so the replacement of Eitel by Faye as the most significant figure in *The
Deer Park* indicates the dramatic evolution of Mailer's thought while
writing his Hollywood novel. In Marion Faye we discover the distinction
Mailer makes between a sexuality which, like that of the movie colony,
appears to be free but is really an enslavement, and the sexuality of Hips-
terism which expresses a new, radical principle of selfhood. The difference is not one of behavior but of consciousness. Whereas all the other
characters in the novel, whether in their political decisions or their sexual
conduct, follow the worn paths of consciousness laid out for them by an
exhausted civilization, Mailer's incipient Hipster hero has settled the new
direction the world must take to save itself: it is the direction of purpose-
ful, as opposed to purposeless, death.[4]

Another breakthrough, as the above quotation suggests, is the central
importance given to sexuality. For the next two novels are organized by
a sexual vision so pervasive that characterization is determined by sexual
quality and the very fabric of external reality is sexually charged.

The most obvious sign of breakthrough is the new metaphorical prose
that begins in *American Dream,* prose that calls attention to itself as it
did not in the earlier novels. Here, for example, is the way Rojack, the
hero of *American Dream,* describes a German soldier he shot in the war,
a soldier whose eyes he cannot forget.

> He had eyes I was to see once later on an autopsy table in a small town in
> Missouri, eyes belonging to a redneck farmer from a deep road in the
> Ozarks, eyes of blue, so perfectly blue and mad they go all the way in
> deep into celestial vaults of sky, eyes which go back all the way to God is
> the way I think I heard it said once in the South, and I faltered before
> that stare, clear as ice in the moonlight. . . . The light was going out in his
> eye. It started to collect, to coagulate into the thick jelly which forms on
> the pupil of a just dead dog, and he died then, and fell over.[5]

Here is how Rojack's wife, the beautiful society girl Deborah Kelly,
looks to him in the morgue after he strangled her, then pushed her out
the window to make it look like suicide. He caught "a clear view of one
green eye staring open, hard as a marble, dead as the dead eye of a fish."
Observing the nightclub singer Cherry, with whom he falls in love a few
hours after the murder, he sees in her substantial bottom the loving
small-town Southern girl concealed beneath the sophisticated face. Her
face he might possess, but not "her bee-hind . . . no one ever had . . . so
all the difficulty had gone down to her feet, yes the five painted toes

talked of how bad this girl could be." "A sickness came off her, something broken and dead from the liver, stale, used-up, it drifted in a pestilence of mood toward my table, sickened me as it settled in." He retires
to the men's room where for the second time that night he vomits, "and
thought that if the murderer were now loose in me, well, so too was a
saint of sorts, a minor saint no doubt, but free at last to absorb the ills
of others and regurgitate them" (76, 100–101).

Such somatic characterization, reminiscent of Lawrence, makes
plausible the events of this American dream, in which the submerged or
potential becomes manifest. In Bellow's *Herzog,* which came out a year
earlier, the hero wants to kill his wife, but does not because he cannot
reconcile with ordinary reality his momentary insights into her supernatural evil. Mailer's hero can do what Bellow's cannot, because his insight
into Deborah's evil transforms reality for him. "I had learned to speak,"
he says, "in a world which believed in the *New York Times,*" but he has
lost his "faith in all of that," because he has learned from Deborah that
the forces that matter are magical. "It was horror this edge of madness
to lie beside Deborah in a marriage bed and wonder who was responsible
for the cloud of foul intent which lifted on the mingling of our breath.
Yes, I had come to believe in spirits and demons" (36–37).

I would call the style of *American Dream* "hallucinated realism,"
because I want to differentiate it from the ordinary realism that contrasts
subjective feeling with the neutrality of the objective world, and because
I want at the same time to call attention to its realism. For nocturnal
New York is sketched in superbly, as are the various kinds of New York
manners. Here, for example, is a bit of dialogue between Steve Rojack
and the producer of his TV show, who has telephoned, after the news of
Deborah's suicide, to persuade Steve to resign.

> "Steve, *anxiety* is loose here [in the studio] today. It hasn't been so
> bad since Kennedy stood up to Khrushchev with the missiles. Poor Debo-
> rah, I only met her once, but she's a great woman."
> "Yes. *Was.*"
> "Steve, you must be in a state of shock."
> "I'm a little rocky, kid."
> "I'll bet. I'll bet. These dependencies we feel on women. When they
> go, it's like losing your mother."
> If Deborah were not dead, but had merely run off to Europe with
> another man, Arthur would have said, "It's like losing mother's tit."
> (137–38)

The surface is rendered in order that it may be psychologically pene-
trated, imbued with magic. When the psychological penetration is deep-

est, the hallucinated realism turns, for those moments only, into allegorical romance.

Through a style that talks with the same words about conscious and unconscious levels of existence, Mailer solves his old problem going back to *The Naked and the Dead*, of the conflict between morality and power. Rojack is the first of Mailer's morally sensitive heroes who can compete with people of power like Deborah and her multimillionaire father. But it is only in the course of the novel that Rojack acquires the strength to compete, because he draws out of himself his own bestiality and thus discovers the source of their power and his. The story tells how Rojack finds his courage and therefore his freedom and humanity.

Rojack, who is professor of something called existential psychology, believes that "the root of neurosis is cowardice rather than brave old Oedipus" (251). By Rojack's criteria, Bellow's Herzog is and remains a coward because he is too nice; he never *does* the unspeakable thing that would teach him what he is capable of. Mailer's story takes place way out beyond the moral experience of the Herzogs, the decent, reasonable people who read the *New York Times*.

That's why it takes place at the top, among *big* people, who are rich, famous, extravagant, who are the equivalent of the kings and princesses of fairy tale. "God and the Devil are very attentive to the people at the summit. I don't know if they stir much in the average man's daily stew, no great sport for spooks, I would suppose, in a ranch house, but do you expect God or the Devil left Lenin and Hitler or Churchill alone? . . . There's nothing but magic at the top" (246). In *Four Postwar American Novelists* (1977), Frank D. McConnell reminds us that it was the 1963 assassination of President Kennedy that made Mailer write *An American Dream* (1965) after nine years away from fiction: Kennedy's name appears in the novel's first sentence. Who knows what thoughts of magic and evil at the top, as well as of heroism, were occasioned by that disaster?

High on a balcony over Sutton Place, Rojack is at the outset tempted to jump by the Lady Moon, who speaks to him with Deborah's voice, urging him to die. Not yet, he thinks, but he knows this was the moment his death began, "this was the hour when the cells took their leap" (13). The middle-aged Rojack is at Dante's "mezzo del cammin," and starts his descent to hell.

He starts downward by strangling Deborah in the upstairs bedroom of her duplex, which is suspended over the East River and is hung with a fabric of tropical flowers that provides the sense of New York chic and the jungle setting appropriate to their moment of truth. Sexually exhilarated by the murder, Rojack descends a flight to vent his hate in intercourse, involving buggery, with Deborah's German maid. This graphically described bang is a tour de force; for it is so thoroughly absorbed in intellectual and moral contemplation that it is transformed—as Coleridge said Shakespeare transformed *Venus and Adonis*—into something other than pornography. Rojack's realization through the intercourse that the maid was a Nazi suggests a significance different from that involved in the same mode of intercourse with the Jewish girl, Denise, in the story "The Time of Her Time" (*Advertisements for Myself,* 1959). I do not find here the homosexual implications the act may have in the story if Denise's accusation is justified. The point here is purely moral, a descent into hell. Denise's orgasm is life-enhancing. But the maid's ferocious orgasm leads Rojack to see first an image of death and then the redemptive imagery of Las Vegas and moon with which the novel closes.

It is only after this further descent into evil that Rojack can reascend to Deborah's room, throw her dead body down to the East River Drive and fabricate the story of suicide. The circle of evil widens at the police station, where we see the criminal mentality of the detectives and learn that one of the cars stopped by Deborah's body contained a Mafia big shot, who has been hauled in with his mistress, Cherry. The Mafia man is released; so finally is Rojack, because of a signal from on high. When the next midnight Rojack ascends the Waldorf Towers to see Deborah's father, he learns who has made the signal. For Kelly is, as he says of himself, "a spider. Have strings in everywhere from the Muslims to the *New York Times*" (237). He has strings in on the CIA and the Mafia, too. The Mafia man is there; so is the German maid, who turns out to be Kelly's mistress, set to spy on Deborah who had herself indulged in some unspecified political spying. Kelly once had Cherry as mistress, and has even had—this is the climactic revelation of evil—an incestuous passion for Deborah. Kelly has called off the police investigation into the murder, perhaps because he fears exposure, more likely because he has his own plans for Rojack.

As in *Barbary Shore,* the claustrophobic closed circle so intensifies the moral atmosphere as to make allegory believable. The main action is compressed into a nightmarish thirty-two hours; and we come to feel, as all threads wind back to Kelly, that he really is the Devil and that the Devil dwells on top, on top of the power structure. It is God who dwells, if anywhere, on the bottom. That is why when Rojack is on his way to the Waldorf Towers, an inner voice tells him to go to Harlem instead. Although we are not allowed to forget Harlem, Mailer fails to make anything morally substantial of it or of the good girl, Cherry, who comes off as a sentimentalized abstraction.

The Devil comes alive in Kelly because Kelly is magnificently attractive, with his intelligence and forcefulness, and because Rojack smells beneath Kelly's cologned surface something else, some whiff of the "icy rot and iodine in a piece of marine nerve left to bleach on the sand" (217). Because Rojack's apprehension of evil is registered as sensation, we understand how he can *know,* without knowing why, that he must to escape evil rush out to the terrace and walk round the parapet thirty stories above the street. This walk round the parapet is the high point of the novel, a triumph of narration. Because we sweat it out with Rojack as wind, rain and psychologically sensed supernatural forces (Deborah's hands, for example) threaten to dislodge him, we believe in the importance of this ordeal, that it is his purgatory, his penance and way to salvation. In his essay "On the Parapet," Tony Tanner says of Rojack:

> If a man becomes aware of those dimensions of nature and super-nature from which he feels that the rest of society has resolutely closed itself off, where does that leave him standing? By analogy we might say on an edge as precarious as the parapet round a balcony.[6]

But Rojack does not walk the parapet a second time, as he knows he should for Cherry's sake. Cherry, whom he followed the night before from the police station to her nightclub and her bed, has become his Beatrice, pointing the way to salvation. They experienced with each other their first genuine emotion of love; and it is Cherry who has transformed the Deborah-inspired impulse to jump into the life-enhancing impulse to walk the parapet. Rojack has already had to pass two tests of courage for Cherry—he has had to defy a Mafia thug and fight her Negro ex-lover, Shago Martin. Now, as he rushes off to possess her, hoping he has fulfilled "the iron law of romance: one took the vow to be brave" (203), he is seized with dread. "You've gotten off easy" (261), he tells himself; and sure enough, he finds Cherry dying, beaten to death by a friend of Shago's. Shago himself has been found beaten to death in Harlem.

Rojack's self-admonition should be answer enough to the reviewers who complained that Rojack does not pay a moral price for the murder. He pays a price in the same way as the ancient Mariner; and, indeed, Mailer's novel is like Coleridge's poem all about the moral price. The killings in both works are merely the occasions for expressionistic portrayal of the *experience* of guilt, penance, and at least partial redemption. The novel, in addition, draws our attention away from the murder to the web of social evil the murder discloses, a web in which Deborah was thoroughly implicated.

In his wartime heroism, Rojack showed a potentiality for courageous action that got squashed in civilian life, where he allowed himself to be used by the Kellys and their like. His marriage went bad because Deborah considered him, and he considered himself, a coward. Now with the murder, an act that disengages him from career and social position, he finds his courage and with it the ability to love. The only really implausible thing in this just plausible novel is the number of Rojack's monumentally long coitions during the night hours that remain after the murder. But this is the American dream—that courage is connected with sexual potency and that a man, when tested, will be found to have infinite supplies of both. The point is that modern American society suppresses the chance of most men to realize this dream by passing—through some traumatic test of courage equivalent to primitive initiation rites—into possession of their manhood. Hence the locked-up seething madness of American life.

In the end, Rojack drifts off to Las Vegas to join "a new breed of man" (269)—presumably a breed recovering the old Wild West virtues by testing their courage at the gambling tables, a breed who if they have not found the good have at least disengaged from the evil. This "solution" is the Hip equivalent (in "The White Negro," Mailer speaks of the Hipster as a "frontiersman in the Wild West of American night life"[7]) of the purgatorial wandering in which the ancient Mariner is finally suspended.

On his way to Las Vegas, Rojack witnesses the autopsy of the old Missouri farmer through whose blue eyes he has evoked the eyes of the German soldier he shot in the war. The old man died of cancer; and we see here how Mailer's psychosomatic theory about cancer seems valid enough when used for symbolic purposes. The old man's terrible smell haunts Rojack's nostrils for the rest of the journey, coming back at him from off the landscape like some quintessential atmosphere of America.

> Cancer is the growth of madness denied. In that corpse I saw, madness went down to the blood—leucocytes gorged the liver, the spleen, the enlarged heart and violet-black lungs, dug into the intestines, germinated stench. . . . some of the real madness went into me. The stink of the dead man went along the dry lands of Oklahoma and northern Texas, through the desert bake of New Mexico, Arizona, on into the valleys of the moon—

where sits Las Vegas, described as the volcanic place where the madness erupts.

Does the eruption make Las Vegas beneficial, and has Rojack saved himself from cancer by expressing his madness? There is in Las Vegas another atmosphere and temperature, that of the air-conditioned interiors which seem to contain air brought "through space" from some "pleasure chamber of an encampment on the moon" (267–68). The moon, which originally symbolized Deborah, seems now to be a good, even a heavenly, thing; for Cherry speaks to him from it, from perhaps (as my colleague Anthony Winner suggests) Dante's lowest circle of Paradise, the lunar circle of nuns who were forced to marry (Cherry conveys regards from Marilyn Monroe; and sure enough Mailer published a biography called *Marilyn* in 1973). Rojack's madly comic oscillation between the "two atmospheres" (of hell and heaven?) seems to do him good. In the last sentence, he is "something like sane again" as he sets off for the jungles of Guatemala and Yucatán. Why there? His spiritual progress has all along been backward and downward. Hence he feels Harlem is the good place, perceives heaven in the hell of Las Vegas, and sets forth to find what he has earlier called "the beast of mystery" in its jungle habitat. This final chapter is too elliptical to be clear, but the symbolism—moving as it does through smell, somatic imagery, and the unearthly moon, to recall all that was contained in the madly cerulean eyes of the German soldier, who was shot in moonlight—brings to a climax the coherence of vision that accounts for the success of this powerfully imaginative novel.

Why Are We in Vietnam? is even more wildly imaginative in its treatment of the American dream and the American madness. Here the Wild West theme is central, for the characters are all Texans; and though the Texans are satirized, it is clearer than in the earlier book that there is something to be said for the American dream of courage and sexual potency and for the barbaric energies it expresses. In this book, imagination shows itself not in the Gothic nightmare way, but through wit and nature poetry. Narrated by an eighteen-year-old Texas hellraiser, named D.J., the book is, considering its horrendous message, curiously lighthearted and young. One feels in its ease of execution that Mailer has finally broken through, has learned how to speak with one voice about the horror and the glory of, to use his phrase, the American "giant."

The wit is not cerebral; it is the expression of physical exuberance, and employs the word "ass" as an all-purpose intensifier. Mailer has borrowed from Joyce and William Burroughs to create an idiom that is genuine, semiliterate, all-boys-together American, heightened most of the time (sometimes Mailer tries too hard) into wit and poetry. Once you get over the first shock at the unceasing obscenities, they take on (if the book works for you) the quality of metaphor, a way of talking about the whole of life like the somatic images of *An American Dream*. Obscenities come to seem the only richly expressive way of talking—the rhythm seems wrong when you leave them out, the expression thin. "There was no villainy in obscenity for him," Mailer says of himself in *The Armies of the Night*, "just . . . his love for America: he had first come to love America when he served in the U. S. Army" and learned that "his obscenity was what saved" the common man.

> Americans were the first people on earth to live for their humor; . . . so Mailer never felt more like an American than when he was naturally obscene—all the gifts of the American language came out in the happy play of obscenity upon concept, which enabled one to go back to concept again. . . . He had kicked goodbye in his novel *Why Are We in Vietnam?* to the old literary corset of good taste, letting his sense of language play on obscenity as freely as it wished, so discovering that everything he knew about the American language (with its incommensurable resources) went flying in and out of the line of his prose with the happiest beating of wings.[8]

The obscenities seem necessary for the giant qualities Mailer wants to portray. Mailer has always admired big, strong characters even when they are bastards. In this book, all the major characters are big, strong bastards.

The idiom is D.J.'s; the others do not all or always talk this way, but D.J. shows through the idiom what they are really saying. "If the illusion has been conveyed that my mother, D.J.'s own mother, talks the way you got it here, well little readster, you're sick in your own drool, because my mother is a Southern lady, she's as elegant as an oyster with powder on its ass, she don't talk that way, she just thinks that way." The idiom is also the means of satirizing D.J. and the others. The point of the satire is that these Texas Yahoos, many of them with Indian blood, are living in "this Electrolux Edison world, all programmed out," and are, like D.J.'s daddy, Rusty, who is a big corporation executive, at the center of the nonvital, anti-individualistic, antiheroic American corporation system. Rusty's God is a G.P.A. or Great Plastic Asshole, excreting "his corporate management of thoughts. I mean that's what you get when you look into Rusty's eyes."[9] The vision is of barbarism equipped with advanced technology.

It is to pit Rusty's God against the vital God of the wilderness, and to pit Rusty against an authentic man like the guide Big Luke, that Mailer sends his Texans to hunt above the Arctic Circle in Alaska. The hunt is being narrated at a Dallas dinner two years later; and to further the satire of our electronic world, D.J. is supposed to be a Disc Jockey broadcasting to the world. He regularly interrupts the action to address us directly in little chapters called Intro Beeps, which are often tiresome. There is entirely too much narrative method for so small a novel; and to confuse us further, Mailer suggests fleetingly that D.J. may himself be a fiction in the brain of a Harlem genius. Mailer cannot get Harlem off his mind.

But the hunt, with its rich recollections of hunts in Hemingway and Faulkner, is the substance of the book and the thing that gives the book its high value. In his critical study of Mailer (1972), Richard Poirier traces the American literary tradition behind the hunt as "the noble effort of a line of heroes stretching back from Faulkner to Emerson and Cooper: the trek to the 'edge' of civilization, there to be cleansed of its contaminations."[10] The point of the hunt is explained by Rojack's lecture in *American Dream* on the primitive view of mystery: "In contrast to the civilized view which elevates man above the animals, the primitive had an instinctive belief that he was subservient to the primal pact between the beasts of the jungle and the beast of mystery" (159). The spiritual essence that in *American Dream* is suggested through somatic and animal imagery is evoked here through the rendition of actual animals. The beast of mystery turns out to be more Devil than God.

We are given murderous little pastorals like this:

> You can tune in on the madness in the air, you now know where a pine tree is rotting and festering somewhere out there, and red ants are having a war in its muck, and the bear is listening to those little ant screams and smelling that rotten old pine, and whoong goes his nose into the rot, and he bites and swallows red ants, slap, bap, pepper on his tongue, he picking up the bite of death in each ant and the taste of fruit in the pulp, digging that old rotten tree whose roots tell him where we are.

When D.J. feels himself "up tight with the essential animal insanity of things" (54, 70), we see that the social madness of *American Dream* is now connected with cosmic madness.

Yet there is a difference between the violence of nature and of these Texans. The Texans violate the wilderness. For Rusty the hunt is a status symbol, a gambit in the game of corporation politics. The Texans don't so much shoot the animals as shatter them with overpowered guns. Worst of all, the Texans get Big Luke to break his professional code by transporting them to the various hunting grounds in a helicopter.

The animals seem noble just by contrast. Even the grizzly bear, who epitomizes all the insane force of nature, has when dying a look in his eyes that makes D.J., who shot him, refrain from finishing him off and step up close to see: "something in that grizzer's eyes locked into his, a

message, fellow, an intelligence of something very fine and very far away"
(146). But Rusty finishes the bear off and later claims possession of the
skin, thus disgusting D.J. and bringing to an end the idyllic episode in
which the father and son, slipping off from the others, discovered love
for each other as hunting companions.

This is the first of two idyllic episodes which are the high points of
the book. Both episodes end in failure. In the second, D.J. and his best
friend, Tex, slips off in disgust at the moral impurity of the hunting party,
and discover for themselves the old Indian purification ceremony. Out of
the same instinct that makes Rojack walk the parapet, they advance into
the wilderness without any weapons. To protect themselves against a
grizzly bear, they climb a tree and from there enjoy a panoramic view of
nature in all her subtly anthropomorphized aspects (Mailer's way with
animals reminds me of Isak Dinesen's in *Out of Africa*). They see nature
as genial when the bear gorges itself on berries; as terrifying when the
bear rips open a living caribou calf to eat her entrails and then, for sheer
assertion of power, kills her and excretes around her body; as sorrowful
when the caribou mother returns to her dead calf.

> She circles about in a dance, but never takes her nose off as if she is going
> to smell on through to the secret of flesh, as if something in the odor of
> her young dead was there in the scent of the conception not ten months
> ago when some bull stud caribou in moonlight or sun illumined the other
> end of the flesh somewhere between timber slide and lightning there on
> the snow, some mystery then recovered now, and woe by that mother car-
> ibou nuzzled in sorrow from her nose while the sky above blue as a col-
> orless sea went on and sun burned on her, flies came, last of the flies trav-
> eling over the snow and now running a shuttle from Baron Bear's pile of
> bauble to the nappy spotty hide of caribou mother, she twitching and
> jumping from the sure spite of the sting but not relinquishing her nose
> and the dying odor of her yearling calf and D.J.'s head full spun with that
> for new percipience, since could it be odor died last of all when one was
> dead? and took a separate route. (193–94)

Even more than in *American Dream*, we are in an intensified Wordsworthian world where smell and the ability to smell is an index of spirit;
so that D.J. moves, through his question about odor, into intimations of
immortality and divinity. Another index of spirit is the recurring imagery
of electromagnetism, the suggestion that the far North is spiritual because electromagnetic, because it draws up all the "messages" or secret
desires of North America. When the two boys go to sleep together that
night, the Arctic Lights, Aurora Borealis, are out; and "the lights were
saying that there was something up here, and it was really here, yeah

God was here, and He was real and no man was He, but a beast" (202). The writing here is mawkish, but the point is important; for it is to merge with this great beast of desire that D.J. puts out a hand to touch Tex and make manifest the latent homosexual feeling between them. "They is crazy about each other," we were told earlier. "But fear not, gentle auditor, they is men, real Texas men" (179).

The satire is directed against their suppression of homosexual feeling. Although Mailer has in the past treated homosexuality as a sign of failure, we have here to follow the story, which seems to suggest that the homosexuality ought to be recognized and outgrown. In "The Homosexual Villain" (*Advertisements*), Mailer regrets his unsympathetic treatment of homosexuality in *Deer Park*. But in *Armies of the Night*, he rejects easy tolerance of it—saying that guilt is necessary as "the existential edge of sex" and that homosexuality has to be overcome in the process by which "you earned manhood" (24–25). For the same reason that Rusty kills and claims possession of Griz #1, Griz #2 kills and excretes on the caribou calf; so some demonic will to power (there has been a running satire on Texas will power) causes the boys to vie in an unspoken contest for the male role. Instead of love, "murder" breaks out between them and they make a pact in blood to be "killer brothers." The effect of the hunt has been pernicious, as we see by the near-criminal behavior of the boys during the two years following in Dallas. And we learn in the last sentence of the book that they are now off to "Vietnam, hot damn."

Only here are we finally brought round to the irritatingly odd title. Why are we in Vietnam? Because we are crazy and nature is crazy, but nature's fall is apparently caused by ours (the Arctic animals are being driven crazy by the noise of airplanes). And why are we crazier and more dangerous than other nations? Because we are bigger, more energetic, more heroic. The whole book sings our potential heroism, what we might have been and how terribly we have gone wrong. Through joking references to the pioneer days, we are reminded of the old American dream of heroic fulfillment in nature. In the Arctic wilderness, the Texans have a chance to start over again. They might have found God there; they find instead the Devil, because of a fatal flaw—the need to express their Faustian pursuit of infinite courage and sexual potency through the desire to dominate and possess. I think we are to understand that this flaw goes back to their origins, but has been aggravated by technology.

"The country had always been wild," says Mailer in *Armies of the Night*, a nonfiction account of the 1967 antiwar march on the Pentagon, which incidentally throws light on *American Dream* and *Why Are We in Vietnam?*

It had always been harsh and hard . . . the fever to travel was in the American blood, so said all, but now the fever had left the blood, it was in the cells, the cells traveled, and the cells were as insane as Grandma with orange hair. The small towns were disappearing in the bypasses and the supermarkets and the shopping centers. . . . Technology had driven insanity out of the wind and out of the attic, and out of all the lost primitive places: one had to find it now wherever fever, force, and machines could come together, in Vegas, at the race track, in pro football, race riots for the Negro, suburban orgies—none of it was enough—one had to find it in Vietnam; that was where the small town had gone to get its kicks. (152–53)

As an analysis of our political reasons for being in Vietnam, the passage is no less deficient than the novel that asks this question; for both attribute the war to popular bloodthirstiness, when there has never been a war more unpopular. But as a metaphorical vision of our culture, employing a parable about Vietnam, the passage has a certain psychological validity—a validity demonstrated by our unhappy precedence over all other advanced nations in crimes of violence, and by isolated cases of American atrocities in Vietnam. The psychology is only valid nonstatistically, however, and at a depth that is best portrayed in fiction, where it need not lead to a doctrinaire position.

Even in his political writings, Mailer cuts through doctrinaire positions—as in *Miami and the Siege of Chicago,* his account of the 1968 nominating conventions, where in preferring the coarsely sensual face of Chicago, represented by its tough mayor, to the "thin nostrils" of Eugene McCarthy's supporters,[11] he expresses metaphorically his temperamental though not political antipathy to the liberal academics whom he sees as new men, natural managers of technology land. Complexity of political judgment is especially apparent in *Armies of the Night,* where Mailer describes himself as a left conservative and reveals the aristocratic bias inherent in the paradoxical cluster of ideas I have earlier associated with the word *culture,* ideas best expressed through forms of imaginative literature. Mailer subtitles *Armies of the Night: History as a Novel, The Novel as History,* to make us read it as imaginative literature. Nevertheless, his political and cultural vision is expressed most profoundly in the novels.

All Mailer's novels are tied to an outstanding event of the time—World War II, the Korean War, Senator Joseph McCarthy's anticommunist investigations, President Kennedy's assassination, the Vietnam war. In spite of his apparently unrealistic new style, Mailer still adheres to the large realistic tradition of the novelist as a chronicler of his time. He remains political, but uses his new style to project those unconscious pathological forces that are, as he sees it, the main determinants of political behavior, especially in America now. In *American Dream* and *Why Are We in Vietnam?* Mailer's psychological and social intelligence combines with a wild, fantastic, unpredictable quality of mind that touches raw nerves in us because it is so alive. We can pick at faults in these and the other novels, but the important point is this—that we sense Mailer's intelligence as a force, passionate and all-pervading, that sees things through to their ultimate causes and consequences. This marks him as a major talent.

Pound and Eliot

P OUND and Eliot. One of the great friendships and col-
laborations of Anglo-American literary history. We
are tempted to find an analogy in the famous friendship and collaboration of Wordsworth and Coleridge.

But there are important differences. First of all, no two friends can
have been more opposite in personality than Pound and Eliot. Pound was
the more "American" of the two—the more democratic, individualistic,
spontaneous, sincere, a radical at heart. Even as a famous old man Pound
remained a bohemian, dressed as he had been all his life in odd and
striking ways. Hugh Kenner describes him as adorned in 1912 with ear-
ring, red beard, and a green velvet jacket. Eliot was at heart conservative,
armored with Boston and English reserve. With his addiction to conservative English tailoring, Tom Eliot projected even as a young man the
image of a stuffed shirt whom the upper-class but bohemian Bloomsbury
group found faintly comic. "Come to lunch," Virginia Woolf wrote to
Clive Bell in the early 1920s, "Tom is coming . . . with a four piece suit." [1]
Eliot's sly form of rebellion was to look like a banker rather than a poet.

In philosophical orientation, Pound and Eliot came to occupy opposite poles, whereas Wordsworth and Coleridge came to argue over
matters of degree in what was essentially the same Burkean position.
Pound remained all his life vociferously and belligerently anti-Christian
and pagan. His later anti-Semitism derived partly from his hatred of the
Hebraic element in Christianity and partly from his hatred of banking.
Eliot, instead, was religious by nature and began, soon after the publication of *The Waste Land* (1922), the movement toward Anglo-
Catholicism which culminated in his conversion and adoption of British
citizenship in 1927.

The transitional poem is *The Hollow Men* (1925) with its echoing of church liturgy. After that all Eliot's major poems and plays are overtly Christian. Only once does Pound in a *published* source mention a non-dramatic poem of Eliot's after *The Waste Land* (my observation is confirmed by Donald Gallup's 1983 Pound bibliography). The exception is Pound's little-known response, published anonymously in *Edge* (May 1957), to Eliot's little known *The Cultivation of Christmas Trees* (1954). "Let us lament," Pound concludes, "the psychosis / Of all those who abandon the Muses for Moses" (12). Pound, does, however, comment in his letters on Eliot's later poems. For example, in a still unpublished letter of 17 December 1934, he writes: "the Possum what onct used to rite a POEN now and then / when I wuz near enough to annoy him / and he not thinking he was a bishop and rife fer ecclesiastikle preferment."[2] In a letter from Rapallo dated 30 January 1935, he makes a similar attack on Eliot's Anglo-Catholicism: "A couple of bawdy songs from father Eliot wdn't go bad with the electorate. I see he has written a play." Of the play he wrote from Rapallo a year later: "Waal, I heerd the *Murder in the Cafedrawl* on the radio lass' night. . . . Mzzr Shakzpeer *still* retains his posishun. I stuck it fer a while, wot whiff the weepin and wailin."[3] Pound objected not only to the Christian content but also to the liturgical style that went with it. The only play of Eliot's he admired was the unfinished *Sweeney Agonistes* (1926–27), especially the part called "Fragment of an Agon," where the style is disconnected, ironic, and modern in idiom with jazz as the musical model.

On the other side, Eliot, while still a student at Harvard, was not impressed by Pound's early poems, which he considered "old-fashioned romantic" and "touchingly incompetent."[4] Eliot changed his mind in 1914 when, as a shy novice, he looked up Pound in London and was so overwhelmed by Pound's enthusiastic recognition of the modernity of "Prufrock," and so impressed by Pound's technical mastery, that he cast himself in the role of disciple though only three years younger than Pound.

No poet can ever have done more for another than Pound did for Eliot in those early years. As London correspondent for the Chicago magazine *Poetry,* he spent six months bludgeoning its editor, Harriet Monroe, into publishing "Prufrock." Pound arranged the poems for Eliot's first volume, *Prufrock and Other Observations* (1917), and without Eliot's knowledge personally borrowed the money to pay for printing the volume. But the price Eliot paid was discipleship. This explains Eliot's almost total acquiescence in Pound's revisions of *The Waste Land* manuscript, revisions which are the most spectacular example of Pound's influence on Eliot's career. In two of the 1922 letters exchanged on the revisions (Pound had by then moved to Paris), Eliot addresses Pound as

"Cher maître," while Pound replies, "Filio dilecto mihi" (170–71). This was of course a joke, but a significant one. Their whole relation was carried on humorously, which is how Eliot came by Pound's fond nickname for him, Possum.

Eliot later recalled that Pound "was so passionately concerned about the works of art which he expected his protegés to produce that he sometimes tended to regard them almost impersonally, as art or literature machines to be carefully tended and oiled for the sake of their potential output."[5] Eliot's biographer Lyndall Gordon writes that

> One observer said [Pound] treated Eliot as a kind of collector's piece. With his prize beneath his eye, he would recline in an American posture of aggressive ease, and squint sideways up at the visitor, over the rims of his pince-nez, to see how impressed he was with Eliot's apt answers.[6]

It does not detract from Pound's unprecedented generosity in acting as unpaid literary agent for Eliot, Joyce, Hemingway, and other young writers to detect in Pound the impresario's desire (he displayed the American talent for publicity) to run the avant-garde literary world, which he did for a time to the benefit of us all. It was when he later desired to run the political and economic world as well that he ran into trouble. Pound's biographer Noel Stock tells us that in 1922 Pound, working from astrological data, "decided that the Christian Era had ended at midnight on 29–30 October 1921: the world was now living in the first year of a new pagan age called the Pound Era."[7] There is doubtless an element of humor in this, but the humor does not negate the element of prophecy as confirmed by the title of Hugh Kenner's excellent book *The Pound Era.*

On 12 November 1917 Knopf issued, in connection with the American edition of Pound's *Lustra,* a small anonymous pamphlet called "Ezra Pound: His Metric and Poetry." The pamphlet was written by T. S. Eliot and is disciple's work. Pound arranged for Eliot to write it, edited the text by making three small deletions, and gave the pamphlet its title. Eliot defends Pound's poetry against the attacks that had been made on it. In answer to the reviewer who wrote that Pound "baffles us by archaic words and unfamiliar metres . . . breaking out into any sort of expression which suits itself to his mood," Eliot replies: "It is, in fact, just this adaptability of metre to mood, an adaptability due to an intensive study of metre, that constitutes an important element in Pound's technique." Against the charge of excessive erudition, Eliot replies equivocally: "to display knowledge is not the same thing as to expect it on the part of the reader; and of this sort of pedantry Pound is quite free." And against the

charge that Pound's example has fathered a lot of sloppy free verse, Eliot
replies soundly: "Pound's vers libre is such as is only possible for a poet
who has worked tirelessly with rigid forms and different systems of met-
rics. . . . Pound was the first writer in English to use five Provençal
forms."[8]

After the publication of *The Waste Land* in 1922, Eliot began breaking the bonds of discipleship. He began mixing praise of Pound with a
certain amount of critical reservation. In reviewing *Personae*, Pound's
collected shorter poems, in the *Dial* of January 1928, Eliot praises Pound
as the greatest living "master of verse form." But the review ends with
"the question (which the unfinished Cantos make more pointed) what
does Mr. Pound believe?" (4–7). This question became the subject of
lifelong contention between the two poets, a contention ranging from
friendly to hostile: it is not always easy to determine the proportions of
the mixture. The very praise—the greatest living "master of verse
form"—implies a reservation that Eliot more or less maintains. Pound is
the greatest living *craftsman*, but pointedly not the greatest living *poet*
because of Eliot's doubts about Pound's content. The dedication of *The
Waste Land* to Pound as "il miglior fabbro" ("the best craftsman") may
contain the same reservation. Pound himself translates this phrase
of Dante's (*Purg.* 26.117) as the "best craftsman" in "Near Perigord,"
pt. 2.[9]

For all its air of praise, Eliot's review of *Personae* is partly an attack
on Pound's content. Eliot begins by saying that Pound has had "an immense influence, but no disciples," for "influence can be exerted through
form, whereas one makes disciples only among those who sympathize
with the content." He describes Pound's influence on his own verse, but
then confesses, "I am seldom interested in what he is saying, but only in
the way he says it." "In form," Pound "is still in advance of our own
generation and even the literary generation after us; whereas his ideas
are often those of the generation which preceded him." His ideas are
compounded of "the Nineties," "some medieval mysticism, without belief," and "Mr. Yeats's spooks." Having said that in the *Cantos*, "Pound's
auditory sense is perhaps superior to his visual sense," Eliot realizes that
he has made Pound sound like Swinburne, so he hastily differentiates
them: "Swinburne's form is uninteresting, because he is literally saying
next to nothing, and unless you mean something with your words they
will do nothing for you" (4–7). Pound, he continues lamely, intends a
meaning even if the meaning is unclear or uninteresting to the reader.
Eliot, nevertheless, may have had Pound in mind when he wrote in his
subtle 1920 essay "Swinburne as Poet": "The bad poet dwells partly in
a world of objects and partly in a world of words, and he never can get

them to fit. Only a man of genius could dwell so exclusively and consist-
ently among words as Swinburne."[10] In my opinion Pound's ear is so
much finer than Swinburne's that as a poet of sound he can be compared
only with the Milton he so much berates.

In his review of *Personae* and elsewhere, Eliot raises what remains
the crucial issue in evaluating Pound—the question of content. In his
1919 review of Pound's volume *Quia Pauper Amavi* and more elabo-
rately in the introduction to his 1928 selection of Pound's poems, Eliot
suggests that in his shorter poems Pound has little of his own to say since
his best poems are translations or adaptations from Provençal trouba-
dours, classic Chinese poets, and the Latin poet Sextus Propertius. The
poems on contemporary life, in which Pound broaches his own ideas, are
less successful. "Pound," writes Eliot in his introduction, "is much more
modern, in my opinion, when he deals with Italy and Provence, than
when he deals with modern life." "If one can really penetrate the life of
another age, one is penetrating the life of one's own."[11] Eliot is applying
the paradoxes he worked out in "Tradition and the Individual Talent"
(1919), an essay for which he must have had in mind so backward-
looking and erudite a poet as Pound, who nevertheless organized the
modernist movement in Anglo-American poetry.

Eliot, in his introduction, finds in Pound a dissociation between his
"personal feeling" (which includes his ideas) and his technique: "there is
the aspect of deeper personal feeling, which is not invariably, so far,
found in the poems of most important technical accomplishment. . . . it
is not until we reach *Mauberley* (much the finest poem, I believe, before
the *Cantos*) that some definite fusion takes place" (xiv–xv).

Most readers will agree that in *Mauberley* Pound's ideas are as interesting as his technique. But the fusion Eliot was hoping for has proved
disappointing in the *Cantos*. If Pound had little of his own to express in
the shorter poems, the ideas he advances in the *Cantos* are often an em-
barrassment that spoils the poetry; while the poetry itself, where it is
good, is better than anything he had written earlier. But the poetry is
good as fragments not as a whole. For writing a long poem, Pound shows
himself deficient in organizing ability.

In 1918 Pound adopted the Social Credit theory of Major C. H.
Douglas. This is a monetary theory which takes a medieval view of banking and interest. Pound uses the word *usura* for excessive interest not tied
to production, and in the medieval manner uses the word as a talisman
of all evil. Pound took Social Credit in a direction of his own when he
combined it with fascism; Douglas was antifascist. Pound latched onto
Douglas's theory with an eagerness that suggests his need to find something to *say*. Social Credit and Confucianism, with Confucianism's West-

ern counterpart, the Enlightenment, were to constitute a "system" analogous to Yeats's *A Vision* and Dante's Aquinian theology, a system which
Pound hoped would give form and meaning to the *Cantos*. "As to the
form of *The Cantos*," Pound replied to an inquirer as late as February
1939, "All I can say or pray is: *wait* till it's there. I mean wait till I get
'em written and then if it don't show, I will start exegesis." He did not,
like Dante, he added, have an "Aquinas-map" to guide him: "Aquinas
not valid now." [12]

According to Hugh Kenner, "it was in the first glare of the Douglas
revelation that Pound wrote *Mauberley*" (1920), which bids farewell to
his aesthetical retreat from society because Pound now had a key by
which to make society conform to the artist's imagination. The *Cantos*
were now reconceived as "nothing less than a vast historical demonstration, enlightened by Douglas's insight." [13] Pound shows good periods in
history when culture flourished, presumably because money represented
productivity, and periods which were bad, presumably because money
merely chased after money. But the monetary explanation is not always
evident as, for example, in Canto 13, the first Confucius canto.

In a Rapallo letter of 11 April 1927, Pound outlines for his father
the "main scheme" of his "rather obscure," fragmented poem:

A.   A.   Live man goes down into world of Dead
C.   B.   The "repeat in history"
B.   C.   The "magic moment" or moment of metamorphosis, bust
            thru from quotidien into "divine or permanent world."
            Gods, etc. (210)

We can easily recognize these motifs in the *Cantos* without understanding
how they cohere. Pound tells his father they are arranged contrapuntally
as in a fugue (hence the double set of letters). This is more confusing than
clarifying, as is Pound's attempt in the rest of the letter to show connections among details in the *Cantos*. In an interview with Pasolini in 1968,
Pound again alludes to musical form to justify the apparent incoherence
of the *Cantos*. "They say [the quotations in the *Cantos*] are chosen at
random, but that's not the way it is. It's music. Musical themes that meet
each other." [14]

Even the famous Canto 45 on *usura* is no exception to what I have
been saying about the lack of fusion between the poetry and the ideas,
especially the ideas about money. We are so overwhelmed by the biblical
cadences and rhetoric (the repetitions and parallel constructions) as to
forget that the content will not bear investigation:

WITH USURA
wool comes not to market
sheep bringeth no gain with usura.

Yet modern banking coincides with unprecedented European prosperity.
We are inclined to agree with Pound that at least in modern times the
arts and sexuality have suffered:

Usura rusteth the chisel
It rusteth the craft and the craftsman
. . . .
Usura slayeth the child in the womb
It stayeth the young man's courting
It hath brought palsey to bed, lyeth
between the young bride and her bridegroom
                CONTRA NATURAM.[15]

Yet population increased enormously during the nineteenth century, and
while the handicrafts declined, literature, music, painting, philosophy
and science flourished. Ruskin railed against much the same social symptoms, but attributed them to an unprecedented complex of causes
brought on by the Industrial Revolution and not to a single cause recurring throughout the past. Ruskin and Pound, like all romantic thinkers,
like Eliot, too, in his social thought, longed nostalgically for the organic
society of the past.

Pound does better with the journey-to-the-dead motif in the superb
Canto 1, where he returns to translating and deals with myth rather than
ideas. Pound translates Andreas Divus's sixteenth-century Latin translation of Homer's chapter on Ulysses' journey to Hades. By translating a
Renaissance Latin translation of an ancient Greek poem into a modern
English that recalls Anglo-Saxon verse ("Men many, mauled with bronze
lance heads, / Battle spoil, bearing yet dreory arms," 4), by layering the
language, Pound shows how myth endures through changes of language
and how the memory of myth and the memory in language of its own
changes sustain cultural continuity.

In accordance with his anti–narrative "ideogrammic" method,
Pound fragments the narrative in order to lyricize it, to give it lyric intensity. "The *Divina Commedia* must not be considered as an epic," he wrote
in 1910. "It is in a sense lyric, the tremendous lyric of the subjective
Dante."[16] In Canto 1 Pound translates the beginning of Homer's Book 4,
yet the first line suggests that, as in a fragment, something has preceded:
"And then went down to the ship" (3); similarly in the last line the canto
breaks off abruptly, suggesting something to follow, "So that:" (5). A few

lines earlier the *Odyssey* itself breaks off, as Pound switches without explanation to a Homeric Hymn in praise of golden Aphrodite. The movement from underworld to golden Aphrodite may be a ritualistic movement, as described by Frazer in *The Golden Bough* (the last line names "the golden bough of Argicida")—a movement from death to renewed sexuality and fertility.[17]

The journey-to-the-dead motif is taken up again in the "hell cantos" (Cantos 14, 15), which Pound in a letter of 1932 describes as "specifically LONDON, the state of English mind in 1919 and 1920" (239). In contrast to Canto 1, these cantos are ideological and full of abstract hatred. Although the first line sets the cantos in Dante's Inferno, the sinners wallow in a swamp of excrement ("Profiteers drinking blood sweetened with sh-t," 61) for which there is only slight precedent in Dante's end of Canto 18 and last line of Canto 21. Like Dante, Pound puts whole classes of people into hell. The difference is that Dante's are moral classes as determined by the Church, while Pound's classes are determined by eccentricities like Social Credit theory and his own notions. There can be no consensus that such occupational groups as "financiers" and "the press gang" belong in hell, or that the politicians identifiable as Lloyd George and Woodrow Wilson (61) belong there. The hell cantos are powerful in that they horrify us, but we are horrified less by the sinners than by the unbridled violence of Pound's bias and hatred. "An intellectual hatred is the worst," as Yeats wrote.

So little did Eliot, after his conversion, approve of Pound's ideas that he placed his good friend among the modern heretical writers—Lawrence, Yeats, Hardy—whom he attacks in *After Strange Gods,* not for their literary quality but for their content. Pound's Confucianism, says Eliot, is typical of "the rebellious Protestant." Pound finds Guido Cavalcanti "much more sympathetic than Dante," because "Guido was very likely a heretic." "With the disappearance of the idea of Original Sin . . . of intense moral struggle, the human beings presented to us both in poetry and in prose fiction today . . . become less and less real." Thus the sinners "Mr. Pound puts in Hell" are unreal. One finds "politicians, profiteers, financiers, newspaper proprietors and their hired men, . . . those who do not believe in Social Credit, . . . and all 'those who have set money-lust before the pleasures of the senses.'" It is a hell, to quote Pound, "'without dignity, without tragedy,' . . . I find," Eliot continues,

> one considerable objection to a Hell of this sort: that a Hell altogether
> without dignity implies a Heaven without dignity also. If you do not dis-
> tinguish between individual responsibility and circumstances in Hell, be-
> tween essential Evil and social accidents, then the Heaven (if any) implied

will be equally trivial and accidental. Mr. Pound's Hell, for all its horrors, is a perfectly comfortable one for the modern mind to contemplate, and disturbing to no one's complacency: it is a Hell for the *other people,* . . . not for oneself.[18]

The last sentence makes one realize that in his poetry Pound seldom struggles with his own deficiencies; he lashes out against other people. The exception, until *The Pisan Cantos,* is the masterly sequence *Hugh Selwyn Mauberley,* where Pound satirizes his own aestheticism: "His true Penelope was Flaubert." But he satirizes himself mainly as poet not as man, and in the second poem of the sequence begins blaming the age as incompatible with poetry: "The age demanded an image / Of its accelerated grimace." In poem 5 of the sequence, he attacks the age, in memorable lines, for having produced World War I:

> There died a myriad,
> And of the best, among them,
> For an old bitch gone in the teeth,
> For a botched civilization.

If we compare *Mauberley* with "Prufrock," in which the persona is also a projection of the author, we see that Eliot's self-examination is unforgiving though he mixes self-satire with pathos:

> But though I have wept and fasted, wept and prayed,
> Though I have seen my head [grown slightly bald]
>   brought in upon a platter,
> I am no prophet—and here's no great matter.[19]

The difference can also be accounted for by Pound's singular lack of interest in *psychological* characterization, which is what distinguishes his Browningesque dramatic monologues from Browning's dramatic monologues. In Pound's early dramatic monologues, like "Cino" and "Sestina Altaforte," he triumphs in Browning's style, but unlike Browning presents in each only one emotion without complication or suggestion of psychological motives. "Near Perigord," not a dramatic monologue though like one, is more enigmatic but not psychologically. The question is whether Bertrans de Born was *politically* motivated in loving Maent. Almost all Eliot's major poems, instead, are self-examining; when we read about the neurotic apathy or aboulie of Eliot's youth, we realize that *he* is the walking dead of *The Waste Land.* The exceptions are the satirical quatrain poems of 1920, written under Pound's influence,

in which Eliot mercilessly satirizes members of other ethnic groups—
Sweeney, Bleistein, Grishkin—who are obviously external to himself.

After all Pound's suffering during the immediate post-World War II
years, when he was arrested by the American army in Italy for his wartime profascist broadcasts,[20] exposed in a cage in the American army
prison camp outside Pisa, and committed to a mental hospital in Washington, D.C., after all this suffering Pound seems in certain passages of
the *Pisan Cantos* to be at last examining himself critically:

> "Master thyself, then others shall thee beare"
>   Pull down thy vanity
> Thou art a beaten dog beneath the hail.
>
> (521)

Even here Hugh Kenner sees a restatement of Social Credit theory:
"*vanus*" is "the false accounting" that makes money out of nothing
(308). If Kenner is right, Pound will again be accusing others and the
lines would lose their beauty; but given the moral imperative of these
lines and the lovely lines above them:

> The ant's a centaur in his dragon world.
> Pull down thy vanity, it is not man
> Made courage, or made order, or made grace.
>
> (521)

I think Kenner must be wrong. Even so Pound remains politically unre-
pentant in the *Pisan Cantos* and concludes the above passage of self-
criticism with a self-defense:

> But to have done instead of not doing
>   this is not vanity
> . . . .
>   To have gathered from the air a live tradition
> or from a fine old eye the unconquered flame
> This is not vanity.
>
> (521–22)

In a September 1946 article in *Poetry,* Eliot writes: "If I am doubtful
about some of the [recent] *Cantos,* it is not that I find any poetic decline
in them, but an increasing defect of communication."[21] F. R. Leavis, in
the *Times Literary Supplement* of 11 September 1970, quotes from a
letter Eliot, toward the end of his life, sent him after reading the "Retrospect 1950" in a new edition of Leavis's influential *New Bearings in*

English Poetry (1932). Eliot expresses his agreement with Leavis's remark about

> the aridity of the *Cantos,* with the exception of at least one item & a few
> lines from one of the so-called *Pisan Cantos* where it seems to me also
> that a touch of humanity breaks through: I mean the lovely verse of
> "Bow [*sic*] down thy vanity" and the reference to the Negro who
> knocked him up a table when he was in the cage at Pisa. And of course
> Pound's incomparable sense of rhythm carries a lot over. But I do find the
> *Cantos,* apart from that exceptional moment, quite arid and depressing.[22]

Pound, on his side, kept up after Eliot's conversion a teasing criticism
of his Anglo-Catholicism—in the opening of Canto 46, for example,
which follows the *usura* canto:

> And if you will say that this tale teaches . . .
>   a lesson, or that the Reverend Eliot
>   has found a more natural language.
>
> (231)

Pound seems to be criticizing the religiosity and the language of Eliot's
later poems. "Curious, is it not," says Pound in Canto 80,

>   that Mr Eliot
> has not given more time to Mr Beddoes
>   (T.L.) prince of morticians.
>
> (498)

The reference to the author of *Death's Jest-Book* (1850) recalls Pound's
often expressed wonderment that Christians are so preoccupied with
death and his account in Canto 29 of the young Eliot's confession to him
(the speaker's name was later changed to Arnaut Daniel): "I am afraid
of the life after death" (145). The Beddoes passage continues with an
address, as Kenner suggests, to Eliot, lover of cats, as a cat: "Prowling
night-puss leave my hard squares alone / they are in no case cat food."
Leave my tough, indigestible poetry alone, he says, continuing with an
intricately syncopated passage that begins by naming the "Battle Hymn
of the Republic":

> "mi-hine eyes hev"
>   well yes they *have*
>   seen a good deal of it
>   there is a good deal to be seen

> fairly tough and unblastable
>   and the hymn . . .
> well in contrast to the *god*-damned crooning
>   put me down for temporis acti [the old days].

(498–99)

I have seen too much tough reality, Pound seems to be saying, to tolerate the Tennysonian crooning of *Four Quartets.*

Pound also reproves Eliot for disagreeing with him politically: "(at which point Mr Eliot left us)," he says in the midst of a political passage in Canto 65 (378). "Yeats, Possum and Wyndham," he says in Canto 98, "had no ground beneath 'em" because they did not believe in Social Credit; "Orage," who did believe, "had" (685). In Canto 74, the first of the *Pisan Cantos,* Pound adapts the famous last lines of Eliot's *The Hollow Men* ("*This is the way the world ends / Not with a bang but a whimper*") to admonish the loyal British subject Eliot (called Possum) that the deaths of Benito Mussolini (called Ben) and his mistress, Clara Petacci— who in 1945 were shot by Italian partisans and exhibited strung up by the heels in Milan—restored heroism to the modern world: "yet say this to the Possum: a bang, not a whimper, / with a bang not with a whimper" (425).

I have said that with one exception Pound never names in published sources any nondramatic poem of Eliot's after *The Waste Land.* He does, however, openly attack Eliot's criticism—in "Credo" (1930), for example: "Mr. Eliot who is at times an excellent poet and who has arrived at the supreme Eminence among English critics largely through disguising himself as a corpse." Note, in "at times," the implied criticism of the later poetry (we know Pound liked the early poetry). The criticism is corpselike because of Eliot's impersonal, academic tone contrasting to Pound's personal tone in criticism. "I believe," Pound continues, "that postwar 'returns to christianity' . . . have been merely the gran' rifiuto and, in general, signs of fatigue."[23]

The attack on Eliot's criticism is even stronger in a Rapallo letter of 1932: "I dunno how you feel about Eliot's evil influence. Not that his crit. is *bad* but that he hasn't seen *where* it leads. What it leads TO. Attention on lesser rather than greater." Pound was probably thinking of Eliot's arguments for minor Metaphysical poets and Jacobean dramatists; Eliot was later to defend minor poetry in an essay on Kipling (1941). Pound probably has Eliot in mind when he goes on in this letter to describe the lowest class of critic: "The pestilence masking itself as a critic distracts attention *from* the best work, either to secondary work that is more or less 'good' or to tosh, to detrimental work, dead or living snobisms, or to indefinite essays on criticism" (240–41).

Amazingly Pound and Eliot remained good friends, perhaps even best friends, through all this disagreement. When Eliot died on 4 January 1965, Pound, old, sick, and poor, flew from Italy to attend the memorial service at Westminster Abbey. "Who is there now for me to share a joke with?" he wrote in the Eliot memorial issue of the *Sewanee Review.* "His was the true Dantescan voice—not honoured enough, and deserving more than I ever gave him." [24] At the Abbey the contrast between the two poet friends must have been striking. One had reaped all the honors the Establishment has to bestow, including the Nobel Prize. The other, for all his fame, was still poor and an outcast, shadowed by imputations of treason and insanity.

Now Pound began to admit that he might have erred. We see the admission in the above suggestion that he had not sufficiently honored Eliot's later poetry, which in being Christian was "Dantescan." We see it in the "Pull down thy vanity" passage in Pisan Canto 81. We see it in his confession to a friend that the *Cantos* were "a botch. . . . I picked out this and that thing that interested me, and then jumbled them into a bag. But that's not the way to make a *work of art*." [25] "I cannot make it cohere," he admits in the late Canto 116. And in the beautifully moving lines, which in the 1972 New Directions *Cantos* are printed last as Canto 120 (1969), he expresses disappointment that he has not completed Dante's scheme, which was one of his models, by failing to write a *Paradise* to follow upon the hell and purgatory cantos. Here is the whole canto:

I have tried to write Paradise

Do not move
    Let the wind speak
       that is paradise.

Let the Gods forgive what I
    have made
Let those I love try to forgive
    what I have made.

(803)

Questions have been raised about the authenticity of these lines and as to whether Pound approved their placement at the end of the 1972 New Directions *Cantos* (they are omitted from the corresponding London, Faber and Faber edition, 1976). Since the lines appeared (as lines 23, 16–18, 24–25) in an early version of Canto 115, first published in 1961 in *Threshold* (Belfast), there can be no question of their authenticity. If Pound removed such beautiful lines from the final version of Canto

115, it must be because he wanted to use them elsewhere. And, indeed, in the year after the final version of Canto 115 appeared in *Drafts and Fragments of Cantos CX–CXVIII* (1968), the deleted lines appeared in their present arrangement as "Canto 120" in *Anonym* (Buffalo, 1969), under the pseudonym "The Fox," but copyrighted by Ezra Pound. Who but Pound would have rearranged and submitted the lines with the pseudonym, and indicated by the title their closing position in the next printing of the *Cantos?* Although the 1972 printing of the *Cantos,* ending with Canto 120, came out the month after Pound's death on 1 November, the edition was prepared while Pound was still living. It is therefore difficult to believe he did not hear about the new ending from his companion, Olga Rudge, who carried on the correspondence with New Directions. Although depressed during his last years, Pound was in control of his faculties and quick, according to his publisher, James Laughlin, to indicate disapproval by way of Olga.

In a fragment dated 24 August 1966, however, Pound had sent Laughlin versified instructions regarding the ending of the *Cantos:*

> That her acts
> Olga's acts
>   of beauty
>   be remembered.
>
> Her name was Courage
> & is written Olga.
>
> These lines are for the
>   ultimate CANTO
>
> whatever I may write
> in the interim.

Laughlin considers these lines too unpoetic to use as instructed (Pound's motives for writing them were clearly not primarily aesthetic). New Directions will therefore relegate both endings to an appendix in their next printing of the *Cantos.* I for one would have them stand by the far more beautiful and equally authentic Canto 120, which as the later idea should have more authority.[26]

Late in life Eliot remarked, as often before, that he owed Pound everything. He repaid the debt handsomely, first by using his editorial connections with the *Criterion* and Faber and Faber to publish Pound's work (Pound disapproved of both the magazine and the publishing house). In a letter of 4 October 1923, Eliot complained to John Quinn of how difficult it was to help Pound now that their roles were reversed: "Apart from the fact that he is very sensitive and proud and that I have to keep an attitude of discipleship (as indeed I ought) every time I print anything of his it nearly sinks the paper."[27]

Furthermore, after Pound's arrest for treason and his commitment to the Washington, D.C., mental hospital St. Elizabeths, Eliot, according to Pound's lawyer, was "the most faithful and concerned" of Pound's friends.[28] Eliot worked out business trips to the United States so he could visit Pound yearly, even though he had to endure lectures attacking his religion and his publishing house. He persuaded the authorities to give Pound more comfortable quarters along with special privileges, and led the campaign to secure Pound's release and to have the treason charge dropped. In addition Tom, as Mrs. Eliot told me, did many things for Ezra that people do not know about. Eliot was on the Library of Congress committee that awarded Pound the Bollingen Poetry Prize of 1949 for the *Pisan Cantos,* in which Mussolini is conspicuously praised. The award raised a storm of controversy. If we had lost the war, we would not have forgiven Pound. But since we won, certain people could afford to understand that politics should not influence literary judgment.

Actually Pound was never so widely appreciated as during his years at St. Elizabeths (1945–58). It became the fashion for young writers to visit him there. He was by now a legendary figure, a survivor of that dwindling generation of early modernists who were already considered classics. Always on the lookout for disciples, Pound was surprisingly accessible; and the contrast between his fame, on the one hand, and his accessibility and pitiable incarceration, on the other, presented an example of the informality appropriate to a poet and of the poet's oppression by society. Thus Pound—like Coleridge when he lived during his last years under surveillance near London—exerted yet another round of influence on a new generation.

What about mutual influence between Pound and Eliot? The influence seems to run one way, from Pound to Eliot. The exception seems to be the confirmation Pound found in "Gerontion" and *The Waste Land* for the "mythical method" that he and Eliot discovered in the manuscripts and the *Little Review* serialization of Joyce's *Ulysses* (March 1918–December 1920). We are told that Pound wrote the *Cantos* with a copy of "Gerontion" and *Ulysses* on his table. Nevertheless, Pound does not in the *Cantos* use the "mythical method" as it is described by Eliot in his review of *Ulysses* (quoted above, 114) and as we find it in *Ulysses* and *The Waste Land.* Pound uses the "mythical method" when he injects modern language into ancient situations, as in his adaptations of the Chinese poets or of the Latin poet Propertius:

> And there was a case in Colchis, Jason and that
>   woman in Colchis;

And besides, Lynceus,
                    you were drunk.

                              (*Homage to Sextus Propertius*, poem 12)

But in the *Cantos* Pound mainly lays historical periods side by side; he
does not fuse antiquity and modernity as they are fused in the Stetson
passage of *The Waste Land* (pt. 1), where the same words describe an
ordinary conversation about gardening between two modern Englishmen
and the mutual recognition between two Phoenician sailors who fought
with Carthage against Rome. In the same way, the splendid metamorphoses in the *Cantos* are epiphanies in the Greek sense—manifestations
of gods in ancient situations (as for example the epiphany of Dionysus
in Canto 2). They are not Joycean epiphanies in that they do not transform commonplace modern situations.

Pound's editing of *The Waste Land* manuscripts is the most famous
example of his influence on Eliot. Pound cut out three long narrative
passages leading, but with a big leap, to the intense lyrical passages that
remain. In other words, Pound changed *The Waste Land* from a poem
mixing passages of low and high intensity to a poem of continuously
high lyric intensity. "The test of a writer," he said in a letter of 1915, "is
his ability for . . . concentration AND for his power to stay concentrated
till he gets to the end of his poem, whether it is two lines or two hundred"
(49). Pound wanted the long poem to yield the same high intensity as the
short poem. Eliot, instead, was working toward a different theory, one
which would permit him to write verse drama. "In a poem of any
length," he said in 1942,

> there must be transitions between passages of greater and less intensity, to
> give a rhythm of fluctuating emotion essential to the musical structure of
> the whole; . . . no poet can write a poem of amplitude unless he is a mas-
> ter of the prosaic.[29]

Eliot uses deliberately prosaic passages even in a nondramatic poem
like *Four Quartets*. Pound had no use for drama, and appreciated only
the lyric effect—which is why he cut *The Waste Land* down in size, and
why in the *Cantos* he uses a sequence of only moderately long poems.
Even the cantos that quote prose letters are, I think, intended to give a
lyric effect through presentation of the prose in fragments intended to set
up poetic vibrations.

Pound turned *The Waste Land* into a Poundian poem of juxtaposed
images, of those jumps and disconnections that he called his "ideogrammic method" as an acknowledgment of his debt to Fenollosa's essay

"The Chinese Written Character as a Medium for Poetry." Fenollosa, who argues that ideograms give Chinese poetry an imagistic concreteness, merely confirmed a method that grew out of Imagism which in turn grew out of the nineteenth-century romantic replacement of rhetoric by immediate sensuous presentation.

Although Pound made *The Waste Land* incoherent in one sense, he insisted on its unity in another sense at a time when Eliot thought of *The Waste Land* as a sequence of poems. He would not let Eliot publish it in magazines in installments, but insisted that it be printed all together. When Eliot in a 1922 letter suggested omitting the beautiful lyric on Phlebas's drowning, since Pound had cut the rest of part 4 when he cut out the narrative about a shipwreck leading to the lyric, Pound replied from Paris: "I DO advise keeping Phlebas. In fact I more'n advise. Phlebas is an integral part of the poem; the card pack introduces him, the drowned phoen[ician] sailor" (171). Pound understood, better than Eliot at that point, the replacement of narrative continuity by continuity of the mythical pattern. How sad that in an earlier letter in which he organizes Eliot's poem for him, he speaks of "never getting an outline" for "my deformative secretions," the *Cantos* (169).

Nevertheless Pound's influence on Eliot was not fundamental; for Eliot had already arrived at his own style in "Prufrock," written during 1910–12, well before he met Pound. "Prufrock" is full of jumps and disconnections:

> Shall I say, I have gone at dusk through narrow streets
> And watched the smoke that rises from the pipes
> Of lonely men in shirt-sleeves, leaning out of windows? . . .
>
> I should have been a pair of ragged claws
> Scuttling across the floors of silent seas.
>
> And the afternoon, the evening, sleeps so peacefully!

Where did Eliot get this style, since it is not in his principal influences at the time—the late-nineteenth-century French poet Laforgue and the seventeenth-century English Metaphysical poets (Laforguian and Metaphysical poems move logically, even if the logic is ingeniously stretched). Eliot, I think, got the style of jumps and disconnections from the same source as Pound, from the romantic poetic tradition. Both poets got the style from poems like Wordsworth's "Tintern Abbey," Coleridge's "Frost at Midnight" and Keats's "Ode to a Nightingale," which move by leaps of psychological association. The poetry, Browning wrote to Ruskin in answer to his charge of obscurity, lies in the leaps. Browning asks

us to make formidable leaps between stanzas in "By the Fireside," as
does Yeats in the great poems beginning with his middle period, in
"Among School Children," for example. The poetry of jumps between
what Pound called "luminous details" derives from the romantic epiphanic mode discussed above. Pound tried to write the first long poem
which would employ not narrative but conjunctions of "luminous
details." [30]

Pound and Eliot collaborated most closely between 1917 and 1920,
when they were determined to improve their poetry through a discipline
that would check the sloppiness free verse was falling into. Pound suggested as model Gautier's strict tetrameter quatrains in *Émaux et Ca-
mées,* and Eliot suggested adding Laforgue's satirical rhyming. The experiment resulted in Eliot's *Poems, 1920* and Pound's *Hugh Selwyn
Mauberley* (1920), volumes in which both poets use Gautier's straitjacket
in order to break out of it. Eliot breaks out through the ruggedness of
satire:

> Apeneck Sweeney spreads his knees
> Letting his arms hang down to laugh,
> The zebra stripes along his jaw
> Swelling to maculate giraffe

and through subject matter. In the last two stanzas of this poem,
"Sweeney Among the Nightingales," he makes the little quatrain express
Frazer's gigantic scheme in *The Golden Bough,* the scheme used in *The
Waste Land,* by assimilating the failed plot against Sweeney to the murder of Agamemnon as type of the murders in the sacred wood at Nemi
of god-kings ("The Convent of the Sacred Heart" includes in the scheme
the sacrifice of Christ) in order to renew the fertility of the land:

> The nightingales are singing near
> The Convent of the Sacred Heart,
>
>   And sang within the bloody wood
> When Agamemnon cried aloud,
> And let their liquid siftings fall
> To stain the stiff dishonoured shroud.

In all his quatrain poems, Eliot adheres to Gautier's meter; but he
modifies, except in one poem, the rhyme scheme from *abab* to *abcb.*
Pound, instead, in poem 1 of *Mauberley* immediately plays a syncopated
variation of the iambic, thus moving toward free verse while, as I hear
it, trying to maintain Gautier's tetrameters:

For thŕee yeárs, out of kéy with his tiḿe,
He stróve to resúscitáte the dead aŕt
Of póetry;

The need to forego, in order to maintain the tetrameter, the expected
accent on "dead" creates an exciting syncopated pause between "art"
and "Of." All hell breaks loose in the transition from the fourth line to
the first line of the next stanza:

Of póetry; to máintáin "the subliḿe"
In the óld sénse. Wŕong from the stárt—

Nó, hárdly.

The iambic tetrameter is almost abandoned with the long pause and syn-
tactical ellipsis between "start" and "No," and with the sequence of three
accented syllables. It is only a step to the syncopated free verse of poem
4 on the war:

These fóught ‖ in any cáse,
and sóme ‖ beliéving,
pro dómo, ‖ in any cáse . . .

In poem 5, also on the war, Pound returns to quatrains, but they are
unrhymed and the tetrameter is only approximated; the second quatrain
is separated into two-line units. In the poems that follow, the quatrain is
more or less maintained but with *abcb* and other variations, with vari-
able meters, and with sometimes a longer stanza.

Pound shows himself a subtler metrist than Eliot. Both poets achieve
triumphs of diction in these volumes. Most spectacular is Pound's line
"walked eye-deep in hell" (poem 4) about soldiers in the trenches. Best
of all is his line about the war dead, "Quick eyes gone under earth's lid"
(poem 5), where the combination of motion with stasis produces a noble
serenity worthy of Homer.

Pound's most sustained triumph of diction is *Cathay* (1915, reprinted in *Personae*), his translations of classic Chinese poetry. Hugh
Kenner in *The Pound Era* says that *Cathay* is about World War I, and he
is right in that the volume contains several poems about ancient Chinese
wars which are treated antiheroically—"Our mind is full of sorrow, who
will know of our grief?" ("Song of the Bowmen of Shu")—in the manner
of literature about World War I. Even more important, Pound perfects in
these translations the modernist style of the war and immediate postwar
years, the style we associate with early Hemingway. Eliot wrote in 1919

that the style of *Cathay* "owes nothing to the Chinese inspiration; it is a development—in fact, the development—of Mr. Pound's style.[31]

The style of *Cathay* is plaintively modern in its understatement, its avoidance of general or value-laden words, its reliance on concrete details but with the poignant admission that the speaker has no ordering principle by which to indicate that one detail is more important than another. Emotions are not named, they are projected through objective correlatives. All this is illustrated in my favorite poem of the volume, "The River-Merchant's Wife: A Letter," in which the wife expresses her sorrow over her husband's long absence:

> The leaves fall early this autumn, in wind.
> The paired butterflies are already yellow with August
> Over the grass in the West garden;
> They hurt me. I grow older.

The poem ends:

> If you are coming down through the narrows of the river Kiang,
> Please let me know beforehand,
> And I will come out to meet you
>   As far as Chō-fū-Sa.

That last line is the key to the poem's style in that the detail is exquisitely precise and yet, for us who do not know where Chō-fū-Sa is, irrelevant; so that the line vibrates.

Eliot does not in his prewar poems employ this style, except in the question of the blank young man in "Portrait of a Lady": "Are these ideas right or wrong?" But the style comes to fruition in *The Waste Land*—in the plaintive opening, "April is the cruellest month," in the snatches of conversation that follow, "In the mountains, there you feel free. / I read, much of the night, and go south in the winter" (1.17–18), in the lament of the seduced girl in part 3, "I can connect / Nothing with nothing" (ll. 301–2), and in the desperate question addressed to the protagonist by the neurotic lady of part 2:

>   "Do
> "You know nothing? Do you see nothing? Do you remember
> "Nothing?"
>   (Ll. 121–23)

Cathay may have helped Eliot develop the war and postwar style.

As for influence from Eliot to Pound, Pound in a letter of 21 August

1917 wrote of *Three Cantos* just after their first publication in *Poetry* (June, July, August 1917): "Eliot is the only person who proffered criticism instead of general objection" (115). But looking back in 1939, Pound wrote: "I have had five, and only five, useful criticisms of my writing in my lifetime, one from Yeats, one from Bridges, one from Thomas Hardy, a recent one from a Roman Archbishop and one from Ford." [32] Eliot is conspicuously absent from the list.

Perhaps the best proofs of mutual influence are the echoes of each other in their writing. Here are a few examples. The opening line of Canto 8 (1925), "These fragments you have shelved (shored)" (28), echoes *The Waste Land* (1922), "These fragments I have shored against my ruins" (5.430). The lines in Eliot's "Journey of the Magi" (1927) "A hard time we had of it" and "The summer palaces on slopes, the terraces, / And the silken girls bringing sherbet" echo Pound's lines in "Exile's Letter" (*Cathay*, 1915): "And what with broken wheels and so on, I won't say it wasn't hard going / . . . And the vermilioned girls getting drunk about sunset." In Canto 20 (1928), the line "Give! What were they given?" (94) echoes *The Waste Land* (1922), "*Datta* [Give]: what have we given?" (5.400). The lines in Canto 7,

> And the old voice lifts itself
>   weaving an endless sentence.
> We also made ghostly visits, and the stair
> That knew us, found us again on the turn of it,
> Knocking at empty rooms, seeking for buried beauty
>
>   (24–25)

sound like "Gerontion," the utterance of an old man, in the lines where the old man says that what were once religious rituals have been taken over by aesthetes and occultists: by Mr. Silvero, caressing porcelain, "Who walked all night in the next room," and

> By Madame de Tornquist, in the dark room
> Shifting the candles; Fräulein von Kulp
> Who burned in the hall, one hand on the door.
>   Vacant shuttles
> Weave the wind. I have no ghosts.

"Gerontion" was written in May–June 1919; Canto 7 was written in November–December 1919; Ronald Bush, in *The Genesis of Ezra Pound's Cantos*, speaks of Pound's debt in Canto 7 to "Gerontion," citing different lines than I do. [33] A sentence in Eliot's famous passage on "dissociation of sensibility" in "The Metaphysical Poets" (1921) resembles a

sentence in Pound's essay "Cavalcanti" (1934). "The difference," Eliot
says, between Tennyson and Browning, on the one hand, and Donne, on
the other, "is not a simple difference of degree between poets. It is something which had happened to the mind of England." Pound writes: "The
difference between Guido [Cavalcanti] and Petrarch is not a mere difference of degree, it is a difference in kind"—the context suggests that the
difference is something which had happened to the mind of Europe.[34] We
cannot be sure who echoes whom, because "Cavalcanti" was written
between 1910 and 1931 and the two poets read each other's work in
manuscript.

Where then do the two poets stand in relation to each other now? Eliot
seems to rate higher than Pound among academics (he is certainly taught
more than Pound), for Eliot's oeuvre is complete and consistent, displaying an easily discernible line of development. His output is remarkably
small but remarkably even. Although his verse ranges from the nonsense
of *Old Possum's Book of Practical Cats* (Eliot would have enjoyed its
success as a musical comedy since he always wanted to make it in the
commercial theater), through plays designed to hold the stage, to the
solemnity of *Four Quartets;* although Eliot worked in so many genres,
his work in each is distinguished in its own kind. Pound, instead, wanted
poetry to be always at the highest pitch; so when a poem falls short, it
seems a failure.

Eliot established himself as the most authoritative critic of his time,
and there is for the academic mind a satisfying consistency between his
criticism and his verse. The great early essays, "Tradition and the Individual Talent," with its argument for a learned, impersonal poetry;
"Hamlet," with its imagist theory of the "objective correlative" for emotion; and "The Metaphysical Poets," with its praise of a witty poetry that
does not dissociate sensibility from thought—these essays account for
his early triumphs in poetry, for "Prufrock," "Portrait of a Lady," "Gerontion," *The Waste Land.* When with his conversion Eliot changed poetic
style, he wrote the essays on Dante (1929) and Lancelot Andrewes
(1926) to explain the change from an imagist poetry of jumps and disconnections to a poetry of vision and statement as in *Ash Wednesday,*
"Journey of the Magi," and *Four Quartets.*

Eliot stands even higher in the English academy than in ours, because as an outsider who enthusiastically embraced English citizenship,
religion, literature, and gentlemanliness, he renewed for the English their
faltering confidence in their own institutions. American academics are
more restless, since there are those who claim Eliot's niche for Wallace
Stevens or William Carlos Williams.

More than Eliot, Pound seems to appeal to poets, especially young poets now. Eliot's oeuvre arrives too signed, buttoned up, and delivered; it leaves no point of entry for young poets. Pound, who was remarkably prolific and remarkably uneven, offers young poets fruitful starting points as they mine the *Cantos* for passages of great poetry that appeal to them. Pound's obscurity enables them to take over a style, a cadence, a kind of music and pour into it their own ideas and feelings. Poets can for their own purposes ignore Pound's fascism and anti-Semitism, but the rest of us should take them into account in evaluating Pound's work because their virulent expression is intellectually disreputable. A well-known contemporary poet, Charles Wright, told me that he picked up a copy of the *Cantos* while a soldier in Italy just after World War II, that he did not understand them but that the rapturous experience of reading them made him want to be a poet. He also said that Pound's criticism provides practical tips for writing that a young poet can find nowhere else.

Pound's published criticism never achieved the authority of Eliot's, because it is often undisciplined in thought and style, and personal to the point of quirkiness. But he was as influential as Eliot if we take into account his conversations and correspondence with other writers, his editing of their manuscripts, and his choice of works to be published in the magazines that employed him. (His letters, humorous and full of pregnant insights, are a delight to read.) Both critics did the important job of revising the literary canon, but Eliot's revisions have been more influential since few readers know enough foreign languages to follow Pound's recommendations.

One might argue that, despite his unevenness, Pound was so prolific that he actually wrote more lines of great verse than did Eliot with his small output. Certainly Eliot never wrote lines so free-flowing musically as these from Canto 20:

> Sandro, and Boccata, and Jacopo Sellaio;
> The ranunculae, and almond,
> Boughs set in espalier,
> Duccio, Agostino; *e l'olors*—
> The smell of that place—
>
> (90)

or these from the first Pisan canto:

> yet say this to the Possum; a bang, not a whimper,
>   with a bang not a whimper,
> To build the city of Dioce whose terraces are the colour of stars.

The suave eyes, quiet, not scornful,
                    rain also is of the process.
What you depart from is not the way
and olive tree blown white in the wind
washed in the Kiang and Han
what whiteness will you add to this whiteness,
                    what candor?

                                        (425)

One almost feels that the obscurity is necessary, that meaning would weigh down the words. Yet the obscurity is annoying in those places where the verse is less successful. And the lines preceding the above Pisan canto passage extol the heroic death of Mussolini, "the twice crucified" (425), so that content again becomes an issue.

Even if we cannot, because of Pound's deficiency in the *Cantos* of valid content, communicativeness, and organizational ability, even if we cannot all agree to call him the greatest English-speaking poet of the first half of the twentieth century (I myself place Eliot above him and Yeats above them both), we can, I think, all agree that he is the greatest single *personal* force in the poetry of that time.

Notes
Index

Notes

FREUD AND SOCIOBIOLOGY

1 Ernest Jones, *The Life and Work of Sigmund Freud*, 3 vols. (New York, 1953, 1955, 1957), 3:302–4.
2 Frank J. Sulloway, *Freud, Biologist of the Mind* (New York, 1979), p. 5.
3 Edward O. Wilson, *Sociobiology: The New Synthesis* (Cambridge, Mass., and London, 1975), p. 4.
4 Stephen Jay Gould, "Cardboard Darwinism," *New York Review of Books*, 25 September 1986, pp. 47, 48, 50.
5 Marshall Sahlins, *The Use and Abuse of Biology: An Anthropological Critique of Sociobiology* (Ann Arbor, Mich., 1977), pp. 7–8.
6 Sigmund Freud, *The Standard Edition of the Complete Psychological Works*, translated under the general editorship of James Strachey, 14 vols. (London, 1978), 7:242.
7 Lionel Trilling, *The Liberal Imagination* (New York, 1950), p. 52.
8 William J. McGrath, *Freud's Discovery of Psychoanalysis: The Politics of Hysteria* (Ithaca and London, 1986), p. 23.
9 Ronald W. Clark, *Freud: The Man and the Cause* (New York, 1980), pp. 208, 424.
10 *The Complete Letters of Sigmund Freud to Wilhelm Fliess, 1887–1904*, translated and edited by Jeffrey Moussaieff Masson (Cambridge, Mass., and London, 1985), 31 October 1895, p. 147.
11 Charles Darwin and Alfred Russel Wallace, *Evolution by Natural Selection* (Cambridge, 1958), p. 277.

CAN WE STILL TALK ABOUT THE ROMANTIC SELF?

1 Samuel Beckett, *The Unnamable, Three Novels* (New York, 1965), p. 386.
2 Michel Foucault, "What Is an Author?" in *Textual Strategies: Perspectives in Post-Structuralist Criticism*, ed. Josué V. Harari (Ithaca, N.Y., 1979), p. 160.

3 Martin Heidegger, "The Origin of the Work of Art," *Basic Writings*, ed. David Farrell Krell (New York, 1977), p. 149.

4 David Hume, *A Treatise of Human Nature*, ed. L. A. Selby-Bigge (Oxford, 1965), Bk. 1, Pt. 4, Sec. 6, pp. 251–52.

5 Paul de Man, "The Rhetoric of Temporality," *Blindness and Insight: Essays in the Rhetoric of Contemporary Criticism*, 2d ed. rev. (Minneapolis, 1983), p. 220.

6 William Wordsworth, *Selected Poems and Prefaces*, ed. Jack Stillinger (Boston, 1965), lines 27–29.

7 Lord Byron, *Manfred* (III.iv. 129–32), *The Complete Poetical Works*, ed. Jerome J. McGann, Vol. 4 (Oxford, 1986).

8 Martin Heidegger, "Language," *Poetry, Language, Thought*, trans. with introductions by Albert Hofstadter (New York, 1975), p. 192.

9 Michel Foucault, *The Order of Things: An Archeology of the Human Sciences*, trans. of *Les mots et les choses* (New York, 1973), p. xxiii. The same statement, in a slightly different translation, appears as an epigraph to Jacques Derrida's "The Ends of Man," *Margins of Philosophy*, trans. Alan Bass (Chicago, 1982), p. 111. The quotation follows quotations from Kant and Sartre in order to show the contrast between their humanism and Foucault's antihumanism.

10 Paul de Man, "Shelley Disfigured," in Harold Bloom, Paul de Man, Jacques Derrida, Geoffrey H. Hartman, J. Hillis Miller, *Deconstruction and Criticism* (New York, 1979), p. 61.

11 S. T. Coleridge, "The Statesman's Manual," *Lay Sermons*, ed. R. J. White, *Collected Works*, Bollingen Series 75 (London and Princeton, 1972), p. 30.

12 S. T. Coleridge, "Dejection: An Ode," *Poems*, ed. E. H. Coleridge (London, 1945), lines 53–55.

13 Geoffrey H. Hartman, *Wordsworth's Poetry 1787–1814* (New Haven and London, 1964), pp. 136–37.

THE EPIPHANIC MODE IN WORDSWORTH AND MODERN LITERATURE

1 William Hazlitt, *Lectures on the English Poets and The Spirit of the Age* (London and New York, 1963), pp. 252–53. My italics.

2 Quoted in Richard Ellmann, *James Joyce* (New York, 1965), p. 169.

3 James Joyce, *A Portrait of the Artist as a Young Man* (New York, 1963), p. 221.

4 James Joyce, *Stephen Hero* (Norfolk, Conn., 1963), p. 211.

5 James Joyce, *Ulysses*, new edition, corrected (New York, 1961), p. 40.

6 *The Workshop of Daedalus*, ed. Robert Scholes and Richard M. Kain (Evanston, Ill., 1965), p. 4.

7 James Joyce, *Dubliners* (New York, 1954), p. 288. My italics.

8 Ralph Waldo Emerson, *Selections*, ed. Stephen E. Whicher (Boston, 1960), p. 90.

9 Ezra Pound, "A Retrospect," *Literary Essays*, edited with an introduction by T. S. Eliot (New York, 1968), p. 4; *Selected Letters, 1907–1941*, ed. D. D. Paige (New York, 1971), 11 April 1927, p. 210.

10 Wallace Stevens, *Collected Poems* (New York, 1961).

11 Quoted in Morris Beja, *Epiphany in the Modern Novel* (Seattle, 1971), pp. 17–19.

12 See Browning's letter to Ruskin, answering Ruskin's charge of obscurity (10 December 1855). Quoted in W. G. Collingwood, *The Life of John Ruskin* (Boston and New York, 1902), pp. 164–65.

13 Unless otherwise specified, verse, prose and notes are quoted from William Wordsworth, *Selected Poems and Prefaces*, ed. Jack Stillinger (Boston, 1965).

14 Joseph Frank, "Spatial Form in Modern Literature," *The Widening Gyre* (New Brunswick, N.J., 1963), pp. 13, 18–19; "Spatial Form: Some Further Reflections," *Critical Inquiry*, 5 (Winter 1978), 284.

15 To Stanislaus Joyce, 11 June 1905, *Selected Letters of James Joyce*, ed. Richard Ellmann (New York, 1975), p. 63.

16 Virginia Woolf, *To the Lighthouse* (New York, 1955), pp. 99–100, 158, 240, 264, 271, 310, 158.

17 See Stephen Parrish, "'The Thorn': Wordsworth's Dramatic Monologue," in *Wordsworth: A Collection of Critical Essays*, ed. M. H. Abrams (Englewood Cliffs, N.J., 1972).

18 William Wordsworth, *Poetical Works*, ed. E. de Selincourt, 5 vols. (Oxford, 1940), 1:61, 63. I quote the 1849 revised text because it makes even sharper the contrast between description and epiphany.

19 Georges Poulet, *Studies in Human Time*, trans. Elliot Coleman (Baltimore, 1965), pp. 23–24, 29–30.

20 Thomas De Quincey, *Recollections of the Lakes and the Lake Poets* (Harmondsworth, 1970), pp. 160–61.

21 See Longinus *On the Sublime* and Edmund Burke, *A Philosophical Enquiry into the Origin of Our Ideas of the Sublime and Beautiful.*

22 William Wordsworth, ["The Sublime and the Beautiful"], *Prose Works*, ed. W. J. B. Owen and J. W. Smyser, 3 vols. (Oxford, 1974), 2:353–54.

23 Henri Bergson, *Essai sur les données immédiates de la conscience*, 11th ed. (Paris, 1912), p. 76. My translation.

24 To Benjamin Bailey, 22 November 1817, *The Letters of John Keats*, ed. Hyder E. Rollins, 2 vols. (Cambridge, Mass., 1958), 1:185. The "imaginative Mind may have its rewards in the repetition of its own silent Working coming continually on the spirit with a fine suddenness"—a precise description of the internal-external doubleness of epiphany.

25 T. S. Eliot, *Collected Poems* (London, 1963), lines 37–41. In this last edition he corrected, Eliot changed "Hyacinth" to "hyacinth," making the scene more realistic and thus more epiphanic. Quotations are from this edition.

WORDSWORTH'S LYRICAL CHARACTERIZATIONS

1 *Henry Moore on Sculpture*, ed. Philip James (New York, 1971), pp. 82, 285.

2 William Wordsworth, *The Prelude*, ed. Ernest de Selincourt, 2d ed. revised by H. Darbishire (Oxford, 1959), p. 624, lines 46–47. In this passage excised from Book 13 (1805 text), the "Borderer" is a horse standing still in moonlight, likened to an amphibian. The fluid line between species accounts for

Wordsworth's way of merging his human border figures with lower forms of existence both animate and inanimate.

3 *Journals of Dorothy Wordsworth,* ed. Mary Moorman (London and New York, 1971), p. 42. I have modernized the punctuation.

4 Unless otherwise specified, verse, prose, and notes are quoted from William Wordsworth, *Selected Poems and Prefaces,* ed. Jack Stillinger (Boston, 1965).

5 Wordsworth and Coleridge, *Lyrical Ballads,* the text of the 1798 edition with the additional 1800 poems and the Prefaces, ed. R. L. Brett and A. R. Jones (London, 1963), p. 271.

6 S. T. Coleridge, *Biographia Literaria,* ed. James Engell and W. Jackson Bate, Bollingen Series 75 (Princeton, 1983), Vol. 2, chap. 22, p. 135.

7 Daniel Albright, *Lyricality in English Literature* (Lincoln, Neb. and London, 1985), p. 40.

8 John F. Danby, *The Simple Wordsworth* (London, 1960), p. 55.

9 To John Wilson, 7 June 1802, *The Letters of William and Dorothy Wordsworth,* ed. E. de Selincourt, 2d ed., revised by Chester L. Shaver, 2 vols. (Oxford, 1967), 1:357.

10 William Wordsworth, *The Salisbury Plain Poems,* ed. Stephen Gill (Ithaca, 1975), p. 281.

11 See Beth Darlington, "Two Early Texts: *A Night-Piece* and *The Discharged Soldier,*" which analyzes and prints the early drafts of both poems, in *Bicentenary Wordsworth Studies,* ed. Jonathan Wordsworth and Beth Darlington (Ithaca and London, 1970).

12 T. S. Eliot, *Four Quartets, Complete Poems and Plays* (London, 1969), p. 196.

THE VICTORIAN IDEA OF CULTURE

1 Quoted in G. M. Young, *Victorian England: Portrait of an Age,* 2d ed. (New York, 1964), p. 87.

2 Sir Henry Taylor, *Philip van Artevelde, Works,* 5 vols. (London, 1883), 1:xiii.

3 W. B. Yeats, "The Tragic Generation," *Autobiography* (New York, 1971), p. 185.

4 Raymond Williams, *Culture and Society 1780–1950* (New York, 1958), p. 4.

5 John Stuart Mill, *On Bentham and Coleridge,* introduction by F. R. Leavis (New York, 1950), pp. 102, 131.

6 David P. Calleo traces Coleridge's historicism to the late-eighteenth-century German writer Herder—"the first to use the word 'culture' (*Kultur*) in its modern sense"—who "believed that each *Volk* possesses its own individual forms of genius. Who can say, Herder argued, that one culture or one age is better than another?" (*Coleridge and the Idea of the Modern State,* New Haven and London, 1966, p. 51). Herder was anticipated by Vico's little known *Scienza nuova* (1744), which Michelet discovered and began translating in 1824, and which Coleridge began reading in Italian in 1825. To show the effect of the new historicism, Jacques Barzun compares Voltaire's choice as historian of "four periods of civilization as alone worthy of record" with the

German historian Ranke's nineteenth-century dictum that "all periods are immediately before God and equal in His sight" (Barzun, "Cultural History as Synthesis," in *The Varieties of History,* ed. Fritz Stern (New York, 1956, p. 401).

7 Edmund Burke, "Appeal from the New to the Old Whigs," *Works,* rev. ed., 12 vols. (Boston, 1865–67), 4:176.

8 Quoted in Williams, *Culture and Society,* p. 62.

9 T. S. Eliot, *Notes towards the Definition of Culture* (London, 1948), p. 107.

10 Matthew Arnold, "The Function of Criticism at the Present Time," *Complete Prose Works,* ed. R. H. Super, 11 vols. (Ann Arbor, Mich., 1962), 3:261.

11 See Phyllis Rose's feminist *Parallel Lives: Five Victorian Marriages* (New York, 1983) and Gertrude Himmelfarb's critique of Rose in the title essay of *Marriage and Morals among the Victorians* (New York, 1986). The most ambitious project is Peter Gay's multivolume study of nineteenth-century middle-class sexuality, *The Bourgeois Experience: Victoria to Freud,* of which two volumes have so far appeared: 1, *Education of the Senses;* 2, *The Tender Passion* (New York, 1984, 1986).

12 S. T. Coleridge, *A Lay Sermon, Lay Sermons,* ed. R. J. White, Bollingen Series 75 (London and Princeton, 1972), pp. 206–7, 126.

13 Burke quoted in Arnold, *Prose Works,* 3:267.

14 John Holloway, *The Victorian Sage* (New York, 1965), pp. 10–12.

Is guido saved?

1 Robert Browning, *The Ring and the Book, Works,* Centenary Edition, introductions by F. G. Kenyon, 10 vols. (London, 1912), Vols. 5–6. I am quoting this edition because it uses Browning's 1888–89 revision, which I find a distinct improvement over the first edition used by Richard D. Altick in the Penguin, Yale *The Ring and the Book* (1971, 1981).

2 Roy Gridley, "Browning's Two Guidos," *University of Toronto Quarterly,* 37 (1967), 51–68.

3 Morse Peckham, instead, ignoring what Browning tells us in Book 1, considers Guido's second monologue no less strategic than the first: "When this does not work he presents himself as a wolf." His final cry to Pompilia is a collapse into nothingness (*Victorian Revolutionaries,* New York, 1970, pp. 93–94).

4 Jacques Lacan, *Speech and Language in Psychoanalysis,* trans. Anthony Wilden (Baltimore and London, 1981), pp. 9–10.

5 Bernard Brugière, "Guido dans *The Ring and the Book* de Robert Browning," *Études Anglaises,* 21:1 (1968), 27, 34. The phrase Brugière quotes is not in "Rabbi Ben Ezra," but the idea is there. "A Bean-Stripe" would be enough to prove my case if we could assume that Browning's 1884 statement of his philosophy of evil applies to his earlier work.

6 *Robert Browning and Julia Wedgwood: A Broken Friendship as Revealed by Their Letters,* ed. Richard Curle (New York, 1937), pp. 144–45, 149–51, 153–54.

7 William Allingham, *A Diary*, ed. H. Allingham and D. Radford (London, 1908), p. 195.

8 *Curious Annals: New Documents Relating to Browning's Roman Murder Story*, translated, edited, introduction by Beatrice Corrigan (Toronto, 1956), p. 93.

9 Browning's letter of 20 February 1883, quoted in Frederick James Furnivall, *A Volume of Personal Record* (London, 1911), pp. lxx–lxxi. The Secondary Source—a contemporary manuscript pamphlet, "The Death of the Wife-Murderer Guido Franceschini, By Beheading"—is translated by Charles W. Hodell and included in his edition of *The Old Yellow Book* (Washington, D.C., 1908), pp. 207–13. For the manuscript letters, including the one by de Archangelis that Browning showed Allingham, see pp. 190–91.

BROWNING AND THE QUESTION OF MYTH

1 See W. B. Yeats, "The Philosophy of Shelley's Poetry," *Essays and Introductions* (New York, 1961).

2 Robert Browning, ["Essay on Shelley"], *The Poems*, 2 vols., ed. John Pettigrew, supplemented and completed by Thomas J. Collins (New Haven and London, 1981), 1:1012. Verse will be quoted from this edition based on the 1888–89 revised text.

3 *The Letters of Robert Browning and Elizabeth Barrett Browning 1845–1846*, ed. Elvan Kintner, 2 vols. (Cambridge, Mass., 1969), 20 March 1845, 1:43.

4 All this has been made abundantly clear by W. C. DeVane in his excellent essay "Browning and the Spirit of Greece," *Nineteenth Century Studies*, ed. Herbert Davis et al. (Ithaca, 1940), as well as in his *Browning's Parleyings* (New Haven, 1927), and his *Browning Handbook*, 2d ed. (New York, 1955).

5 *Letters R.B.–E.B.B.*, 13 January 1845, 1:7.

6 See, for example, Kerényi's "Prolegomena," in C. G. Jung and C. Kerényi, *Essays on a Science of Mythology*, trans. R. F. C. Hull, rev. ed., (New York and Evanston, 1963).

7 See DeVane, "Browning and the Spirit of Greece," pp. 485–90.

8 Hence Joyce's interest in Vico's cyclical theory of history. In commenting on Vico's cyclical theory, Yeats writes: "though history is too short to change either the idea of progress or the eternal circuit into scientific fact, the eternal circuit may best suit our preoccupation with the soul's salvation, our individualism, our solitude. Besides we love antiquity, and that other idea—progress—the sole religious myth of modern man, is only two hundred years old" (introduction to "The Words upon the Window-Pane," *Explorations*, London, 1962, p. 355).

9 Park Honan, *Browning's Characters* (New Haven, 1961), p. 37. J. Hillis Miller, *The Disappearance of God* (New York, 1965), p. 90.

10 Quoted in W. G. Collingwood, *The Life of John Ruskin* (Boston and New York, 1902), pp. 164–65.

11 A. C. Swinburne, *George Chapman* (London, 1875), pp. 16–17. For a de-

tailed analysis of associationism and speed in Browning, see Robert Preyer, "Two Styles in the Verse of Robert Browning," ELH, 32 (March 1965).

12 See Blake's poem "With happiness stretched across the hills," in his letter to Thomas Butts (22 November 1802).

13 S. T. Coleridge, "The Statesman's Manual," *Lay Sermons,* ed. R. J. White, *Collected Works,* Bollingen Series 75 (London and Princeton, 1972), p. 30. Roma A. King, Jr. derives from the Prometheus passage the title of his book *The Focusing Artifice* (Athens, Ohio, 1968); see chap. 7 on the *Parleyings.*

14 Kenneth Clark, *The Nude: A Study in Ideal Form* (New York, 1956), p. 370.

15 To Dr. F. J. Furnivall, 11 October 1881, *Letters of Robert Browning,* collected by T. J. Wise, ed. T. L. Hood (New Haven, 1933), p. 200. Browning's argument would be stronger had he not confused Darwinian theory with the Lamarckian, which actually does find intelligence in the evolutionary process.

16 William Blake, *The Marriage of Heaven and Hell,* "Proverbs of Hell."

17 To Lady Elizabeth Pelham, 4 January 1939, *The Letters of W. B. Yeats,* ed. Allen Wade (London, 1954), p. 922.

18 T. S. Eliot's introduction to Ezra Pound, *Selected Poems* (London, 1935), p. xiii.

19 Douglas Bush, *Mythology and the Romantic Tradition* (Cambridge, Mass., 1937), pp. 365–66.

A NEW LOOK AT E. M. FORSTER

1 Quoted by Oliver Stallybrass, introduction to E. M. Forster, *The Life to Come and Other Short Stories* (New York, 1976), p. xvii.

2 E. M. Forster, *Where Angels Fear to Tread* (New York, 1920), pp. 19, 26.

3 E. M. Forster, *Abinger Harvest* (New York, 1936), pp. 5, 8.

4 P. N. Furbank, *E. M. Forster: A Life* (New York and London, 1977), p. 30.

5 E. M. Forster, *Aspects of the Novel* (New York, 1954), p. 126.

6 Interview in *Paris Review,* 1 (Spring 1953), 39–40. Of Jane Austen: "I was more ambitious than she was, of course. I tried to hitch it [the humor] on to other things." Of Proust: "He gave me as much of the modern way as I could take. I couldn't read Freud or Jung myself; it had to be filtered to me."

7 Wilfred Stone, *The Cave and the Mountain: A Study of E. M. Forster* (Stanford, 1966), p. 216.

8 E. M. Forster, *The Longest Journey* (Norfolk, Conn., 1922), pp. 318, 312, 319.

9 Lionel Trilling, *E. M. Forster* (Norfolk, Conn., 1943), p. 124.

10 E. M. Forster, *Howards End* (New York, 1954), p. 24.

11 Frederick Crews, *E. M. Forster: The Perils of Humanism* (Princeton, 1962), p. 30.

12 E. M. Forster, *Goldsworth Lowes Dickinson* (London, 1934), p. 116.

13 E. M. Forster, *Two Cheers for Democracy* (Harmondsworth, 1965), p. 79.

14 G. K. Das, "*A Passage to India:* A Socio-Historical Study," in *A Passage to*

India: Essays in Interpretation, ed. John Beer (Basingstoke and London, 1985), p. 1.

15 E. M. Forster, *A Passage to India* (New York, 1924), pp. 69, 114, 123–24.

16 Gillian Beer, "Negation in *A Passage to India,*" in *A Passage to India: Essays in Interpretation,* pp. 45, 52, 58.

17 W. B. Yeats, *A Vision* (New York, 1961), p. 25.

18 W. B. Yeats, "The Unicorn from the Stars," *Collected Plays,* new ed. (New York, 1962), p. 245.

THE IMPORTANCE OF TRILLING'S *The Liberal Imagination*

1 Lionel Trilling, *The Liberal Imagination: Essays on Literature and Society* (New York and London, 1950), p. xv.

2 *The Works of Lionel Trilling,* Uniform Edition, 12 vols. (New York and London, 1978–80). Books on Trilling: Robert Boyers, *Lionel Trilling: Negative Capability and the Wisdom of Avoidance* (Columbia, Mo., and London, 1977); William M. Chace, *Lionel Trilling: Criticism and Politics* (Stanford, 1980); Edward J. Shoben, Jr., *Lionel Trilling: Mind and Character* (New York, 1981); Mark Krupnick, *Lionel Trilling and the Fate of Cultural Criticism* (Evanston, 1986).

3 Lionel Trilling, introduction to the 1975 reissue of his novel *The Middle of the Journey* (1947) about his break with communism; the introduction is reprinted in the *New York Review of Books,* 17 April 1975.

4 Lionel Trilling, "T. S. Eliot's Politics," *Partisan Review* (September–October 1940), posthumously collected, *Speaking of Literature and Society,* ed. Diana Trilling, Uniform Edition (1980), p. 158.

5 Lionel Trilling, excerpts from notebooks, selected by Diana Trilling, *Partisan Review,* 51 (1984–85), 503, 505–6, 508–9.

6 Both the unfinished essay "Why We Read Jane Austen," and the lecture "Art, Will, and Necessity," are published in Lionel Trilling, *The Last Decade,* ed. Diana Trilling, Uniform Edition (1979). The published lecture omits the stirring conclusion I heard.

THE NEW NATURE POETRY

1 Wallace Stevens will be quoted from *Collected Poems* (New York, 1961).

2 Marianne Moore will be quoted from *Collected Poems* (New York, 1952).

3 John Ruskin, "Of the Pathetic Fallacy," *Modern Painters,* Vol. 3, pt. 4, chap. 12; in *Complete Works,* ed. E. T. Cook and A. Wedderburn, 39 vols. (London, 1903–12), 5:205–9.

4 Robert Frost will be quoted from *Complete Poems* (New York, 1949).

5 Reuben A. Brower, *The Poetry of Robert Frost* (New York, 1963), pp. 76–77, 93.

6 Richard Poirier, *Robert Frost: The Work of Knowing* (New York, 1977), p. 246.

7 Thomas Hardy, *Complete Poems,* ed. James Gibson (London and Basingstoke, 1978).

8 Reginald Cook, *The Dimensions of Robert Frost* (New York, 1958), p. 35. In *Connoisseurs of Chaos* (New York, 1965), Denis Donoghue derives Frost's ideas from the Social Darwinism that taught survival as the only relevant value (p. 182). Thus conviction reinforced temperamental *sabiduría*.

9 John Stuart Mill, *Autobiography* (New York, 1944), chap. 5, p. 105; Matthew Arnold, "Memorial Verses."

10 Dylan Thomas, *Collected Poems* (New York, 1957).

11 Theodore Roethke will be quoted from *Collected Poems* (New York, 1966).

12 D. H. Lawrence, *Complete Poems,* ed. Vivian de Sola Pinto and Warren Roberts (New York, 1971).

13 Ted Hughes, *New Selected Poems* (New York, 1982).

14 See Frank Kermode, *Wallace Stevens* (Edinburgh and London, 1967), pp. 35, 38. See also Donoghue's illuminating discussion of Stevens's aestheticism in *Connoisseurs of Chaos,* chap. 7.

15 Richard Wilbur, *Poems* (New York, 1963).

16 Richard Eberhart, *Collected Poems 1930–1960* (New York, 1960).

17 W. S. Merwin, *Green with Beasts* (1956), reprinted in *The First Four Books of Poems,* (New York, 1975).

MAILER'S NEW STYLE

1 *New York Times Book Review,* 17 September 1967, p. 4. See, for example, Granville Hicks in *Saturday Review,* 28 December 1968, p. 30.

2 Read at Modern Language Association; published in *Commentary,* March 1966, p. 39.

3 Norman Podhoretz, introduction to Norman Mailer, *Barbary Shore* (New York, 1963), pp. xi–xii.

4 Diana Trilling, "The Moral Radicalism of Norman Mailer," *Claremont Essays* (New York, 1964) p. 192.

5 Norman Mailer, *An American Dream* (New York, 1965), p. 5.

6 Tony Tanner, "On the Parapet," in *Modern Critical Views: Norman Mailer,* edited with an introduction by Harold Bloom (New York, 1986), p. 42.

7 Norman Mailer, "The White Negro," *Advertisements for Myself* (New York, 1960), p. 305.

8 Norman Mailer, *The Armies of the Night* (New York, 1968), pp. 47–48.

9 Norman Mailer, *Why Are We in Vietnam?* (New York, 1967), pp. 22, 8, 36–37.

10 Richard Poirier, *Norman Mailer* (New York, 1972), p. 139.

11 Norman Mailer, *Miami and the Siege of Chicago* (New York, 1968), pp. 90–91. See also *Armies of the Night,* p. 15.

POUND AND ELIOT

1 Quoted in Clive Bell, "Encounters with T. S. Eliot," *Old Friends: Personal Recollections* (New York, 1957), p. 120.

2 The quotation from Ezra Pound's typed letter to F. V. Morley, 17 December 1934 (Beinecke no. 1421), is published by permission of the Collection of

American Literature, Beinecke Rare Book and Manuscript Library, Yale University.

3 *The Selected Letters of Ezra Pound 1907–1941*, ed. D. D. Paige (New York, 1971), pp. 266, 277. See also Christina C. Stough, "The Literary Relationship of T. S. Eliot and Ezra Pound after *The Waste Land*," Ph.D. diss., University of Southern California, 1980.

4 Quoted in Donald Gallup, *T. S. Eliot and Ezra Pound: Collaborators in Letters* (New Haven, 1970), pp. 4, 9.

5 T. S. Eliot, "Ezra Pound," *Poetry* (September 1946); reprinted in *Ezra Pound: A Collection of Critical Essays*, ed. Walter Sutton (Englewood Cliffs, N.J., 1963), p. 18.

6 Lyndall Gordon, *Eliot's Early Years* (Oxford and New York, 1977), p. 67.

7 Noel Stock, *The Life of Ezra Pound*, expanded edition (San Francisco, 1982), pp. 246–47.

8 T. S. Eliot, "Ezra Pound: His Metric and Poetry," reprinted in Eliot's *To Criticize the Critic* (New York, 1965), pp. 165–68.

9 Ezra Pound's shorter poems will be quoted from *Personae: The Collected Shorter Poems* (New York, 1971).

10 T. S. Eliot, *Selected Essays*, new ed. (New York, 1950), p. 285.

11 Ezra Pound, *Selected Poems*, edited with introduction by T. S. Eliot (London, 1928), pp. xiii, xii.

12 Quoted in Stock, *Life of Pound*, p. 359.

13 Hugh Kenner, *The Pound Era* (Berkeley and Los Angeles, 1971), p. 408.

14 The interview, taped for Italian radio, is transcribed and translated by David Anderson in *Paideuma*, 10 (Autumn 1981), 333–42.

15 Ezra Pound, *The Cantos* (New York, 1981), pp. 229–30.

16 Ezra Pound, "Dante," *The Spirit of Romance* (1910; reprinted New York, 1968), p. 153.

17 Hugh Kenner sees here the beginning of the monetary theme in that gold is still "innocent stuff . . . ornamenting Aphrodite" (*Pound Era*, p. 425). If Kenner is right, this would be an example of fusion between the poetry and the monetary theme. But I wonder how many readers find the monetary theme here, even after having read Kenner.

18 T. S. Eliot, *After Strange Gods: A Primer of Modern Heresy* (New York, 1934), pp. 44–47.

19 T. S.Eliot's poems will be quoted from *Collected Poems 1909–1962* (London: Faber and Faber; New York: Harcourt Brace Jovanovich, 1963); copyright 1963 by Harcourt Brace Jovanovich, Inc.; copyright 1963, 1964 by T. S. Eliot. Reprinted by permission of the publishers.

20 See *"Ezra Pound Speaking": Radio Speeches of World War II*, ed. Leonard W. Doob (Westport, Conn., and London, 1978). In the broadcasts all anti-fascists are Jews, especially the British. Pound speaks of "the Anglo-Jew empire" (p. 4), and of Churchill's, Stalin's, and Roosevelt's "hebraicized governments" (p. 11).

21 T. S. Eliot, "Ezra Pound," reprinted in *Pound: Critical Essays*, ed. Sutton, p. 23.

22 F. R. Leavis, letter in *Times Literary Supplement*, 11 September 1970, p. 998.

23 Ezra Pound, "Credo," *Selected Prose 1909–1965* (New York, 1973), p. 53.

24 Ezra Pound, "For T.S.E.," in *Sewanee Review*, A Special Issue for T. S. Eliot (1888–1965), January–March 1966, p. 109.

25 Quoted in Stock, *Life of Pound*, pp. 457–58.

26 Bibliographical information comes from Donald Gallup, *Ezra Pound: A Bibliography* (Charlottesville, 1983), pp. 80, 352; and from Christine Froula, *To Write Paradise* (New Haven, 1984), pp. 174–75. I am indebted to James Laughlin of New Directions for information and for letting me see and published Pound's still unpublished "FRAGMENT (1966)." I am indebted to Michael Coyle for calling my attention to the early version of Canto 115 and to Pasolini's interview with Pound.

27 Quoted in Gallup, *Eliot and Pound*, p. 30.

28 Quoted in Stock, *Life of Pound*, p. 422.

29 T. S. Eliot, "The Music of Poetry," a 1942 lecture reprinted in Eliot's *On Poetry and Poets* (New York, 1957), pp. 24–25.

30 "Pound," writes George Bornstein, "separates the image [or epiphany] from the quest for it . . . traces product rather than 'process'" (*The Postromantic Consciousness of Ezra Pound*, Victoria, B.C., 1977, pp. 51–52). The "process" is the action of romantic dramatic lyrics, like "Tintern Abbey," that dramatize the evolution of an epiphany.

31 T. S. Eliot, review of Pound's *Quia Pauper Amavi*, in *The Atheneum*, 24 October 1919, p. 1065.

32 Ezra Pound, "Ford Madox (Hueffer) Ford; Obit," *Nineteenth Century and After* (August 1939), pp. 178–79.

33 Ronald Bush, *The Genesis of Ezra Pound's Cantos* (Princeton, 1976), pp. 220–21. See also Gordon, *Eliot's Early Years*, p. 100; and Myles Slatin, "A History of Pound's Cantos I–XVI, 1915–1925," in *American Literature* (May 1963), p. 188.

34 Eliot, *Selected Essays*, p. 247. Ezra Pound, *Literary Essays*, ed. T. S. Eliot (New York, 1968), p. 153.

Index

Abrams, M. H., 34
Adorno, Theodore, 3
Aeschylus, 121
Albright, Daniel, 64 and 224 n.7
Allingham, William, 93 and 226 nn. 7,9
Altick, Richard, 90
Anderson, Sherwood, 151, 155
Annan, Noel, Lord, 78
Aquinas, Thomas, 200
Aristotle, 44, 59, 154
Arnold, Matthew, 24, 78, 79, 82, 83, 84,
    85, 86 and 225 n.13, 112, 125, 139,
    141, 148, 152, 153, 154, 167 and
    229 n.9
    Culture and Anarchy, 86
    "Function of Criticism, The," 84 and
        225 n.10
    Merope, 111
    Poems of 1853, 111–12
    Sohrab and Rustum, 111
    "To a Friend," 139
Auden, W. H., 148
Austen, Jane, 132, 135 and 227 n.6, 140,
    157–58, 228 n.6

Bagehot, Walter, 79 and 224 n.1
Barzun, Jacques, 149, 224 n.6
Beach, Joseph Warren, 159
Beckett, Samuel, 20–21, 26, 38
    Unnamable, The, 21 and 221 n.1
Beddoes, Thomas L., 205
Beer, Gillian, 144 and 228 n.16
Beja, Morris, 34, 40, 223 n.11
Bell, Clive, 195 and 229 n.1

Bellow, Saul, 183, 184
Bentham, Jeremy, 79, 80, 82, 83 and 224
    n.5, 84, 100
Bergson, Henri, 51 and 223 n.23
Blackmur, R. P., 147
Blake, William, 46, 110, 111, 120 and
    227 n.12, 124
    "Auguries of Innocence," 39
    Book of Thel, The, vii
    Marriage of Heaven and Hell, The, 32,
        227 n.16
    "Tyger, The," 54
Bornstein, George, 231 n.30
Boyers, Robert, 228 n.2
Breuer, Josef, 12, 13, 15, 17, 18
Bridges, Robert, 215
Brooks, Cleanth, 147, 149
Brower, Reuben, 163 and 228 n.5
Browning, Elizabeth Barrett, 111 and
    226 nn.3,5, 116, 117
Browning, Robert, 40 and 223 n.12, 64,
    81, 82, 89–96, 100, 108–119, 203,
    211, 216, 226 nn.2–5, 227 nn.11,15
    "Andrea del Sarto," 128
    Balaustion's Adventure, 125–28
    "Bean-Stripe, A," 91, 225 n.5
    "Bishop Blougram's Apology," 114
    "Bishop Orders His Tomb, The," 90,
        113
    "By the Fireside," 212
    "Childe Roland," 125, 128
    "Cleon," 114
    "Essay on Shelley," 110
    "Fifine at the Fair," 114

233

Browning, Robert (*continued*)
"Fra Lippo Lippi," 108
Letters, R. B.–E. B. B., 117, 226
nn.3,5
Men and Women, 114
"Mr. Sludge, the Medium," 114
"Numpholeptos," 128, 129
Paracelsus, 112–14
Parleyings, 120, 121 and 227 n.13,
123, 124; "Bernard de Mandeville,"
91, 120; "Charles Avison," 116–17,
120; "Christopher Smart," 122;
"Daniel Bartoli," 121; "Francis Fu-
rini," xiv, 122–23; "George Bubb
Dodington," 122; "Gerard de Lai-
resse," 111, 119–20, 128
Pauline, 115, 117
"Prince Hohenstiel-Schwangau," 114
"Rabbi Ben Ezra," 92 and 225 n.5
Ring and the Book, The, xiv, 89–109,
114–16, 125, 126, 225 n.1
Sordello, 113, 114, 117–18
Brücke, Ernst, 12
Brugière, Bernard, 91–92, 225 n.5
Burke, Edmund, 50 and 223 n.21, 82, 83
and 225 n.7, 84–86, 152, 195, 225
n.13
Burroughs, William, 188
Bush, Douglas, 126 and 227 n.19
Bush, Ronald, 215 and 231 n.33
Byron, George Gordon, Lord, 24, 81
Manfred, 24 and 222 n.7

Calleo, David P., 224 n.6
Carlyle, Thomas, 80, 83, 86
Past and Present, 80, 85
Sartor Resartus, 80, 81
Cavalcanti, Guido, 202, 216
Cervantes, Miguel de, 41
Chace, William M., 228 n.2
Chapman, George, 119 and 227 n.11
Chekhov, Anton, 38, 43, 58
Clark, Kenneth, Lord, 123 and 227 n.14
Clark, Ronald W., 14 and 221 n.9, 15,
18
Freud: The Man and His Cause, 4
Cobbett, William, 82
Coleridge, Samuel Taylor, 8, 29–30, 34,
40, 63, 79, 82, 83 and 224 nn.5–6,
84–86, 120, 121 and 227 n.13, 148,
185, 195, 209

Ancient Mariner, The, 63, 149, 186,
187
Biographia Literaria, 34
"Dejection," 30 and 222 n.12
"Frost at Midnight," 29, 211
Lay Sermon, A, 225 n.12
"Statesman's Manual, The," 222 n.11
Collingwood, W. G., 223 n.12, 226 n.10
Confucius, 200, 202
Conrad, Joseph, 38–39
Cook, A. K., 90
Cook, Reginald, 166 and 229 n.8
Cooper, James Fenimore, 190
Corrigan, Beatrice, 94 and 226 n.8
Coyle, Michael, 231 n.26
Crews, Frederick, 141 and 227 n.11, 146

Danby, John F., 67 and 224 n.8
Dante, 40, 161, 184, 188, 198, 200–202,
207, 216
Darlington, Beth, 224 n.11
Darwin, Charles, xiii, xiv, 3–11, 13, 15,
17–19, 31, 78, 123 and 227 n.15,
159, 164, 165, 167, 168, 221 n.11,
229 n.8
Das, G. K., 142 and 227 n.14
de Born, Bertrans, 203
de Man, Paul, 31
Blindness and Insight, 29
"Rhetoric of Blindness, The," 29
"Rhetoric of Temporality, The," 22
and 222 n.5, 25, 29–30
"Shelley Disfigured," 29 and 222 n.10
De Quincey, Thomas, 49–50, 223 n.20
Derrida, Jacques, 29, 222 n.9
Descartes, Renè, 9, 19, 22
DeVane, W. C., 90, 113, 121, 123, 125,
226 nn.4,7
Dickens, Charles, 79, 81
Dickinson, G. Lowes, 140–41, 227 n.12
Dinesen, Isak, 191
Disraeli, Benjamin, 87, 122
Divus, Andreas, 201
Donne, John, 216
Donoghue, Denis, 229 nn.8,14
Dostoevsky, Fyodor, 103, 155
Douglas, C. H., 199, 200
Dreiser, Theodore, 151, 155
Durkheim, David-Emile, 6

Eberhart, Richard, 229 n.16
"Groundhog, The," 175

Eckstein, Emma, 12
Einstein, Albert, 13
Eliot, George, 87, 132
Eliot, T. S., 8, 20–22, 24, 55–57, 82,
    110, 114, 115, 117, 126 and 227
    n.18, 147, 149, 150, 157, 161, 195–
    218, 228 n.4, 229–31 nn.1,3–6, 8,
    10,18–19,21,24,27,29,31,33–34
  After Strange Gods, 202
  Ash Wednesday, 216
  Cultivation of Christmas Trees, The,
    196
  "Dante," 216
  "Ezra Pound," 230 n.21
  "Ezra Pound: His Metric and Poetry,"
    197–98, 230 n.8
  Four Quartets, 55–57, 76, 206, 210,
    216, 224 n.4
  "Gerontion," 209, 215, 216
  "Hamlet and His Problems," 216
  Hollow Men, The, 195–96, 206
  Idea of a Christian Society, The, 153
  "Journey of the Magi," 55, 215, 216
  "Lancelot Andrewes," 216
  "Love Song of J. Alfred Prufrock,
    The," 196, 203, 211, 216
  "Metaphysical Poets, The," 215, 216
  Murder in the Cathedral, 196
  "Music of Poetry, The," 231 n.29
  *Notes towards the Definition of Cul-
    ture,* 84 and 225 n.9
  Old Possum's Book of Practical Cats,
    216
  Poems, 1920, 212
  "Portrait of a Lady," 214, 216
  Prufrock and Other Observations, 196
  "Rudyard Kipling," 206
  Selected Essays, 231 n.34
  Sweeney Agonistes, 196
  "Sweeney Among the Nightingales,"
    212
  "Swinburne as Poet," 198–99
  "Tradition and the Individual Talent,"
    199, 216
  Waste Land, The, 55 and 223 n.25,
    115, 116, 195, 196, 198, 203, 206,
    209–12, 214–16
Eliot, Valerie, 209
Ellenberger, Henri
  Discovery of the Unconscious, The, 3
Ellis, Havelock, 11

Ellmann, Richard, 222 n.2
Emerson, Ralph Waldo, 37 and 222 n.8,
    190
Engels, Friedrich, 81
Epiphany, epiphanic, xiii, xiv, 25, 33–57,
    97, 119, 124, 167, 210, 223 n.11,
    231 n.30
Euripides, 121, 125–27

Faulkner, William, 39, 181, 190
Fenollosa, Ernest, 210–11
Fenwick, Isabella, 63, 67
Ferenczi, Sandor, 16, 17
Fitzgerald, F. Scott, 39
Flaubert, Gustave, 20, 27, 28, 203
Fliess, Wilhelm, 11, 12, 14–18, 221 n.10
Ford, Ford Madox, 215 and 231 n.32
Forster, E. M., 78, 87, 130–46, 227
    nn.4,7,9,11
  Abinger Harvest, 227 n.3
  "Ansell," 134
  Aspects of the Novel, 134, 227 n.5
  Howards End, 130, 131, 136, 138–40,
    227 n.10
  Life to Come, The, 130 and 227 n.1
  Longest Journey, The, 134, 136–37,
    139, 227 n.8
  Maurice, 130, 131, 135
  Passage to India, A, xiv, 130–32, 134–
    37, 139–46, 227 nn.14–16
  Room with a View, A, 130, 131, 136–
    38
  "Story of a Panic, The," 134
  Two Cheers for Democracy, 79, 141
    and 227 n.13
  Where Angels Fear to Tread, 132–34,
    135–36, 138, 227 n.2
Foucault, Michel
  Order of Things, The, 25, 26 and 222
    n.9
  "What Is an Author?" 21–22, 25–29,
    221 n.2
Fragmentation, xiii, 40, 43, 44, 87, 118,
    211–12, 216
Frank, Joseph, 43 and 223 n.14
Frazer, Sir James George, 114, 167, 174,
    202, 212
Freud, Sigmund, xiii, xiv, 3–19, 31, 84
    and 225 n.11, 146, 149, 152–54,
    167, 227 n.6
  Autobiographical Study, 14

Freud, Sigmund (*continued*)
  Beyond the Pleasure Principle, 19
  Civilization and Its Discontents, 10
  Complete Letters, The, 15
  Interpretation of Dreams, The, 14
  Moses and Monotheism, 11
  Origins of Psychoanalysis, 15
  "Project for a Scientific Psychology,"
    19
  Studies in Hysteria, 12
  Three Essays on the Theory of Sexuality, 8 and 221 n.6
  Totem and Taboo, 10
Frost, Robert, 159, 161–67, 172, 173,
    178, 228 nn.4–6, 229 n.8
  "Acceptance," 164
  "After Apple-Picking," 163–64
  "Build Soil," 166
  "Come In," 162–63
  "Desert Places," 165–66
  "Design," 164–65, 171
  "Going for Water," 162
  "In Hardwood Groves," 163
  "Mowing," 163
  "Need to be Versed in Country Things,
    The," 161–62
  "Old Man's Winter Night, An," 163–
    64
  "On a Bird Singing in Its Sleep," 164
  "Servant to Servants, A," 164
  "Stopping by Woods on a Snowy Evening," 162
  "Storm Fear," 163
  "Wood-Pile, The," 162
Froula, Christine, 231 n.26
Frye, Northrop, 59, 155
Furbank, P. N., 130, 134 and 227 n.4,
    137
Furnivall, Frederick James, 94 and 226
    n.9, 227 n.15

Gallup, Donald, 196 and 230 n.4, 231
    nn.26–27
Gautier, Théophile, 212
Gay, Peter, 225 n.11
Gide, André, 157
Godwin, William, 110
Goethe, Johann Wolfgang von, 81, 83
  Faust, 81, 192
  Wilhelm Meister, 81

Gordon, Lyndall, 197 and 230 n.6, 231
    n.33
Gould, Stephen Jay, 6 and 221 n.4
Gridley, Roy, 90 and 225 n.2, 91

Haeckel, Ernst, 5
Hallam, Arthur, 81
Hardy, Thomas, 31, 87, 159, 165 and
    228 n.7, 202, 215
  "In a Wood," 165
  "Shelley's Skylark," 165
Hartman, Geoffrey, 31 and 222 n.13, 62
Hazlitt, William
  The Spirit of the Age, 33 and 222 n.1
Hegel, Georg, 148
Heidegger, Martin, 22, 24–25
  "Language," 24 and 222 n.8, 25
  "Letter on Humanism," 24
  "Origin of the Work of Art, The," 21
    and 222 n.3
  "Thing, The," 25
  "Thinker as Poet, The," 25
Helmholtz, Hermann von, 12
Hemingway, Ernest, 39, 181, 190, 197,
    213
Himmelfarb, Gertrude, 225 n.11
Hitler, Adolf, 6, 150
Hobbes, Thomas, 100
Hodell, Charles W., 90
Holloway, John, 86–87, 225 n.14
Homer, 114, 201–2, 213
Honan, Park, 90, 118 and 226 n.9
Hopkins, Gerard Manley, 117, 119
  "Andromeda," 117
  "Windhover, The," 54, 118, 119
Hughes, Ted, 172, 229 n.13
  "Ghost Crabs," 172
  "Pike," 171
Hume, David, 22, 30
Husserl, Edmund, 22

Ibsen, Henrik, 82

Jakobson, Roman, 43
James, Henry, 38, 64, 149, 152–55
  Princess Casamassima, The, 151–54
James, William, 164–65
Jones, Ernest, 16
  Life and Work of Sigmund Freud, The,
    3–5, 221 n.1

Jones, Henry, 90
Joyce, James, 34–38, 41, 44 and 223
    n.15, 50, 58, 59, 110, 114, 115, 117
    and 226 n.8, 149, 157, 188, 197,
    210
    "Clay," 44
    "Dead, The," 38, 40, 50
    Dubliners, 35, 36 and 222 n.7, 43, 44
    "Encounter, An," 59
    Portrait of the Artist as a Young Man,
    A, 20, 35 and 222 n.3, 37, 41, 42
    Stephen Hero, 35 and 222 n.4, 36, 41,
    42
    Ulysses, 20, 35–37, 42–43, 110, 114,
    209, 222 n.5
    Workshop of Daedalus, The (Scholes
    & Kain, eds.), 35 and 222 n.6, 41
Joyce, Stanislaus, 41, 223 n.15
Jung, Carl G., vii, 14, 18–19, 227 n.6

Kafka, Franz, 27, 28, 157
Kant, Immanuel, 222 n.9
Keats, John, 21, 53–54, 81, 82, 149,
    164, 223 n.24
    "Bright Star," 54
    "Ode to a Nightingale," 29, 211
    "On First Looking into Chapman's
    Homer," 53–54
Kennedy, John F., 184, 193
Kenner, Hugh, 195, 197, 200 and 230
    nn.13,17, 204, 205, 213
Kerényi, C., 226 n.6
Kermode, Frank, 229 n.14
Keynes, John Maynard, 78
King, Roma, 90, 91, 227 n.13
Kingsley, Charles, 161
Krafft-Ebing, Richard, 11, 12
Kris, Ernst, 15
Krupnick, Mark, 228 n.2

Lacan, Jacques, 3, 90–91, 225 n.4
Laforgue, Jules, 211, 212
Lamarck, Jean de, 5, 7, 227 n.15
Langbaum, Robert, 34, 67, 89
Laughlin, James, 208 and 231 n.26
Lawrence, D. H., 31, 38, 82, 86, 137,
    157, 169–71, 172, 183, 202, 229
    n.12
    "Fish," 170, 172–73

"Snake," 170–71
Sons and Lovers, 20
Leavis, F. R., 204–5, 231 n.22
Lewis, Wyndham, 206
Locke, John, 22
Longinus, 50 and 223 n.21
Loucks, James F., 90
Lueger, Karl, 14
Lumsden, Charles J., 6

Macaulay, Thomas Babington, 78–80
Macaulay, Zachary, 78–79
McCarthy, Eugene, 193
McCarthy, Joseph, 181
McConnell, Frank D., 184
McGrath, William J., 12
    Freud's Discovery of Psychoanalysis,
    221 n.8
Machiavelli, Niccolò, 122
Mailer, Norman, 180–94, 229 nn.1–11
    Advertisements for Myself, 185, 192
    American Dream, An, xiv, 180, 182–
    88, 190–92, 194, 229 n.5
    Ancient Evenings, 180
    Armies of the Night, 180, 189, 192–
    93
    Barbary Shore, 181, 185
    Deer Park, 181–82, 192
    Executioner's Song, The, 180
    "Homosexual Villain, The," 192
    Marilyn, 188
    Miami and the Siege of Chicago, 180,
    193
    Naked and the Dead, The, 180–82,
    184
    "Time of Her Time, The," 185
    Tough Guys Don't Dance, 180
    "White Negro, The," 181, 187
    Why Are We in Vietnam?, xiv, 180,
    188–94
Mallarmé, Stéphane, 20, 25, 27–28
Mann, Thomas, 146, 157
Marcuse, Herbert, 3
Marx, Karl, Marxism, xiv, 3, 10, 13, 81–
    82, 149, 156
Masood, Syed Ross, 131
Masson, Jeffrey Moussaieff, 15
    The Assault on Truth: Freud's Suppres-
    sion of the Seduction Theory, 11–12
Meredith, H. O., 131

Merwin, W. S., 229 n.17
   "Mountain, The," 176–77
Michelet, Jules, 83 and 224 n.6
Mill, John Stuart, 80, 82–83 and 224
   n.5, 84 and 225 n.8, 141, 167 and
   229 n.9
Miller, J. Hillis, 118 and 226 n.9
Milton, John, 50, 52–53, 100, 149, 199
Moll, Albert, 11
Monroe, Harriet, 196
Monroe, Marilyn, 188
Moore, G. E., 79
Moore, Henry, 60 and 223 n.1, 62
Moore, Marianne, 168, 174, 228 n.2
   "Fish, The," 169
   "Grave, A," 160–62
   "Jerboa, The," 174
   "Plumet Basilisk, The," 168, 174–75
   "Snakes, Mongooses," 177
   "Steeple-Jack, The," 174
More, Hannah, 78
More, Sir Thomas, 79
Morris, William, 84, 86
Mussolini, Benito, 206, 209, 218
Myth, mythical method, xiii, xiv, 4,
   110–29, 209–10

Newman, John Henry, Cardinal, 86
Newton, Sir Isaac, 13, 120, 159
Nietzsche, Friedrich, xiii, 26–27, 32

Oedipus, Oedipus complex, 11, 12, 17,
   184
Orage, A. R., 206
Orwell, George, 82, 88
Owen, Robert, 82

Parrish, Stephen, 45 and 223 n.17
Pascal, Blaise, 146
Pasolini, Pier Paolo, 200, 231 n.26
Pater, Walter, 35, 37, 81, 86
Pavlov, Ivan, 9
Peckham, Morse, 225 n.3
Petacci, Clara, 206
Petrarch, 216
Plato, Platonic, 24, 110, 137, 140
Podhoretz, Norman, 181 and 229 n.3
Poirier, Richard, 164, 190 and 229 n.10,
   228 n.6

Poulet, Georges, 49 and 223 n.19
Pound, Ezra, 38, 125–26, 166, 195–218,
   222 n.9, 227 n.18, 229 nn.2–5,7–9,
   11–17,20–28,30–34
   Cantos, 38, 198–211, 215, 217–18,
     231 n.33
   Cathay, 213–14
   "Cavalcanti," 216
   "Cino," 203
   "Credo," 206 and 231 n.23
   "Dante," 230 n.16
   Ezra Pound Speaking, 230 n.20
   "Exile's Letter," 215
   "Ford Madox (Hueffer) Ford; Obit,"
     231 n.32
   "For T.S.E.," 231 n.24
   "FRAGMENT (1966)," 208 and 231
     n.26
   Homage to Sextus Propertius, 199,
     209–10
   Hugh Selwyn Mauberley, 199, 200,
     203, 212–13
   Literary Essays, 231 n.34
   Lustra, 197
   "Near Perigord," 203
   Personae, 198 and 230 n.9, 199, 213
   Quia Pauper Amavi, 199, 231 n.31
   "River-Merchant's Wife: A Letter,
     The," 214
   "Sestina Altaforte," 203
   "Song of the Bowmen of Shu," 213
   Spirit of Romance, The, 230 n.16
   Three Cantos, 215
Preyer, Robert, 227 n.11
Proust, Marcel, 20, 27, 28, 38, 39, 41,
   135 and 227 n.6, 157
Pugin, A. W. N., 84

Ranke, Leopold von, 224 n.6
Ransom, John Crowe, 147
Richards, I. A., 21
Ricoeur, Paul, 3
Roethke, Theodore, 168
   "Meditation at Oyster River," 172
   "Minimal, The," 168
   "Root Cellar," 168
   "Snake," 172
Rose, Phyllis, 225 n.11

Rossetti, Dante Gabriel, 54
  "Silent Noon," *House of Life,* 54
Rousseau, Jean-Jacques, 29, 154
Rowse, A. L., 79
Rudge, Olga, 208
Ruskin, John, 84, 86, 118 and 226 n.10,
      161 and 228 n.3, 201, 211, 223
      n.12
  "Of the Pathetic Fallacy," 228 n.3

Sacks, Peter M., 75
Sahlins, Marshall, 8
  *The Use and Abuse of Biology: An An-
      thropological Critique of Sociobiol-
      ogy,* 6 and 221 n.5,7
Sartre, Jean-Paul, 222 n.9
Scholes, Robert, 35
Schorske, Carl E., 14
Shaw, George Bernard, 82, 86, 157
Shelley, Percy Bysshe, 31, 81, 82, 110
      and 226 nn.1–2, 111, 136, 137, 140
  Alastor, 136
  Epipsychidion, 137
  "Mont Blanc," 29
  "To a Skylark," 31
  Triumph of Life, The, 29
Shoben, Edward J., 228 n.2
Slatyn, Miles, 231 n.33
Sophocles, 139
Spenser, Edmund, 75, 77
Stalin, Josef, Stalinism, 150–51, 156,
      158, 230 n.20
Stallybrass, Oliver, 227 n.1
Stephen, James, 78
Stephen, Leslie, 78
Stevens, Wallace, 38 and 223 n.10, 168,
      173–74, 216, 228 n.1, 229 n.14
  "Anecdote of the Jar," 173
  "Idea of Order at Key West, The," 173
  "Latest Freed Man, The," 38
  "Snow Man, The," 38, 160–62
  "Sunday Morning," 178–79
  "Tattoo," 173
  "Thirteen Ways of Looking at a Black-
      bird," 173
Stock, Noel, 197 and 230 nn.7,12, 231
      nn.25,28
Stone, Wilfred, xiv, 131, 135–36, 137,
      140, 146, 227 n.7

Stough, Christina, 230 n.3
Strachey, Lytton, 78, 79
Sulloway, Frank J., 8, 11–18
  Freud, Biologist of the Mind, 3–6, 221
      n.2
Swinburne, Algernon C., 119 and 227
      n.11, 159, 198–99
Symons, Arthur, 90

Tanner, Tony, 186 and 229 n.6
Tate, Allen, 147
Taylor, Sir Henry, 81 and 224 n.2
Tennyson, Alfred, Lord, 81, 82, 128,
      140, 141, 149, 206, 216
  1830 Poems, 81
  Idylls of the King, 111
  "Kraken, The," vii
  "Tithonus," 128
Thomas, Dylan, 167, 229 n.10
  "force that through the green fuse,
      The," 167
  "Refusal to Mourn, A," 167–68
Thornton, Henry, 78, 141
Trakl, Georg, 25
Trilling, Diana, 152, 156, 181–82, 229
      n.4
Trilling, Lionel, 131, 138 and 227 n.9,
      147–58, 228 nn.1–6
  "Art and Fortune," 157
  "Art and Neurosis," 154
  "Freud and Literature," 8 and 221 n.7,
      147, 152
  Last Decade, The, 228 n.6
  Liberal Imagination, The, 147–58,
      228 n.1
  "Manners, Morals, and the Novel,"
      154–55, 157–58
  "Meaning of a Literary Idea, The,"
      157
  Middle of the Journey, The, 157, 228
      n.3
  notebooks, 156–57
  "Princess Casamassima, The," 151–54
  "Reality in America," 151
  "Sense of the Past, The," 157
  Speaking of Literature and Society, 228
      n.4
  "T. S. Eliot and Politics," 153

Valéry, Paul, 174 and 229 n.14
Vaughan, Henry, 39
Victoria, Queen, 80, 81, 225 n.11
Voltaire, François Marie, 224 n.6

Wallace, Alfred Russel, 18 and 221 n.11
Warren, Robert Penn, 147
Wedgwood, Julia, 92–93, 225 n.6
Wilberforce, William, 78, 80
Wilbur, Richard, 229 n.15
  "Death of a Toad, The," 175
Wilde, Oscar, 28
Williams, Raymond, 82 and 224 n.4
Williams, William Carlos, 216
Wilson, Edmund, 148, 154
Wilson, Edward O., 7, 9
  Genes, Mind, and Culture, 6
  Insect Societies, 6
  Promethean Fire, 6
  Sociobiology: The New Synthesis, 3, 6
    and 221 n.3
Winner, Anthony, 188
Wolfe, Thomas, 39
Woolf, Leonard, 78
Woolf, Virginia, 39, 43, 78, 195
  To the Lighthouse, 44–45, 223 n.16
  Waves, The, 43
Wordsworth, Dorothy, 59, 61 and 224
  n.3, 62, 64
Wordsworth, William, xiv, 8, 19–22, 24,
  28–30, 33–57, 58–77, 79, 81, 142,
  149, 163, 165–68, 191, 195, 223
  nn.13,18,22, 224 nn.4,5,9
  "Animal Tranquillity and Decay," 65–
    67
  Borderers, The, 59
  "Composed upon Westminster
    Bridge," 53
  Descriptive Sketches, 48
  "Elegiac Stanzas," 63
  Excursion, The, 60, 65
  Guilt and Sorrow (Salisbury Plain), 65,
    70 and 224 n.10

"Idiot Boy, The," 67–70
"It Is a Beauteous Evening," 53
"Lines Composed a Few Miles above
  Tintern Abbey," 22, 29, 31, 58, 63,
  71, 211, 222 n.6, 231 n.30
"London, 1802," 53
Lyrical Ballads, (Preface, 27), 33–34,
  36, 43–44
"Michael," 47
"Night Piece, A," 48–49, 70–71, 224
  n.11
"Ode: Intimations of Immortality," 63,
  148
"Old Cumberland Beggar, The," 65–
  67, 70, 73–74
Prelude, The, 23, 31, 34, 37, 39, 41,
  49–52, 59–60, 63, 70–75, 158 n.2
"Resolution and Independence," 58–
  66, 70, 73–74
Ruined Cottage, The, 65
"Simon Lee," 43–44
"Slumber Did My Spirit Seal, A," 30,
  168
"Strange Fits of Passion Have I
  Known," 40–42, 58
"Sublime and the Beautiful, The," 50
  and 223 n.22
"Thorn, The," 45–48, 63–67
"White Doe of Rylstone, The," 59, 75–
  77
Wright, Charles, 217

Yeats, W. B., 22, 35, 82, 110 and 226
  n.1, 111, 114, 116–17, 122, 124
  and 227 n.17, 145 and 228 nn.17–
  18, 146, 157, 166, 198, 202, 206,
  215, 218, 226 n.8
  "Among School Children," 212
  "Art and Ideas," 82
  Autobiography, 82 and 224 n.3
  "Leda and the Swan," 54
  Vision, A, 200
Young, G. M., 224 n.1